WHERE
THE BEE
SUCKS

Where the Bee Sucks

WORKERS, DRONES AND QUEENS
OF CONTEMPORARY AMERICAN POETRY

Robert Peters

Santa Maria
Asylum Arts
1994

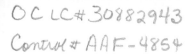

Acknowledgments

For permission to quote from poems, thanks to the poets and/or their publishers:

Edward Field, John Ashbery (APR), Robert Bly (Univ. of Michigan), James Broughton (Jargon Society), Charles Bukowski (Black Sparrow), Paul Christensen, Sharon Doubiago (West End), Lawrence Ferlinghetti, Tess Gallagher, Allen Ginsberg (City Lights), Alfred Starr Hamilton (Jargon Society), Greg Kuzma, Lyn Lifshin (Cherry Valley), Paul Mariah (ManRoot Books), Michael McClure, Judith McCombs (Dustbooks), Rod McKuen, W.S. Merwin (Atheneum), Charles Plymell (Scarecrow Press), Gary Snyder, Jack Spicer (ManRoot), Carolyn Stoloff (Scarecrow Press), Mark Strand (Atheneum), Paul Trachtenberg (Cherry Valley), Diane Wakoski (Black Sparrow), William Wantling (Dustbooks), John Weiners (Good Gay Poets Press).

Each of these essays first appeared in various of the four volumes of my *Great American Poetry Bake-offs*, Scarecrow Press, 1979, 1982, 1987, and 1991, and are here, most revised, through the generous courtesy of the original publisher. There, since I gratefully acknowledged the editors of the various journals first publishing the individual essays (many of these magazines and tabloids are now defunct), here I shall simply refer readers to those volumes—all are still in print. The piece on "Language Poets," the newest contribution, appeared in *Asylum Annual 1994*. Also, since the list of poets focused on in *Bee* is manageable, and since the works by each are named, I am eschewing the bibliography generic to volumes of criticism. Since many of these individual works are long out of print, and even the publishers may have disappeared, interested readers may locate the addresses for individual poets and write to them for their books. See the latest *Directory of American Poets and Writers*.

Finally, three people among others deserve my special thanks: first, Greg Boyd, my indefatigable editor, publisher, and bee enthusiast, whose expertise and enthusiasm have been first-rate; second, Carolyn Stoloff, whose tenacity and perspicacity much improved my introduction; and Paul Trachtenberg, for his affection and support through my years of working on the *Bake-offs*, *Hunting the Snark: A Compendium of New Literary Terminology*, and *Where the Bee Sucks*. I am blessed.

ISBN 1-878580-63-9
Library of Congress Catalogue Number: 94-70673

Contents

AUTHOR'S PREFACE:
FOR *HYMETTUS*

1.

The essays I have included here are among the most important assessments of contemporary writers I have written over the past twenty-five years. Readers familiar with my *The Great American Poetry Bake-off* volumes, the *Peters Black and Blue Guides to Current Literary Periodicals*, and my *Hunting the Snark: A Compendium of New Poetic Terminology* may recall earlier versions of some of these. All are here revised, some drastically. The earliest essay is from the 'seventies, and is on Charles Bukowski; the latest, written for this volume, and the longest of the contributions, is on Language Poetry.

Why such a prolific and long commitment? Very simply, poetry matters to me more than any of the other arts. Even so, there are times when I despair, seeing little in the major literary magazines and in the lists of such publishers as Wesleyan, Pittsburgh, Boa Editions, Ecco, and Copper Canyon worth more than a cursory reading, as their poets wing through the flowers garnering prizes, fellowships, and awards. A vast grayness prevails. A suffocating sameness, a contaminating cloud, floats over all of our writing programs. Safe forms, safe language, safe themes. Then, *The New Yorker, New York Review of Books, The Atlantic Monthly. The Nation, The American Poetry Review*, and *Poetry*, journals most poets en route to trade publishers and academic sinecures, ache to appear in, embed the art in cement. The verse ossifies into worthless amber. One discerns much self-congratulatory piety and smugness in both publisher and writer. There's precious little engagement with broad cultural issues national and international, unless they are deemed fashionable. And I cringe now anticipating floods of poems on Michael Jackson. The fashionable norm for poets currently is a tranquilized personal experience, with a concomitant lack of real verse music and forms that gratify either the intellect or the passions. Thank God for the individualist talents who are at work in the swamps and suburbs of verse, and who continue to excite us as excellent poetry always has. Some of these talents, as

Where The Bee Sucks will make clear, are reclusive; you may be reading about them for the first time here, as I detail what, for me, makes them memorable. They turn up in Milwaukee, Wisconsin; Cherry Valley, New York; Juneau, Alaska; Hanford, California; or Columbus, Georgia. Journals in which they appear are apt to be scruffy, occasional, and poorly supported and distributed. I seek these out. Some poets are young and some are old. Two of the latter I call "unacknowledged American Treasures," William Elizabeth McDaniel and Alfred Starr Hamilton. Hamilton is in his nineties, and McDaniel in her seventies. The anthologists have almost all bypassed them. Among younger poets of distinction are Jesse Glass, Jr., Holly Prado, Paul Trachtenberg, Thomas Meyer, Harry Northup, Brian Daldorph, Laurel Ann Bogan, and Penelope Reedy.

2.

Like bees poet hymenoptera plunk themselves deep inside wild and domesticated blossoms, flowers of life, flowers of evil, flowers of beneficence, cramming poet bee stomachs and bee leg pollen bags with fluids and aromatic dusts for digesting into poems. A volume of verses is not unlike a honeycomb, each cell stuffed with a single poem, or with a verse for a multi-celled poem. Bees, like poets, arrange themselves into strata. An elite suck substances from rare orchids, trailing arbutus, century plants, and flashy yuccas. Plebeian hymenoptera work on a descending scale, from roses, camellias, orange blossoms and violets, down to Queen Anne's lace and clover, dandelion, and thistle. Most gatherers, returning to the hive, deposit their contributions freely, dumping their leg pouches of pollen and regurgitating nectar from their minuscule nectar stomachs. Inadmissible are those bees who imbibe fluids from the eyelids of cattle and from streams of urine. Soldier bees, I suspect, slaughter workers returning to the hive with such noxious cargoes. Their queen insists on quality. I know of no bees who sip putrefying flesh.

3.

My models for translating poets into a fable of insects are Bernard Mandeville and Jonathan Swift. A truly gifted poet may translate substances imported from carrion, garbage cans, and city jungles into verse and song as sweet as those sipped from Princess Di's favorite rose, orchids at the Getty Museum or the Taj Mahal. No poet can ever isolate his work; for, once published, he either damages or lends luster to the hive. Most poets, like most bees, are at neither extreme, functioning as pallid stuffers of honeycombs, sufficient for nurturing larvae and for keeping the hive fed during the winter. A crammed hive, at any time a bee keeper examines it, will symbolize the state (the mellifluousness) of contemporary verse.

I hope that my sampling of American poetry will reveal the honey I find there. If poetry lovers are disappointed with my sampling they should encourage poets to select better pollen sources and to improve their poetic skills so that the honey improves. My critic's role resembles the sweet singer of Shakespeare's wonderful song; the critic is a humble bee snuggled inside flowers where poet pollen and nectar is being gathered.

4.

For this collection, I start with a piece on opening lines, establishing the idea of beginnings; this works also in honey-gathering terms, for initial sips reveal the abundance (or lack thereof) to ensue. The individual writers who follow appear alphabetically, since isolating names according to renown would keep readers from making discoveries of poets new to them. Among this latter group are Paul Christensen, Sharon Doubiago, Alfred Starr Hamilton, Greg Kuzma, Paul Mariah, Judith McCombs, Bert Meyers, Carolyn Stoloff, Paul Trachtenberg, and William Wantling. Among the more visible poets I assess are W. S. Merwin, Mark Strand, Gary Snyder, Allen Ginsberg, Lawrence Ferlinghetti, John Ashbery, and Robert Creely. The quiz I've devised to foster fairness for Rod McKuen is a slap at the smug pretensions of most "serious" poets. My unsubtle, yet, I hope, funny attacks on poetasters Ray Bradbury and Leonard Nimoy are diversions emphasizing the cancerous influence of celebrity scribblers on serious verse. No responsible soldier bee would allow them near the home hive. My concluding essay, on Language Poetry, attempts to describe and evaluate a current fad now occupying many writers, journals, and presses anxious for anything remotely avant garde.

Finally, by posing as a spy deep inside flowers where authentic poet bees are going about their gatherings I realize I've taken a risk. Honey-lovers outraged by my dismissals of some of their favorite bees may translate themselves into vicious wasps and barrel down on me where I loll inside yet another cowslip bell, awarding me lethal thoracic stabs.

WHERE
THE BEE
SUCKS

WHAT'S MY OPENING LINE,
OR A MATHEMATICS FOR THE MUSE

"But was the language alive?"—Robert Friend

Examining only the first lines of poems is possibly a superficial critical exercise. It's akin to a doctor's taking your pulse but not your temperature, or to his thumping your chest but not proceeding to your nether parts where the trouble is; or, it's like a vet's dropping flea powder behind a poodle's ear when the whole creature is infested; or, finally, it's like a bright student who supplies the opening sentence of an essay and asks you to intuit what he or she knows from that sentence.

So, I am aware that what I undertake implies some risk. In the interests of serving poetry and the fledgling writers of verse who may see this essay, I shall be fearless. For my purposes, I have taken Edward Field's anthology *A Geography of Poets* since it was an ambitious presentation of poets known and unknown from all over the country. [A second, more limited, edition has since appeared.] Moreover, as the poets were still alive when the book was new, we had a guarantee that the poems reflected a spectrum of poetry as it was occurring.

Until I started copying first lines and classifying them, much as old Charles Darwin classified beetles and finches, I had no idea that they would group themselves as neatly as they do. Much of the monotony of current poetry is due to the dullness of opening lines. Generally, the language is declarative, plain-language, and detrital. Eschewed are old-fashioned starts, the overt alliterative line, and the highly inspired opening moment we associate with the ode or epic—"Arms and the man I sing," "Lost midway this path of life in a dark wood," "Of man's first disobedience..." etc. Modern launchings often seem purloined from newspapers, or from letters back to dear old granny on the farm, or from tacky autobiographical details. I hope that my examples (I mean to be entirely scientific) will startle poets into testing out their first lines before they print them. If they sound stupid and indulgent they probably are.

I will be accused of being unfair for not presenting entire opening verse sentences rather than first lines. I hereby throw down a scented glove. Since most contemporary poets using the fashionable free-verse modes swear by their line-breaks as necessary, pregnant, and even gorgeous, they should gladly submit to scrutiny. Obviously, a sentence cut off in mid-air, as most of my examples are, often appear ridiculous without their lower parts, legs, feet, and slippers. Unintentional double-entendres occur: One poet offers her man "head." Some sound more pompous than they should. Others do intrigue us over what is to come. My apologies to any poet (and several are friends) who may be offended by finding their lines parading around sans fig leaf. Like all satirists, I hope that my bolus will effect cures, and that future poems by these poets will have better starts. As you will see, the more prestigious the poet, the sappier these lines. There are moments, too, where they wonderfully evoke one another, making comments and completions never intended by their authors, their critics, the gods, or anyone else.

To be fair, I invite another critic to inspect an earlier anthology—say one by Selden Rodman, Oscar Williams, or Louis Untermeyer, and make a similar study. We may find that opening lines have always been lousy. At the same time, we may find empirical evidence for evaluating poetry then and now. The more data and related instruments of measurement the better. Since poets as a gens are pretty self-obsessed, we need to remove their work from the critical market-place, and freeze, dissect, classify, and analyze. I caution though against using any laser-beam technology—our poet-science is unsophisticated. Rudimentary steps first, please! We are in our infancy. I turn now to the major classes of opening lines, with examples and interpretative commentaries.

Reportage:

Reportage is common. Some of the assumptions by poets who see themselves as reporters are: l) Poetry is for plain folks—so throw out anything that smacks of the literary; 2) Limit your subject matter to families and friends, and to humdrum events. I doubt that the confusion of poetry with journalism is so endemic it will never disappear. American poetry will continue to sound like conglomerations of gears and cotter pins, all alike as to function; colors and sizes may vary.

There are two main sub-classes of reportage. In the first, the poet narrates about people other than himself. In the second, he tells you about himself. Here are examples of Type A. Notice how Simpson's line squints at Soto's grandmother and Ortiz's sister. Hitchcock lets us know that Kinnell's bear is doing more than defecating or eating blackberries. Finally, Dickey delivers Gildner's bitch of its pups. I have grouped the lines that tie-in:

"My oldest sister wears thick glasses" (Simon J. Ortiz)
"Grandma lit the stove" (Gary Soto)
"Her face turned sour" (Louis Simpson)

"A black bear sits alone" (Galway Kinnell)
"He sits in a deckchair reading Colette" (George Hitchcock)

"The boxer bitch is pregnant" (Gary Gildner)
"Next door they've finally brought home the new baby." (William Dickey)

Type B, Personal Reportage falls into five sorts, all possibly suspect unless they predict some devastating irony or drama to be worked out. It is almost impossible to detect lyrical beauty in any of these—although some lines scan. Here are the five sorts:

a. *What I Look Like:* Here we have a choice of physiognomies. For evocativeness, I prefer Le Sueur's:

"I have a wide, friendly face" (Paul Zimmer)
"I am a crazy woman with a painted face" (Meridel Le Sueur)

b. *What I'm Doing:* This one allows for a delicious poetic license—unless you imagine the poet composing as he bends over a stump and stares out at the trees:

"I bend over an old hollow cottonwood stump...." (Robert Bly)
"I am looking at trees" (W. S. Merwin)

c. *What I'm Really Like:* These starts seldom help us. King, Ortiz, and Stafford are pretty straightforward, and we might see Stafford's love for flat country as a paradigm for his poetry. Browne's "green books" aren't helpful though— Graham Greene's novels? Books Browne hasn't read and which, therefore, remain green? Or, has he literally painted all his books green as part of a decorating scheme? I like the ambiguity.

"I like a man around" (Linda King)
"I happen to be a veteran" (Simon J. Ortiz)
"In scenery I like flat country." (William Stafford)
"In my house I keep green books" (Michael Dennis Browne)

d. *My guilts and traumas:* This sub-class overlaps with a larger class, "problems." I include them because they deal frankly with autobiographical facts. I assume that Haines never became a cauliflower—which may be a metaphor for his having left Alaskan snow and ice (cauliflowers are polar bear-piss yellow). Norse deals with his gay feelings for an elusive Mr. Right of the Golden Calves. Meltzer supplies a religious turn: centuries of Jewish religious life confront him, and we are anxious to know his sin. Kunitz's speaker makes us wonder on whose side he is, and how heavy the guilt trips are.

> "I wanted to be a cauliflower" (John Haines)
> "A pair of muscular calves" (Harold Norse)
> "The Rabbi is before me." (David Meltzer)
> "My mother never forgave my father" (Stanley Kunitz)

e. *Irrefutable Facts About Me:* These might appear with sub-group "c", but separating them seems appropriate. Reed Whittemore's event, entirely factual, is so casual it means little more than what it says. May Swenson's news about herself is shocking—and refreshing. Mei-Mei Bersenbrugge's line nicely begins with first things—honkings? Alta's confession, unfrosted with guilt, seems almost metaphysical and, as such, anticipates McClure's scream of joy, a scream all poetry and art moves toward—the intense, personal apotheosis:

> "At breakfast I had french toast." (Reed Whittemore)
> "I took my cat apart" (May Swenson)
> "I was born the year of the loon" (Mei-Mei Berssenbrugge)
> "I'm frigid when i wear see thru negligees" (Alta)
> "I HAVE INHERITED THE UNIVERSE!" (Michael McClure)

Placings

Some poets place themselves in unexpected locales. I admire these because they promise more than journalistic drivel. The most free-wheeling is Nathan's appearance in the Indian Ocean. Barker and Lawson write while borne aloft. Huff is ethnic and earth-located. Brinnin's panegyric to suburban life (actually a threnody on Dachau) turns more melancholy in Levine's line and achieves violence in Barker's, although the violence is that of movie illusion. In all these cases, we know where the poet was when the poem was conceived:

> "I come sailing through the Indian Ocean" (Leonard Nathan)

"Here in the open cockpit" (David Barker)
"We're up in a balloon" (Paul Lawson)

"Sitting down near him in the shade" (Robert Huff)
"Such a merry suburb!" (John Malcolm Brinnin)
"In a coffee house at 3 am" (Philip Levine)
"On these sunny steps / they stabbed Sal Mineo" (David Barker)

Flamboyancies

Flamboyant openings draw us in through sheer style, or by saying something outrageous to arouse (or offend) our grosser instincts or our socio-political senses. Of three sub-groups here, the first is the most traditional: Wagoner and Jong love alliteration. The sibilants roll trippingly from their lips. Duncan is much less serpentine—his joy is cathartic; naming is a celebration, and he loves the dance of syllables. Ashbery employs sibilants to evoke delicious breakfasts past:

"On sloping, shattered granite, the snake man" (David Wagoner)
"Stiff as the icicles in their beards, the Ice Kings" (David Wagoner)
"A man so sick that the sexual soup" (Erica Jong)
"Most beautiful! the red-flowering eucalyptus" (Robert Duncan)
"A pleasant smell of frying sausages" (John Ashbery)

Here are some much less-daring alliterations:

"The planet that we plant upon" (Knute Skinner)
"There was a brightness in the branches" (Ron Loewinsohn)

The second sub-group means to jar by presenting human universals semi-tragically or grossly—scroti and abortions appear:

"They [genitals] droop like sad fuchsias from our bodies" (Henry Carlile)
"Cell by cell the baby made herself..." (George Oppen)
"My sweet-faced, tattle-tale brother was born blind" (Mona Van Duyn)
"After she finished her first abortion" (Judy Grahn)

In *sub-group three* fall lines with a funky, folksy, or intimate touch. Their colloquial tone is anti-poetic. Genitals and breasts are zippy beginnings for Ochester, Stetler, Barker, and Koch. Sometimes these starts are surreal (Edson) and sometimes funny (Broughton):

"Ordinarily I call it 'my cock ' but" (Ed Ochester)
"Karl, my friend, caught the crabs" (Charles Stetler)
"I know those tits. They are" (David Barker)
"Happy the man who has two breasts to crush against his bosom"
(Kenneth Koch)
"He had hitched a chicken to a cart" (Russell Edson)
"In Zen you can't yen for anything" (James Broughton)

Since poets are so inclined to be assertive and bossy, I am surprised to find so few poems opening with *imperatives*. This may, of course, reflect the wisdom of the editor. But, there area few. Wagoner tells us to "stand still," Meinke says "stop"; alta, helped by Contoski, informs us how to behave once we have followed Meinke's command. Field is about to show us what to do when drums appear at the door. Bronk hates turn-on stuff and waxes nicely metaphysical:

"Stand still. The trees ahead and bushes beside you" (David Wagoner)
"STOP: if you're racing at night" (Peter Meinke)
"hunger for me hunger hunger for me" (alta)
"Kiss the one you love." (Victor Contoski)
"When the drums come to your door" (Edward Field)
"Yes, look at me; I am the mask it wears" (William Bronk)

Ejaculations and Apostrophes

Ejaculatory starts are rare in Field's anthology, demonstrating how far behind we have left the English Romantics and the writers of Neoclassical odes. Only three instances of the rotund apostrophe appear. Kuzma's line has sexual overtones; his sex life is no longer as vigorous as it once was. Rakosi is ambiguous—a circle of friends? a circle of early poets presided over by rare Ben Jonson? a fairy circle of mushrooms on a lawn? Rukeyser's line is a refreshing comment on this study:

"Oh to be moving as we once were" (Greg Kuzma)
"o rare circle" (Carl Rakosi)
"O for God's sake" (Muriel Rukeyser)

You Do This, You Do That

One of the most pretentious of all starts is the "You do this, you do that" one. I am happy to report only a scattering of these in *A Geography of Poets*—evidence,

I hope that this once immensely popular form (nourished by workshops) is waning. The device was useful particularly for evoking dead people—dead fathers and grandmothers once despised by the poet. Sometimes historical figures are addressed. What sounds so phony is that the persons are told what they once knew—if they are stone-dead and unresurrected, the effect is of talking to a tombstone. Corpses aren't prescient:

> "When you walked down the stairs / to touch my root" (Steve Orlen)
> "You drive down MAIN STREET" (Jim Heynen)
> "As you are walking / down the street" (William J. Harris)
> "You remember the name was Jensen. She seemed old." (Richard Hugo)
> "You raise the ax" (Ai)
> "You follow, dress held high above / the fresh manure" (Lucien Stryk)
> "you know" (Charles Bukowski)

Direct Address

A related form, and one of the most common, is the Direct Address opening where the poet zeroes in on a listener, often with dramatic effect. There are three subspecies here. The first treats sexual matters. Taken together the examples create a short story of sexual favors and vengeances:

> "Do you love me? I asked. " (Gerald Locklin)
> "darling here's my head" (Judith Johnson Sherwin)
> "Haunt him, Mona! Haunt him, demon sister!" (Larry Rubin)

The second sub-class addresses parents and siblings. Kumin recalls her mother's girlhood. Scott reassures his parent that her life-teaching was effective. De Frees tries to love a son who may have good reason to doubt her affection. Ai arraigns her man for abandoning her in a truck, while Huff, enamored of passing years, addresses an old ventriloquist. Dickey says goodby to his teeth, items more intimate and necessary to one's life than parents. Shelton brings a dear-departed up to date. Aubert, almost divining Dickey's problem, blames Jean for the loss of teeth. Did Jean, Dickey's mom, feed him too much refined sugar?

> "Mother my good girl / I remember this old story" (Maxine Kumin)
> "Mother Dear, I am being careful. " (Herbert Scott)
> "It's right to call you son. That cursing alcoholic" (Madeline De Frees)
> "You keep me waiting in a truck" (Ai)
> "Four years ago, dear old ventriloquist" (Robert Huff

"Now you are going, what can I do but wish you" (William Dickey)
"Five years since you died and I am" (Richard Shelton)
"you should have, jean, stopped them" (Alvin Aubert)

The third sub-class (the reader may wish to flesh this one out with examples from other anthologies) flashes certain political apostrophes (Knight), lines directed to people in general (Corso), and apostrophes to devils and supernatural entities (Clifton):

"And, yeah, brothers" (Etheridge Knight)
"Folks, sex has never been" (Gregory Corso)
"Demon, Demon, you have dumped me" (Lucille Clifton)

The Pregnant Problem / Question

We arrive finally at lines preoccupied with stating a problem the poet is obliged to work out. Poems traditionally deal with strivings and spiritual struggles. For, as philosophers and linguists keep pointing out, these age-old conundrums perpetually snow white hairs on our heads. Or, to switch metaphors mid-stream, if time is but the stream we go a-fishing in, as Thoreau said, we should drop a series of baits, hoping to lure the bass of wisdom. Starts and castings from *A Geography of Poets* reveal our dismal failure to resolve such preoccupations.

Finkel and Di Prima, by asserting the whoeverness of self, symbolize *the first sub-class*. Ammons has a more responsible grip on the issue and pursues both unity and difference. By ignoring the point, Alan Dugan actually absolves himself from making a quest. Miller Williams has more courage, framing his conclusions around an image of banging. Watson moves through "invisible glass"—a nice Wonderland metaphor. Gregor, a passive poet, is in a dilemma over which role to choose in the face of the Existentialist angst. Shapiro begs the question by assuming there is a "dawn." The concensus is that no amount of poet-haggling will resolve our eternal "dusk":

"Whoever I am..." (Donald Finkel)
"who is the we, who is" (Diane Di Prima)
"I want to know the unity in all things and the difference" (A. R. Ammons)
"I never saw any point" (Alan Dugan)
"No one knows what the banging is all about" (Miller Williams)
"Was I moving through the invisible glass" (Robert Watson)
"If I could choose a role" (Arthur Gregor)

"What dawn is it?" (Karl Shapiro)

A *second class* develops the problem of lost cultures and decaying societies--problems of a different magnitude than metaphysical ones. Bloch worries about lost tribes. Schulman evokes the Cassandra-wail, and writes stiltedly in the manner of a nineteenth-century Oresteia. This is the only overt imitation of a dead style in Field's anthology. Heyen seems unsure of the folk needing to be saved—the implication is that since we can't save ourselves we shouldn't save others. Tate provides an epitaph for our own age, seen from a scary perspective, one uncannily foreseen by Josephine Miles: "Shall I pull the curtains...."

> "What happened to the ten lost tribes" (Chana Bloch)
> "What happened to Cassandra? She who cried" (Grace Schulman)
> "I do not think we can save them" (William Heyen)
> "They didn't have much trouble" (James Tate)
> "Shall I pull the curtains against the coming night?" (Josephine Miles)

The most problematical line (*in a third sub-class*) is personal rather than grandiose. Extremely solipsistic at worst, and generally anemic in imagination, these lines are best when they transcend snivelling, contain surprises, or are funny. A series of these counter-point one another. Poverty is the theme for Howard Moss who is awakened by his refrigerator. James Wright whistles in the wind. Cid Corman dips into his history, as does Vern Rutsala. Nathan's question, though refreshingly literal, is confusing, we can't tell whether he's well-off or not. Does he merely hope to experience poverty by simply wearing a poor dude's shirt?

> "The argument of the refrigerator wakes me." (Howard Moss)
> "I still have some money" (James Wright)
> "I had so little" (Cid Corman)
> "We had more than / we could use" (Vern Rutsala)
> "What is it like to have just one shirt" (Leonard Nathan)

Other lines of a highly personal-problem sort treat pregnancy, alcohol, and pseudonyms:

> "I have this bulging belly because" (Ann Darr)
> "If I needed brandy alone / there would be no problem" (Keith Wilson)
> "I was content with the pseudonym" (Vassar Miller)

As I pull the curtains on this arcane, scientific excursion into the core of poetry, I hope that poets will analyze their openings. How silly do these lines strike you taken by themselves? Do line-breaks really matter? Do you risk writing nonsense if you observe the breaks and read individual free verse lines as if they were single-line poems? Are you too much enamored of the ephemeral and the solipsistic? Have you done well to abandon a style that appears literary because it sounds like a grandfather wrote it? If you are writing journalism (which much poetry seems to be) why should you expect your scribblings to endure longer than daily newspaper columns? Other questions will come to mind, I am sure. Obviously, there are other beginnings not evident in *Geography:* the nonsense line, for example, or the language-syllable line which makes no sense as ordinary syntax, or the overtly scatalogical line, or the baldly parodic line. I can foresee new studies of second, third, and fourth lines. The consummation of all such studies would be, of course, a monumental Arithmetic of Poetry, or a Muse's Math, which would take the teeth out of Jonathan Williams' first-line command: "Stop all the literary shit," or would provide an affirmative response to Robert Friend's opening query: "But was the language alive?"

DICK AND JANE, AT HOME IN CALIFORNIA,
TRY TO SAY SOMETHING SIMPLE
ABOUT JOHN ASHBERY'S "LITANY"

I employ Dick and Jane, those primer siblings, in an effort to say something simple about John Ashbery. I've sent the pair to college (Jane to Vassar, Dick to law school at USC—from which he's dropped out to be a plumber, and, astonishingly enough, I have married them. Mother, Father, Spot (the dog was trained to bark out critics' names), and Puff the kitten are dead. Baby, a non-poetry lover, lives with her husband and her Baby in Newport Beach, California. She plays a lot of golf. I owe a debt also to Gary Trudeau, and keep hearing Joanie Caucus, Jr. and pals talking more than I want to. I am, I stress, trying to say something fresh about Ashbery's work.

Dick and Jane are seated on their Southern California patio. Dick is tanned and bare-chested. Jane is wearing a flowered bikini and a scarlet hibiscus over her right ear. Behind them, as background, is a terraced vegetable garden, an apricot tree, a Santa Rosa plum, a Japanese persimmon tree, and three hummingbird feeders. On a glass-topped patio table is a copy of *The American Poetry Review* for July/August 1979, the first appearance of "Litany."

JANE: Slow down, Dick You're drinking your strawberry margarita too fast. Anything wrong?

DICK: Ashbery's Litany. I'm afraid to read it. The critical crap that's been written on him is as confusing as he is.

JANE: Trust me; stay away from libraries. If you need commentaries to understand a poet then that poet can't be much good. [She pauses to marvel at the smog-haze sunset]. Dick, ever since you dropped out of law school and took up plumbing, and realized that poetry also begins with "p," you've been an aficionado. I love you for it!

19

DICK: Reaming eucalyptus roots from sewer lines is simpler than deciphering Ashbery.

JANE: He does make my head spin. I never got through his books in those Vassar lit courses. I preferred playing tennis to reading "The Tennis Court Oath."

DICK [Replenishing their margaritas]: Since "Litany" is arranged for two voices, I'll read the left column and you read the right.
[They alternate their reading with commentaries along the way].

DICK: Remember when Baby saw his first airplane? All he could say was "See. See." Well, Ashbery's poems resemble that biplane whizzing over.

JANE: He's a poet of marshes and estuaries.

DICK: He seems to regard time as a horizontal process.

JANE: True, if there are no vertical processes (lines), how can anything run up to God?

DICK: Time is seamless, without beginning or end. We swim on an onward sweeping time-wave.

JANE: He's ripped off Swinburne's "Thalassius."

DICK: He often evokes childhood. Our favorite blanket, he writes, "buries us in a joyous tumult." As children our sorrow "is precipitated out."

JANE: You make him sound like Wordsworth. Child as father of the man. Impulses from a vernal wood. "Except as ye are little children," or however it goes.

DICK: I see a lot of Wordsworth in Ashbery—and some of that other old William, Blake. And babbling—I'm not being pejorative—is in that tradition. The Prelude is loquacious speech. You feel distressed: Byronic displacements, Shelleyan exaltations, Keatsian triumphs over blood and expectorated lung cells. We feel threatened. We still our fears through singing and babbling. We fill the Universal Void.

JANE: A hundred and fifty years have passed since the Romantics. You make

Ashbery sound like a Camus Existentialist—and except for a handful of poets (Kinnell and Merwin) the mode is passé.

DICK: Where Kinnell constructs a verse rhetoric against absurdity by asserting a vigorous will, Ashbery inveighs against a Sysyphean universe, fashioning looser poetic forms. He's writing, he says, "Poems that are as inexact as mathematics."

JANE: Well, that's a conundrum.

DICK: I don't agree that his babble-poems aim for a mathematical purity. Something clicks.

JANE: In the prayer section of Litany he asks for "shrewd, regular knowledge" to counteract a meaningless universe. He hungers "for something to calm his appetite," some "positive chunk" of faith counteracting "the freedom of too much speculation."

DICK. That's as smug as anything T. S. Eliot ever said in Ash Wednesday where he urged us to "sit still" and keep the faith.

JANE: Yet, Ashbery is more humane, friendlier. He sits there beside us on the edge of the abyss, chatting, and dangling his legs while we dangle ours.

DICK: He decoys us from our mystical plight by reciting a lyrical flow of childhood memories and delivering thoughts on environmental pollution, death, sex, eternity, Casey at the bat, and criticism.

JANE: Whitman was also threnodic. "Out of the Cradle Endlessly Rocking," amazingly orchestrated, segues from topic to topic, often without transitions.

DICK: A potpourri is an extended prayer.

JANE: "The way to nothing," Ashbery says here, "is the way to all things."

DICK: As part of that "riddle of the skies" (the "meaningless / rolling and lurching" of the universe), our mind surges, falls, lifts, and ebbs in a thematic chaos.

JANE: And, as we know from Whitman and Swinburne, the sea, verbal and symbolic, flashing endlessly silvered meanings.

DICK: And some of Litany winks at Alexander Pope. There's also an Edward Lear-like creature, a beast in a pen. There is campy verse—"Honey, it's all Greek to me." And there are Walter Paterian "filaments of silence."

JANE: Oh, Baby would have so loved him!

DICK: Our minds lack justified right margins. As in a life, with a single fixed margin, what transpires in a poem are elusive flappings, constrictions, and expandings. Ashbery knows this well and composes a parody on the theme using a "Beatitudes" vernacular:

> And so
> I say unto you: beware the right margin
> Which is unjustified; the left
> Is justified and can take care of itself
> But what is in between expands and flaps
> The end sometimes past the point
> Of conscious inquiry, noodling in the near
> Infinite, off—limits.

JANE: Our minds seldom proceed from point A to B to C without meandering. And yet, poets since Chaucer have shown us that the well-made poem is an unfortunate perversion of how our minds work, a deceit even.

DICK: Metaphysically, our left margins are fixed by God, society, and family. The right approximate our free will.

DICK: I prefer parallels with photography better than metaphysics.

JANE: Well, he suggests the parallel. "Litany" begins: "I photographed all things" Whitman again. Encyclopedic?

DICK: He's the Edward Steichen of American verse.

JANE: Or the Cecil Beaton.

DICK: He doesn't much like portraits—they're boring. He prefers landscapes. Photography records elusive hints of meaning snatched from the ether. "Preludes" is the word he uses. He writes a series of snapshots, superb pictures, visual poems. And you can have fuzzy pictures, right, by rubbing vaseline over your lens.

JANE: A Watteau shimmer says a lot more than a Chardin glow. It depends on how reflective you want to be.

DICK: In another passage, "I have heard that in spring the mountains change," a landscape stimulates reflections and a serial poem unfolds. A man chews "on darkness like a rind," finding no "comfort" in the "crevices between us."

JANE: Does he fear he won't find pictures?

DICK: And end up repeating himself? Listen to these lines: In "We fucked too long," his lovers, after sex, decide it's "too late to stay home" and so go to a film they've already seen a dozen times. They are the movie; movie life transcends theirs. It's too easy to play possum with life.

JANE: His social nostalgia draws him into playing ostrich.

DICK: He never preaches and shares my Existential dark. His wit and casual manner ingratiate:

> Anyway, I am the author. I want to
> Talk to you for a while, teach you
> About some things of mine, some things
> I've put away, more still that I remember
> With a tinge of sadness....

JANE: I'd like to meet him.

DICK: Don't let him fool you. He may have ulterior motives. Like the rest of us, he wants to "get something out of life." If we fail to share his quest, he warns, "the night has no end." His fatigue is my fatigue.

JANE: He likes commonplace objects: coffee pots and taxis. Here's a marvelous parody of a bad song by William Morris or Dante Rossetti:

> The lovers saunter away

It is a mild day in May
With music and birdsong alway
And the hope of love in the way
like Chaucer or bad Rossetti.

DICK: When he satirizes, parodies, or burlesques he's never vicious. And we are amused when we see the absurd in what has amused him.

JANE: Yes, I love the fun he finds amidst the ashes.

DICK: Abandon the still-life, he advises: "those oranges / And apples, and dishes, what have they to do / With us...?" Plenty, he says, paradoxically, turning from them to landscapes of the mind—to capes and peninsulas, to sea gales: "We can see / Into them and come out on the other side..."

JANE: That's a good metaphor for his poetry; his expansive forms resemble landscapes.

DICK: Visions require space; jolts of recognition do not. To meditate on a pair of peasant's shoes, or a sick hawk on one's back porch, is not the same as being lost in a sea-scape.

JANE: We're at those margins again.

DICK: This may be Ashbery's contribution to esthetics—his return to the long poem; we no longer see poems as "verbal constructs."

JANE: Strange how a poet so arcane has won all the literary prizes there are.

DICK: Try this idea: let's say that the "duration" of a poem is determined by the number of miles you'd have to walk in order to read through a poem. As we plod, reading, our mind wanders to the path, to the scenery off to one side, to the sky. We can, therefore, describe some of the poem but not all of it. Though we began at point A and stop at point B, we miss much in between.

JANE: Yet, we've understood enough so that what we haven't understood doesn't bother us. After all, nature has its rewards, its concavities and convexities.

DICK: Our old need to translate poems into exact ideas or prose equivalents no longer obtains. And, obviously, as elusive as Ashbery is, he's getting through to many readers.

JANE: He's not aloof; that may be his secret. When we paint wooden tulips and little jockeys for our lawns he's there to help. He even brings his own brushes.

DICK: He's so right about our lives being collections of perhapses, almosts, and only ifs. Transversals (another of his words) define our lives. Ecstasies are "unfinal."

JANE: Are you implying he's a sexy poet?

DICK: That's a silly leap.

JANE: You hinted earlier at his androgyny—much of his writing seems feminine, and much seems masculine.

DICK: He's child-like.

JANE: I'm never threatened sexually.

DICK: Remember when we were kids? Those doctor games? Just listen to these allusions to boys and their "meat"; that's kinky. So is this passage on the dangers of gay cruising, in campy end-rhymes:

> The sleeve detaches itself from the body
> As the two bodies do from the throng of gay
> Lovers on the prowl that do move and sway
> In the game of sunrise they play
> For stakes no higher than the gray
> Ridge of loam that protects the way
> Around the graveyard that sexton worm may
> Take to the mound Death likes to stay
> Near so as to be able to slay
> The lovers who humbly come to pray
> Him to pardon them yet his stay
> Of execution includes none and they lay
> Hope aside and soon disappear.

JANE: What can I say? A fun verse romp.

DICK: His versicles here runneth over.

JANE: Both genders appear in "Field full of people in gentle raiment." Prowling lovers, enjoying the "contagious" air, seem special, as lovers do. As they promenade near the sea, the waves stand on tiptoe around the ball / of land where they all are." That's lovely.

DICK: The paired voices, heard simultaneously, are facets of Ashbery's consciousness. Voice A is reflective and conceptual, more concerned with public issues. B is intimate, personal, more conversational. At an actual recital, both voices, together, would borrow latching points one from the other.

JANE: I'd like now to read the entire book.

DICK: Remember my equation between reading poems and walking? Tomorrow we'll hike up Mt. San Gorgonio? That's over nine miles, right? The highest peak in southern California. We'll cover a lot of verse.

NEWS FROM ROBERT BLY'S UNIVERSE

Mountains, rivers, caves, and fields quicken us in solitude. We leap toward connections lost to our rational selves and defy logic. This, as Bly explains in *Leaping Poetry: An Idea with Poems and Translations* (1975), occurs when the newest of our three brains is activated. This, the Reptile Brain, acts coldly to preserve us against dangers real or imagined. The Mammal Brain, constituting the cortex, creates our institutions, affections, and sexual fervors. The third, and least-used brain, one lying as a one-eighth inch thick layer over the Mammal Brain, is the New Brain, the neo-cortex; this generates "wildness" and produces the "leaping poetry" written by Lorca, Rilke, Neruda, Takahashi, and Vallejo.

This activated New Brain evokes verbal miracles. "Watery syllables" well up from mythic depths, from the Dordogne caves and the aboriginal South Sea islands where men lived "under the cloak / of an animal's sniffing." Ancient angers explode. One of Bly's poems, "Words Rising," echoes howls once declaimed by ancient priests in furs holding aloft luminous barley heads. They generate verbal wildness. We are "bees" with language for "honey." We express the inexpressive, the archetypal, what was residual long before the invention of the wheel. Both celebrant (priest) and sufferer (aborigine and political victim) dwell within our words:

Wicker baskets and hanged men
come to us as stanzas and vowels.
We see a million hands with dusty
palms turned up inside each verb,
lifted. There are eternal vows
held inside the word "Jericho"*

---

*Reprinted by permission from *Robert Bly: When Sleepers Wake*, ed. by J.Peseroff, University of Michigan, 1984, pp. 304-314.

As mystery, language reflects profound events unlimited by space. During meditation, cortextual cells generate dance and ecstasy.

I simplify, and urge readers to turn to Bly's provocative essays (in addition to "Leaping Poetry" see "I Came Out of the Mother Naked" in *Sleepers Joining Hands* (1973), and the prose sections of his Sierra Club anthology, *News of the Universe*). I wish here to employ his main distinctions as a way of perceiving his new poems. His verse techniques reflect his theories. No matter how good Bly was in the past—and he was good—this poetry is an impressive advance. The *Man in the Black Coat Turns* was one of the seminal works of the eighties.

Some readers complain that Bly's poems are almost completely devoid of living persons other than himself. Clear the stage is Bly's refrain. The creative occurs in a nurturing isolation. Forest, pasture, clearing, the isolated building, all suit him for meditation. His writing-shack is so private that even his wife doesn't know where it is, and he carries his own drinking water with him in jars. He recalls Thoreau with whom he has many similarities, and tangentially, Wordsworth. He would not hesitate to eat Thoreau's woodchuck raw if it would intensify his perceptions; and he would welcome the stark fear induced in Wordsworth by that shadow looming suddenly over the water at Mt. Skiddaw. "Urge and urge and urge," wrote Whitman: "Always the procreant urge of the world."

Bly is unlike other contemporary nature poets who seldom take themselves off very far from the boat landing or the fire tower. In him there's nothing genteel. His reclusiveness is itself a metaphor for toughness. He is no Sunday dabbler, taking nature trails through museum-forests which some placid ranger has marked for easy recognition. His secret places are invested with agents of psychic confrontation: mythic mothers and fathers bearing-fangs; the male instincts to kill, waste, and subdue are omnipresent in our psyches, in conflict with our gentler, creative selves. Only in solitude is our mental subsoil activated, proving equal to these conflicts, stilling the nagging, demanding Father who speaks for order, reason, and obedience. You can't build a birdhouse or haul much manure sitting on your haunches in a forest, or in the lotus position beside a stream.

To achieve quietude, Bly has explored various disciplines, including Tibetan ones. No matter the guides, he remains himself, quizzical, self-reliant, choosing from an eclectic feast only what will enhance his spirit. There is no wastage.

We observe Bly on his own mind-stage with minimal properties, peopled with a few souls acting out scenes as he invites them in. Like Whitman (about whom Bly has written a most valuable and perceptive essay, [in *Walt Whitman: The Measure of His Song*, ed. Jim Perlman, Holy Cow Press, 1981] we "loaf" with him and share his urges and leapings, which drift to us like bird feathers, or leap with the brilliance of arcing trout, or does in meadows. Energy and largeness, two of Whitman's favorite concepts, for Bly induce ecstasy and insight. To adapt one of Mary Baker Eddy's images, Bly is utterly at ease in those natural vestibules where the material sense of things disappears.

Before scrutinizing Bly's new work, I should like to speculate briefly on Bly the Surrealist. Despite the fact that he sees his poems deriving from, or inspired by, poets he calls Surrealist—Rilke, Vallejo, Lorca, and Neruda, among others—I don't find the term useful when applied to him. Most obviously, Surrealism refers to that movement in the arts initiated by André Breton, c. 1924, attracting Aragon, Eluard, Desnos, Cocteau, Dali, and Tanguy, among other writers and artists. They sought juxtapositions of irrational images, often derived from easy associations. The result was an often trivial, zany melange produced by an imagery of pyrotechnics rather than one emergent from a substratum of psychic fears and joys, from dream and archetypal energies. Bly's surrealism is of these deeper perceptions. No Tinker Bell waves her wand over a gaggle of pastel oblivion ha-has. No snickering, skeleton-bone, Halloween belly-riffs here. Bly's images emerge from a neocortical loam, with an unpredictability and speed distressing to readers prizing the linear, the rational, the easily deciphered—readers with Mammal brains. Bly is a whirl of color in a field of cabbages.

"Visiting the Farallones" will clarify what I mean. Here Bly revisits concerns that have occupied his energies for years—the pollution of the environment and the insane destruction of natural life. While his fervor has not diminished, his approach has. He seems more content now to allow his rage a less programmatic, less didactic, breath. Imagery, rather than direct statements. He trusts his readers more.

Clubbing seals initiates the poem, followed by the decimation of whales and tortoises. The latter are crammed into shipholds. Often for Bly, the daily news triggers memories of past disasters. The plundering of the tortoises is a leap back to the nineteenth century (a.k.a. "The Age of Darwin") when sailing ships used tortoises for ballast and food. There are more connections, as Bly arraigns decadent human cultures. The Roman empire was the first universal culture to rot. The American frontier, symbolized by a wagon breaking to pieces on boulders, is gone, the landscape is now littered with beer cans and the air is befouled. "Darkness," Bly says, is reality—as is the feather he spies lying near him on snow, leading his gaze to the carcass of a half-eaten rooster. For most of us, a maimed bird is revolting, no matter how rich the thematic evocations. But if we are to be enlightened, Bly believes, we must scrutinize the gross and painful as well as the scenic and palatable. "Crumbling" is the word he employs to interweave these disparate materials. Animal species have crumbled, as have empires, and once vital frontiers.

Thus far, Bly has seen objects clearly. Now he turns to a fresh image, one not literally seen, contemporary, emblematic of all crumblings. In an old folks' home, life crumbles, wasted and brutalized. A sadistic society tucks these ancients out of sight, much as sailing ships stowed the turtles. There's a perversion / inversion here of a life principle. The death-mother works in loathsome ways her wonders to perform.

In "Snowbanks North of the House," the mysterious man in black of the book's title starts up a hill, changes his mind, and returns to the bottom. Is he a minister? An undertaker? Is he Bly's father? Is he Death? What would he have found on the hill? Once more, Bly generates thematic leaps by an initial meditation on something concrete—here it's a great snowdrift stopped about six feet from a house, a phenomenon I witnessed often when I was a boy in northern Wisconsin. In meeting the house, vectored air currents kept the snow back. If the sweeps had piled themselves tight against the building, that building would be insulated and warm. This house, though, contains failed marraiges and memories of children who don't write home. A son dies. The bereaved parents never speak to one another again. The church too fails, as the wine sours, and the minister "falls." These failures seem debris in some ocean of life, lifting and falling (failing) all night long. The saving image is the moon, as it proceeds through clouds and stars, achieving a splendid isolation, a symbol for the self apart, for a lone sufficiency bathed in moon-radiance.

Like the snow drifts, the man in the black coat, who eschews the hilltop, symbolizes the poet in isolation. He seems an "advocate of darkness" (see "For My Son Noah, Ten Years Old"), an associate of the Earth death-mother who appears to ease our way through life. He also suggests what Bly terms "the masculine soul" or "Father consciousness." In its "middle range," the masculine soul is "logic and fairness"; in its higher leapings it "hurries toward the spirit." Like the feminine consciousness, its counterpart and opposite, it is a "good," can't be eradicated and remains ever mysterious. It is a "veil," Bly says, drawn against the death so feared by men. The best we can hope for, Bly writes, is to meld these two consciousnesses and experience what lies beyond the veil. Bly's best images possess a koan-like quality of unresolved suggestiveness—so also with the black-suited man. I shall return to him.

In another poem, "the walnut" of Bly's brain glows in solitude. Even when thus charged, his insights are not all they might be; he has mere intimations of the visionary, of deciphering the vast enigmas behind Shelley's veil. Even Albert Einstein reputedly utilized only a small part of his neocortex. By stimulating his third brain, Bly releases a genie who, alas, flies off to hover over some "car cemetery" and won't return to his bottle. We must accept the presence of such contradictions and our dimly realized visions. By accepting, we may be preparing for later insights of a hitherto unknown grandeur.

One of the best of Bly's efforts to reflect the glowings of that "walnut brain" appears in "The Dried Sturgeon," a prose poem. Insight, ecstasy, growth, and death are the primary motifs. On an October walk along a riverbank, Bly finds a dried-out sturgeon which he examines. A "speckled nose-bone" leads back to an eye socket, behind which is a "dark hole" where soft gills once grew. This hole, a sort of cave, the poet enters to confront his female self. A hunchback appears and is made whole by the "sweet dark," a virgin with magical black stones in her cloak.

These seem elements in a fairy tale, evocative of the narrative inconsistencies children love. Our poet, himself flawed, enters his healing meditation via images of fish corpse, pine needle, sand, and hunchback. Underground, he thrills to the proximity of Death, a duende experience he prizes in other poets. As he returns to light, to Father consciousness symbolized by the sturgeon's scales which are "dry, swift, organized, tubular, straight and humorless as railway schedules, the big clamp of the boxcar, tapering into sleek womanly death," he is invigorated. In a sense, he closes up the rich female concavities of the "dark hole." Reason prevails, symbolized by the straight line, by schedules, by speed—antitheses for the female underworld. To this "womanly" region we shall return at our deaths, completing the circle that began on leaving the womb, on peregrinations to and through our father-selves.

Another striking presence of shadow/duende is in "Mourning Pablo Neruda," written in brief lines reminiscent of the Chilean poet's own. Bly is driving to his shack. Beside him on the seat is a sweating jar of water. Glancing down, Bly observes that the jostling jar creates a wet shadow on the seat, a paradigm for Neruda's death, a shadowing itself of subtle, tragic effects. Bly drives through granite quarries, filled with blocks soon to be shaped into gravestones. A leap: our memories of the dead are watery traces within us, mere hints of the moisture still resident within granite. If we accept this diminution, we see that the dead have merely flowed "around us" to the Gulf Stream and out to the Eternal Sea.

Bly's techniques of moving from the concrete to the universal are well-realized in "Finding an Old Ant Mansion," another prose poem. Asleep on a floor, he dreams that a rattlesnake is biting him . He rises, dresses, and goes to a pasture where he senses the ground beneath his shoes, their rubbery texture allowing feel in a way leather would not. He likes these "rolls and humps," and marvels that the earth "never lies flat." It must accommodate a varied debris both falling down upon it (trees) and emerging from its depths (stones). He passes through a strip of hardwoods to another pasture, and finds a chunk of wood on the ground, strangely etched into some sixteen layers by ants. He fetches the piece home and props it on his desk.

The cavities in the wood create doors into "cave-dark" places—Persephone redivivus. Leaps evoke memories: the shadows recall the "heavy brown of barn stalls" he knew as a boy, and other dark insights—a daughter understands her mother's silences. The ant artifact is a universe all its own, a paradigm for our psyches, so antlike and male, in their obsessions. We scurry to execute our father's hopes and wishes: "infant ants awaken to old father-worked halls, uncle-loved boards, walls that hold the sighs of the pasture, the moos of confused cows...some motor cars from the road, held in the same wood, given shape by Osiris' love." According to designs taught us by our great benefactor and primal father image, himself son of Nut and Geb, the legendary Osiris, we shape our lives.

The ant-riddled wood suggests primeval forces (it recalls, perhaps, in its unchewed state, the erect father) and provides residences, "apartments," for spirits to inhabit. The ants, thus, have wrought "a place for our destiny" that sweep of time within which "we too labor, and no one sees our labor." Uncannily, and with a delicate compassion, Bly retrieves the specific from the universal, returning the motif to himself. He recalls his own father whose labors he has symbolically discovered in this chunk of wood. What follows? Who will discover Bly's labors when he dies? His wood will lie somewhere in a pasture "not yet found by a walker." This poem moves me: the gentle voice, so mature and exploring, is the exfoliation of a man large in both physique and spirit. Bly's leap into that image of our lives as wood pieces waiting for discovery resolves the poem profoundly in areas of the psyche hitherto untapped. To most observers, that anteaten, riddled hunk of dead fibers would deserve, if noticed at all, to be thrust aside by a boot.

Bly's gatherings of objects include many we normally feel squeamish about: a partially devoured bird, a dangling eyeball. A "sick" rose, as William Blake knew, is as conducive to insight as a healthy one. To see whole, Bly implies, we must encompass all of Experience we can, the positive and the negative, the creative and the destructive. In "Kennedy's Inauguration," a Sister hands Bly the seed of a witch hazel tree, a globular fruit with hornlike projections. When it ripened, it discharged its seed in an explosive burst. The pod is as fertile, one feels, as Persephone's pomegranate. Now pinecone dry (an echo of the desiccated sturgeon), the pod is the size of a cow's eyeball. The seeing once possible there, like that in the eyeball, has "exploded out through the eye-holes," leaving behind a husk of spikes and dark vacancies resembling hen beaks "widening in fear."

Bly next reviews his day. He went on errands twice, both times avoiding the funeral parlor. He held three "distant" conversations (by phone?). The gift of the seed followed. Now, as he starts to meditate, the cow's eye reminds him of a Lorenzo shot by a cannonball that left his eye dangling from his face, a horror. Like the seedpod, history, exploding, is both germinative and sterile, humanizing and destructive. In this poem, though, it "seeds" the worst—mayhem and torture: a Papal candidate is murdered by an enemy. Belgian King Leopold's plantation overseer (ca. World War I) chops off the hands of an African youth and deposits them near his father. Fascists destroy contraceptive clinics and carry the women off to breeding brothels. Our drugged sex-mistress, Marilyn Monroe, lies dead on her bed. Young men are decimated in purposeless war, viz., the Vietnam conflict which Bly, as we know, protested vociferously and courageously. A Marine whose head and feet are shot off "cries" for a medic. John Kennedy, a vigorous, youthful man, stands in the cold, taking his oath of office. Nearby waits the old poet Robert Frost. Bly hopes that the inauguration will produce a new national destiny. Hindsight, of course, has it otherwise. The Reptile brain kills and wastes. A father ejects his seed from his loins, delaying his son's return to his primal mother. She, in imitation of Persephone, carries a round red fruit in her hand. Both figures draw us into magnetic fields; both must be departed from, abandoned, and returned to. The father, finally, may be the more difficult of the pair to please.

In "The Prodigal Son," a son kneels on dried cobs in a swine pen and reflects on his hostile father. He hears the latter's death-fearing plea to the doctor: "Don't let me die!" and recalls a particularly venomous altercation. As he was dragging his father over the floor, the father saw a crack in the boards and shouted for him to stop: "I only dragged my father that far!" Brutal conflict seems the norm. As the son resists the father, he pursues his own maleness. His departure vexes not only the father but also the mother—both feel deserted by him (cf. the parents in "Snowbanks North of the House"). Before he can accept his father as an equal, the son must dance to his own music, honor his own dreams, and write poems.

In "The Ship's Captain Looking Over the Rail," Bly observes that to tell a captain or a father that they are "good" is to say nothing; for these men conceal their true scars, limps, and blemishes from underlings—sailors and children. In "Kneeling Down to Look Into a Culvert," the final poem in the book, Bly merges his own father and his sons. The culvert (as reason, rod, conduit) is a masculine image from which the female water is eleased into merry light. Bly imagines his children splashing in the brightness at the culvert's end, where they sense his presence, and where he performs a similar commemorative act for his own father.

"My Father's Wedding 1924" links Bly's father with that puzzling figure in the black coat. Once again a prosaic object, another chunk of wood, stripped of its bark, triggers leaps and recollections. What was Bly's father like, as a younger man? Was he a masked birdfather, Bhutanian, with giant teeth and a pig nose, dancing ritually on a bad leg? Was he really as assured as he seemed? No. He concealed a limp from his son. When he, Bly, fathered his own children, he saw that his father's limp reflected his craving to be loved. Showing affection has not been a desirable masculine trait. Like the log which once held bark, Bly's father kept people at a distance, even members of his family. He covered his vulnerabilities with a gnarled, rough exterior. At his wedding, his true bride was not the woman of flesh and blood beside him; rather, she stood invisible between him and his bride interposing herself as a kind of Fata Morgana. This strange ceremony was performed by a man in a black coat, a preacher who lifted his "book" and called "for order."

Who is the preacher? Possibly he serves as a father-spirit who marries us to our mythic mother, Death, as she waits in those shadowy concavities, death-spaces, burnished through eye sockets, wood, and culverts. The father in black appears when we wed ourselves to Death, which we do when we allow our emotions, our feminine selves, full play, thereby resolving our struggles with our father. Thus, partially fulfilled, we are able to proceed to our Mother (Death) with minimal fear. Male and female spirits balanced.

I don't pretend that my reading of the black figure as a kind of Robert Mitchum Bible-thumper who initiates our journey back to the womb is the only possible reading. The image remains complex. To read the figure merely as Death is facile. Finally, my efforts to sort meanings have made me aware of how male directed are my critical acts.

RAY BRADBURY:
THE COMPLETE POEMS

Readers who value the art of poetry will be encouraged by the title of this book. *Complete Poems* means, let's hope, that no more poems are forthcoming from this author. For these rambling, self-indulgent, anachronistic writings are awful! They have as much to do with contemporary poetry as those lace and velvet cuffs Romantic poets used to wear have to do with nail-studded leather wrist-bands. Even on their own terms, as anachronisms, they are bad. Perhaps I am unfair to expect better from mortals as famous as Bradbury who somehow (as many celebrities seem to do) feel that their fame as fiction writers, after-dinner speakers, conference ornaments, pulp screen-writers, and millionaires means zilch until they arrive as "POETS."

Serious poets would be less exercised had Bradbury foregone displaying his ignorance about contemporary poetry in a self-serving introduction. He arrays himself with Melville, Poe, and Dickinson as he condemns the serious, professional poetry around him. Celebrity Hounds will, of course, buy the book, as they have bought the three previous ones (here gathered into a single tome), and Bradbury will get richer, be invited to dine out more, and be asked to read his wretched verse in public. He might better have imitated James Michener who, rather than self-aggrandize by writing embarrassing verse, gave thousands of his fiction royalty dollars for publishing serious poetry. Almost a sainted act, one is tempted to say.

Lest my severity appear as little more than a diatribe, let me point out some of Bradbury's specific flaws. Here echoes of Robert Service, Edgar Guest, and Clement Moore abound:

> And the creeps and the shades and the shambles
> Gave a shake and a mourn and a yawn
> And with moaning, ochoning, lamenting
> Ran off down the red crack of dawn.

There are also lavish, bad echoes of Shakespeare, Milton, Melville, and Swinburne:

"O vast insucked gasp of loss," "in soughing whistled whining all a whisper," "his earth-dark finger traveling the pages," etc. There's a smorgasbord of wrenched, almost funny inventions: a polar wind comes on "to hair his spine," Ahab's whale (he turns up a lot) is "builded out of steel and loxxed with energy." Bradbury is most inept when he is philosophical; cliches are firewheels. When he scribbles family and childhood recollections he is often winsome.

I don't protest Bradbury's desire to be a poet but rather his disservice to poetry. He draws readers who already hate the form; and once they have put good old Ray back on the shelf, they'll go right on hating it. His poems sound the way they know bad poems should—genteel, pompous, sing-songy, cute, and clever. He won't inspire a single reader to ask "Is that all there is?" And that's sad, especially since most of the serious poets of America continue to go largely unread and unpublished by trade houses who specialize in the most noisome regurgitations of celebrity best-sellers.

JAMES BROUGHTON

A LONG UNDRESSING: THE EARLY POEMS

James Broughton's early poems best delineate the function of poetry as he sees it, in a world inimical to beauty, fantasy, freedom, and sexual love. "Desperate Love," witten in the 1950's, establishes a labyrinthine, entrammeling, and suffocating world. Caught in labyrinths, "plugged in" by "inert sorrow," we hobble about on driftwood crutches. In a society where the bellies of citizens are "pre-shrunk" to famished imaginations, the Keatsian poet (Broughton declares he'd "like to bake a nightingale pie.") is despised. Broughton wants "to revise the local menu." In "A Forced Sojourn in Moribundia" the measure called for is dual: first, something drastic must occur; second, a new measure of music must be created to free us. Baubles will suffice, aerifications of "small surprises," "little poems."

Broughton shares with William Morris, W.B. Yeats and W.H. Auden the view that poetry "makes nothing happen" in a materialist world. Few aficionados of Beauty will feel blessed by the angels of art. Like Morris, who saw himself as the idle singer of "an empty day," Broughton proceeds as though the universe desires songbirds and lovers. He is inventively playful; in fact, no other poet is quite like him. Fairies dance, sprites cavort, magical godmothers regale us with ballads, unicorns rest their loving heads in our laps, winged steeds swim through star-lit skies, a zodiac of tutelary gods, goddesses, and angels amuse us, and singers of nursery rhymes and nonsense poems extol lost Blakean worlds of fancy and imagination. And, yes, there are Boschian demons and witches ensconced in their gingerbread houses, orchestrating natural cataclysms.

Models and Influences

Broughton's work stands outside prevailing fashions of free verse, poems of direct experience, confessional poetry, and poems of genteel gloom conditioned by feelings of private and societal failure in a nuclear age. His spirit-kin are Blake (especially of *The Songs of Innocence and Experience*), Shakespeare (of the songs, particularly those sung by fools, fairies, and madmen), Mother Goose (in both her scary and joyous selves), anonymous ancient balladeers (with their arrangements of questions and responses used to unravel bloody dreams), various lyricists from The Greek Anthology (particularly evident in Broughton's most recent hymns to Priapus), the author of "Sir Gawain and the Green Knight," Dante Alighieri, Spenser (of the "Shepherd's Calendar"), Christina Rossetti (of "Goblin Market"), Dante Gabriel Rossetti (of the ecstatic transposition of high Catholicism to the service of erotic love), Edward Lear and Lewis Carroll (of the great nonsense poems), Robert Louis Stevenson (of *A Child's Garden of Verses*) and, closer to our own time, Stevie Smith, Robert Duncan, Helen Adam, and Michael McClure.

Despite these connections, Broughton never servilely imitates models. His diction can be simple, lucid, matter-of-fact, and even archaic—when he wishes to suggest the Songs of Solomon, old ballads, Shakespearean songs, or Blake's poems. His verse moves through complex meters as well as through broader free verse forms. While his tone is predominately witty and playful, there are sable darks and psychological distresses. He ranges from colloquial idioms to ornate and elusive voices. Occasionally there is doggerel, usually in pieces which seem like Mother Goose rhymes written for playful and satiric effects.

Blake

As one reads the *Selected Poems, A Long Undressing*, published by Jargon Press, in 1971, one thinks often of William Blake. The book, incidentally, includes poems written over two decades, from 1949-1969, and is a must for any reader wishing to know Broughton's verse. The title comes from Walter De La Mare: "They say death's a going to bed; I doubt it; / but anyhow life's a long undressing."

Like Blake's child born into innocence, as one moves through experience towards death, life is a perpetual "undressing." One grows increasingly vulnerable. In *Musical Chairs* (1950), Broughton marks the devastating relationship of parents and children: "Being a child is no excuse. / Being a parent is a form of abuse." In "Mrs Mother Has a Nose," a sensitive child assesses her mother, borrowing from Grimms' Tales to make her point: mother's huge nose resembles a sniffing rat: Mother, child decides, has three atrocious noses:

> What a big nose Mrs Mother has,
> the better to smell her dear.
> Sniff sniff sniff it comes round the door,
> detective of everything queer.
>
> Two big noses Mrs Mother has,

the better to quell her dear.
"I smell something odd, I smell something bad,
what is that smell in here?"

Three big noses Mrs Mother has,
they grow and grow in the night.
Sniff sniff sniff her naughty naughty dear!
And she also can smell with her ears.

Still innocent, Broughton's wise child sings of quasi-sexual matters dimly
perceived. In "Papa Has a Pig" he's fascinated by the father's penis: "Papa has a
pig, / And a big pig too. / Papa plays a piggy-toe that I can't do." Papa's pig is the
"fattest...you ever did feel."

The most destructive legacy of adults is guilt. When Blake's nurse changes
her tune (in "Nurse's Song," from *The Songs of Experience*), she no longer
encourages her charges to romp and laugh, crossly deciding they have wasted
their day. In Broughton's "Backyard Elegies," a child addresses a misbehaving
apple acting outside the norm for late-season apple behavior:

What are you doing here, little apple?
    The blossoms are faded,
    the leaves are no more,
    the cart's gone to market,
    the worm' s in the core,
    God's left for the winter,
    the world's a backdoor.
Where are you rolling to little apple?

In "Little Boy's Nasty News," a miserable lad possessed of a pimple finds a wart
on his fingers, "baubling" them with "tell-tale bumps." Somehow he has betrayed
adult norms; i.e., he has played sexually with a "nasty" boy.

In "The Sweet-Tooth Witch," a not so generic witch inverts adult values to
the delight of all recalcitrant children. This creature eats only good little girls. If
you wish to be spared being eaten, misbehave. What a contrast with the genteel
norms extolled by Robert Louis Stevenson in *A Child's Garden of Verses* where
children are always proper and mindful of their elders:

I've an appetite for curls and dimples in a chin.
Awhiz through the midnight stratospherey
on my lickety spittle I zeppelin,

pursuing little girls who are good as gold
to cook them up for supper in my eerie.

> I marinate and lard them,
> I roast their thin-skin hides,
> I bake a custard pudding
> of their saccharine insides,
> and since they have no spines at all
> I pickle their backsides.

I love a dainty blush and neatly washed ears.
Mother's darling helpers, Daddy's perfect dears,
nice proper prissies who never had a wicked wish,
all good little girls who do what they're told
are just my dish.

Here Broughton weaves a highly sophisticated metrics, eschewing the rocking horse rhythms of conventional nursery rhymes. The basic foot is anapestic. The lines weave through hexameters, pentameters, tetrameters, and trimeters, with an occasional unstressed syllable closing a line, viz., "the midnight stratospherey." Another device is the sudden appearance of a line that has no evident caesura half-way through, as in lines 1, 12, 13, and 14, all in hexameters.

In "Fruits of Experience," as Broughton's maturing child peregrinates through the world, fine residues of innocence remain. While he believes that pomegranates derive from "red hot pearls" and that cherries are "the hearts of baby girls," he is clearly aware of the nay-saying adult world: "A copy says No / a priest says No / but a little boy hardly ever." As he proceeds, only vaguely daunted, he imagines the "true-eyed pilgrim" he hopes to be, striding straight up a road filled with starving cats, carrying a deep sea net, with "field flowers in his mouth":

> Nothing has to be this way,
> everything can be any way.

He is a paradigm for Broughton's reader, the sensitive pilgrim who maintains innocence as he moves through worlds of experience. The concluding stanza of the concluding poem of *Musical Chairs* (1950) sets a pilgrim tone, and is an invitation not dissimilar from that of Blake's "Laughing Song." The passage from Blake precedes Broughton's below:

When the painted birds laugh in the shade
Where with cherries and nuts is spread,
Come live & be merry and join with me
To sing the sweet chorus of Ha, Ha, He. (1789).

Dump out the lead, the cold fears in your boots.
With a warmy ha ha keep stirring your stumps.
Audacity's the buddy for your long-term trip.
Don't waste a single sorry on the tch tch frumps.

> You're never as bad as they say, O they!
> You're never as bad as they say.

Scorpion Sorrows

With the *Sorrows of Scorpio,* dedicated to Anais Nin, Broughton departs the world of children. This work was apparently unpublished before it appeared in *A Long Undressing;* yet, since the arrangement of the Selected Poems is chronological, *Scorpio* falls between *Musical Chairs* (1950) and *An Almanac for Amorists* (1955). The work is unexpectedly dark. The speaker has been lanced through, rot has set in, and the dance of life he'd hoped to run, terminates. He's left enraged, lost in a fumbling lifelimp.

One poem, "Bridge to the Innermost Forest," has four hexameter quatrains with brilliant slant and end rhymes. Like Dante, fruitlessly seeking the bridge that will lead to that "innermost forest," Broughton finds himself lost in a glen of ruins and thistles. Here is the poem in its entirety. There is some faltering in the final stanza:

Bridge to the Innermost Forest
I could not match the labels where the span held the patch
in its doubling of layers on the cables of starch.
For the cape on the arch of the statuary perch
exuded all question of door and path.

I would cover it with spank or with shield or with glass,
but the multiforming gate that would never fix
kept hedging its formula for the wiry copse.
And the tensity of pitch could never be disguised.

I could not catch and mix the meaning of this glen

where the wiser and the meager had already lain.
For the capture of the curtain's thistling stone
excluded all answer of lock and hinge.

I would cover it with fear or with plaster or with noose,
but the multiforming gate would admit of no release
nor admire an oasis in the squamous woods.
And the density of ditch could never be surmised.

Much of the visual matter, filmic, belongs to the period of Broughton's career that produced the Cannes award winning film "The Pleasure Garden" filmed in the ruins of London's Crystal Palace, built by the Victorians in 1851, destroyed by fire in 1936, and finally demolished in 1941, since it served as a landmark for raiding German planes. Broughton's film lingers over ruined statuary and gardens, employing a poetic surrealism. His poem,"The Roads To The Crossroads," with its overtones of Oedipus at the famous juncture where he murders his father, is in couplets, each containing a camera-ready image. A weather cock wobbles back and forth; there's a blind hag, possibly a ruined statue; and dolls lie in a ditch. Aphrodite's garden, now burnt slag, "still crannies flowers." A cross "grows greening" with vegetation. The poet leaves the ruined garden, and, in extremity of spirit, takes shelter in a madman's house before moving to a sanitarium for shock treatment. His distress is almost overwhelming: "the smaller the night hours the larger the scissors!" The weasel is a predatory creature rare in these poems:

Likeness of the weasel
nibbling the bush-tit,
so frets the old fire under fur.

In a series of "Wrong Songs" Broughton is at his technical best, ranging from a cacophonous poem of three six-line stanzas alternating between dimeters and trimeters, and dulled repetitons of "wrong" in end-of-line positions, to a new poem lamenting the world's traps and cages. The three stanzas, quatrains, opening with pentameter and hexameter lines lean out, concluding in a modified ballad form. Another poem is a riddle alternating trimeters and dimeters. In a fourth, made of two dactyllic eight-line stanzas with an insistent end-rhyme pattern, the imagery seems appropriate for hells envisioned by Bosch, Brueghel, or *Mother Goose.*

Thorns will be worn for the masquerade kill:
knot the thistle tight underneath your chin.
Nettle-lined vest for the spine's old chill,
pin up the knees where the blood runs thin.
Stings on your fingers and welts on your toes,
burrs for your bottom sharpening the itch,
bifocal bramble-patch clamped to your nose:
thorns will be worn stitch by stitch.
Skewer new stigmata to the roots of the hair,

pierce the ear with needlepoints inch by inch.
Briery for tongue and prickly-heat prepare,
barb the tender nerve where the old shoes pinch,
Pangs for your cheeks and dagger for your eye,
porcupine your finery quill by quill,
bleeding-heart medals dress you up to die:
thorns will be worn for the masquerade kill .

In *An Almanac for Amorists* (1955) a resurgence of love and a spate of energetic lyrical writing inspired by Troubador and Renaissance songs, overcome all horrors. Musical motifs—rounds, arias in sotto voce, epithalamions, nocturnes, Shakespearean mad songs, Scottish piper songs, and scherzos—appear. All are to be sung. The series is actually followed by a masque, "A Tapestry for Voices," yet another borrowing from a once-popular Renaissance form. In San Francisco, in the late '50's, influenced by Broughton, Robert Duncan, Helen Adam, and Michael McClure, masques were written by various poets to amuse local literati. Only McClure's plays have reached a wide audience.

Broughton's "A Round For Princess Printemps" is a joyous lyric reminiscent of Provençal lyrics, with personal touches supplied by Broughton—he is never controlled by his models. Here, the puns on "round"—the musical form, the leapfrog (possibly a disguised prince?), and Apollo's sons shooting apples—are wonderfully idiosyncratic:

A Round for Princess Printemps
Spring
   spring
      runs round a green riddle,
follows a round robin cruel and gay.
   The virgins of April
    heed the call of the leapfrog
and go on a roundtrip till the middle of May—

> for the sons of Apollo
> rush out to shoot apples
> around the round riddle
> hey diddle
>
> hooray!

"The Clever Troubadour of Amoret Country" riffs on Shakespeare's "My mistress' eyes are nothing like the sun," Broughton delighting in his rustic hero's preference for illiterate, tongue-tied women. The hero boasts: "I'm a tricky toodledoo for a cock and bull race / and Delicate Crazy is my home town." A more convincingly rustic gardener's son seems lifted from a Shakespearean underplot: he boasts of his cap, "trouser," shovel and greensleeves. He will "bed a wild dove" and "will queen a kingdom" when "the rose is new." A "Jimmy" waxes metaphysical when he's disillusioned by a love mathematics he contrived as a metaphor of the earth's four corners. "A Passionate Peacemaker" declares to his "Love" that he'll return—on his terms: she may bring her "scathing needlework" and her "monkey wrench," but must secure her bloodhound and must keep her cats in their bag. Though she may now unpack her "gun-powder talcum," her "driftwood nightgown," and her "garden-party tools," he is quite sure that some further contretemps awaits.

In another "ditty," Psyche extols life to Cupid as a joyous love dance: "Sing nimble, sing careless / of impulsive exuberance, / sing loud the disgraces of exuberant love." Once again, a main theme recurs: abandon one's self to love, be spontaneous, and eschew societal mores. For Psyche "the disgraces of exuberant love" are both delicious to report and to experience. By the 1980's Broughton's poems become even wilder snubbings of conventional sexuality. "Epithalamion Of Old Uncle Ovid," a technical bravura piece, has four stanzas consisting of two six line stanzas (1 and 3) and two five line stanzas (2 and 4). The meter opens with a dactyllic line and then proceeds to supple anapests. Lines 2 and 6 alone rhyme (wed / dead). In the opening stanza, free verse, Ovid's observations on the nature of love are off-the-wall: the merriest (i.e.,freest) of lads are scarce. Sturdy ones and dull ones hastily marry. "The "epithalamion" celebrates the nuptials of a lass lucky enough to wed a spontaneous lover:

> Merry fine lads grow fewer each day
> and the sturdier ones make haste to wed,
> so it's far between and it's way roundabout
> when it comes to that specially well-met fellow
> who will row you away in a strong houseboat,
> who will row past the land of the dead.

Stanza two is a cacophonous interlude. Five lines alternate between trimeters and tetrameters. The anapestic first line followed by a trochaic second predicts a commonplace ballad resolution which Broughton avoids. The third and fourth lines are regular anapests, concluding with a final trimeter hastened on by the insertion of an anapestic foot. Here Ovid reassures the suitor that if she hopes to find a "merry lad," the romance will be bumpy. Yet, the reward will be the moon's honey kept in its golden pot:

> The way to any wedding
> doesn't take a ready road
> through the bumpy hills of desire,
> but the moon keeps its honey in a pot of gold,
> the honey in the moon runs hot.

Stanza three provides a surprising technical turn, an exact rhyming echo of stanza one. Lines 1, 3, and 6 merely employ the same end words as in the opening stanza. "A seaworthy pillow" is a delicious near-rhyme for "well-met fellow," as is "a jewel afloat" for "a strong houseboat." There are subtle goings-on inside these stanzas; viz., "shrewder ones" echoes "sturdier ones"; and "row" becomes "steer." This stanza perfectly counters the first; it extols the girl admired earlier by Ovid:

> Good pretty girls grow older each day
> and the shrewder ones take the first to wed,
> so its hit or miss but a sharp lookout
> for that one shepherdess on a seaworthy pillow
> who will steer your daring like a jewel afloat,
> who will smile down the land of the dead.

Finally, there are lovely linkages between stanzas 3 and 4, the latter, with a couple of variations, being a mirror of the former:

> The route to wedding treasure
> doesn't go an easy map
> through the zigzag forest of the heart,
> but the moon keeps its honey in a pot of gold,
> the honey in the moon runs hot.

The Unicorn

Masques are spectacular mixes of poetry and theater intended for an elite of courtiers or intellectuals. Origins and etymology are obscure, probably deriving from early Renaissance carnival entertainments. Henry VIII introduced the form into England on Twelfth Night, 1512, when he and eleven others, disguised in masks and dominoes, appeared in the banqueting hall and invited court ladies to dance. Performances became increasingly dramatic. The earliest extant masque dates from 1594; Proteus and the Adamantine Rock was performed by gentlemen of Gray's Inn, London, as a compliment to Elizabeth as empress of hearts and of the ocean.

With the arrival of Ben Johnson and Inigo Jones, came Italianate stagings—a scene in perspective now appeared on the stage, eventually leading to scene changes. *The Masque of Queens,* 1609, began with an anti-masque of witches symbolizing evil, a foil to the main masque symbolizing virtue. Gradually the grotesque or realistic antimasque had little relevance to the central theme and was a pure diversion. Audiences remained courtiers.

In addition to Shakespeare's incorporations of masques into his plays, particularly in *A Midsummer Night's Dream, Twelfth Night,* and *King Lear* (a spectacle of characters gone mad), John Milton's *Comus* is of vast literary interest. Performed in 1634 to commemorate the ascension of the Earl of Bridgewater to the office of Lord President of Wales, *Comus* was Milton's first dramatizing of his great theme, the conflict of good and evil. In the masque, sensuality (in the person of Comus, son of Circe and Bacchus) threatens the Lady who as chastity embodies the positive love of the good that is both Christian and Platonic. The fervent exchange of ideas between the two principals still maintains its powerful intellectual appeal. For Milton, the play was not the thing—the lady's passionate argument for "the Sun-clad power of chastity" was.

Broughton's masque *True & False Unicorn: A Tapestry of Voices* (1957) was written for an elite audience of poets—the unicorn aims to breathe "new blood into wilder game / for the reforestations of poetry." The subtitle itself suggests a form medieval in its origins, and evokes the medieval tapestries in the Cluny Museum, Paris. The issue throughout Unicorn is ideological: is the unicorn myth or reality? If the creature is a mix, hermaphroditic (as Broughton suggests), what implications are there for a society mistrusting, fearful of, and even persecuting any one who is colorful and intellectually, creatively, and sexually outside cultural norms? In the late fifties, smothered as those times were by Joseph McCarthy, to handle such themes required courage. To employ the archaic masque for sensitive issues, and by performing before an elite of Bay Area artists and intellectuals was armor against persecution. Allegory has always been a device through which poets have saved their skins.

Broughton's unicorn, puzzled to madness by the true nature of his identity, is on the chase, pursued by an assortment of characters who hope to capture him for their egocentric designs. Here the unicorn expresses his dilemma:

If I am fantasy, I am also its flesh.
Am I less real than my own anguish?

Whether my feelings be false or true,
how can I say till I see what I do?

What is a unicorn? And is that I?
I am the unicor . But who am I?

A voluble lion reviews the unicorn's reputation: in China he is "King of the Beasts," he nests on the uplands of Utopia, he defends "Cinderella kingdoms," he donates his blood to the Holy Ghost. Next, a colorful figure Sigmund [Freud] of Vienna, provides a scholastic underpinning: "We are all hunters of the unicorn," is his refrain. Of all the figures, he best approximates the poet's views:

In the nature of things there is usually a question,
in the vision of things unusually an answer.
    We are all hunters of the unicorn.

Another figure, Tom Fool, shares with Shakespeare's fools a wisdom lacking in other folk. He first observes the unicorn's hermaphroditic nature. Tom's own separateness, oddness, and eccentricity enable him to see these affinities. He shouts "hosanna" to all the world's oddities:

Hosanna to the odd bird much maligned,
    queer fish, fool,
        exception to the rule—
Glory be to God for the one of a kind!
Hooray for prodigy, fluke, and freak.
    Nonesuch, hail, eccentrically prevail—
Hallelujah for the living thing unique!

Part 11: "Horn and Hounds" suits the tradition of the masque as pageant and mummery, advancing Broughton's themes. The unicorn hears a medley of voices. A youthful Sagittarius romps past, singing a lyric inspired by Edward Lear and Lewis Carroll: "In the misty land where horns abound / in the land where the unicorns grow." A plaintive virgin represents female innocence, although she is sexually, if dimly, aroused by fantasies of the unicorn's "long horn." She loves his hermaphroditic nature. On the other hand, a bizarre "Empress of Byzantium" is a libidinous, obsessed, and destructive woman who will murder to slake her thirst "for the male cornucopia." A humorous touch is the appearance of Queen Victoria who sings à la Lear, Carroll, and Gilbert and Sullivan; her closing bit of gay camp, "Mother [knows] best," is special:

> O pretty pony, naughty pet,
> > you pale poetic chap,
> you stay out late at night too much
> > without a proper wrap.
> Come live with me a neater life
> > secure from all mishap.
>
> .   .   .   .
>
> If you're to be a gentleman
> > and not a little pest,
> quips and pranks and running wild
> > had better be suppressed.
> Remember, God and Mother know
> > exactly what is best .

His Honour the Mayor, in a plebeian insensitive voice, declares that his town is full of stags—"clean he-men...proud to be commonplace." The unicorn, "very much too baroque," is "a menace to decent folk." A Blakean Europa, lamenting a joyless, dulled, and war-ridden present, lives "dwindling in the hampers of the lame." Mold, she declares "collects faster than the larks arrive." She craves that the unicorn restore the glorious days of chivalry:

> O unicorn, recaper! Bring knighthood to reflower!
> Abduct me, wed me, re-renaissance my life!
> Else doom will take me in his cold wet arms,
> Doom will seduce me in a drowning bed.

Big Black Sambo is stereotypical of old minstrel shows. Both hilarious and poignant, he is Broughton's satiric thrust at racial prejudice. The opening stanza is a tour de force of Negro spirituals:

Look down, sweet Unicorn, come down my Savior,
I is lookin for to gallop you Home.
When I gets to Heaven gonna shine up my Lord,
gonna ride my Lord all around, O Lord,
gonna win every Holy Derby.
Man, there's honey in that horn for me!

Once he reaches Heaven, how shall Sambo behave? Well, much as the film producers had Paul Robeson behave in *Show Boat*, as a black in a bigoted minstrel tradition, a form of masque:

I been huntin everywheres for you, White Savior,
I wants to be your jockey, I wants to be your groom,
Got strong black arms for any whitewashin needs
like sweepin after angels or movin round clouds.
Though I is black as the Congo, I aint no devil,
I just needin that good job, Lord, with you.
Lemme clean out your stable the rest of my days!

In Part 111: "Snare and Delusion," the Unicorn sees that for each of the pursuing voices he represents drastically varying needs and is more confused than ever. He craves to be free. Yet, logic holds that since he is mythological, his "reality" derives entirely from improvised visions of him in the psyches of others. He feels "white" and naked, like "an undressed Absolute." White is a "final pure negation." He remains a creature of wrenching paradoxes: both "dispossessed and unpossessable," "animate and inanimate," "savior and scapegoat," an "ambiguous steed" in "Jabberwock land, or Elysium." And where, he demands to know, is his unicorn? His horn is a useless symbol of nameless guilt. Could he survive in an open veldt "with antler, billygoat, or rhinoceros?" Shall he ever mate? He tires of seeing his reflection in a well. Is he "merely some fragile lost absurd, / a eunuch's beautiful monster-child?" He pleads for a huntsman to carry him home as a Snark! He's a natural history joke.

At a temple in a clearing wait those figures who have pursued him. Sigmund of Vienna advises that he "accept the mixture caked in the mirror. / Absolute clarity is the mystery beyond." Tom Fool lauds his uniqueness as an "odd bird." The Lion most lavishly corrects the unicorn's self-view: he will prevail "and outwit and outlive the hounds." "Monocerous mystery," declares the affectionate lion, "you are no man's gazelle, / you are your own and your angel's fox...." Behind the Sun's back the unicorn collects talismans. The Moon signs his "metamorphic sleep / with owl, with moth, and with nightingale." He is apprised of such natural mysteries as "the webworking trick of the spider" and "the serpent's grasp on the bough of life." He is the "three-faced" Muse's mascot, and, most important, "the poet's hermaphrodite." Because he foretells "wisdom and love in the night," he shall elude the hounds, those insensitive pursuers whose separate needs would stifle, restrict, and dispossess him of magic.

To express his relief and joy, the unicorn echoes William Blake's "Tiger":

Lion Lion, burning gold,
burn hot, burn bold,
   burn burn
   O Coeur de Leon
burn bright my flickering cold.

The Lion is a lover who shall "ripen" him. "Thou," he exclaims, "are my need. / Succulent harvest, fruit of the Lion, / O shower me in golden seed."

Tom Fool and the Virgin perform amatory lyrics. The Virgin's lullaby is reminiscent of Tennyson's songs:

Sweet sweet sweet desire,
sleep fair, rock your nest,
dream again of when you rise
   again again
   for beauty's eyes.

The unicorn submits to the "burden" of his legends, becoming the sum of his substance:

... ride me out of history, ride me through fact,
ride me to the marriage of heaven and hell.

As the reforester of poetry, he retains his own mystery: "I am myself my own true and false. / I am myself my real unreal / He is my unicorn, and I am he."

The theme of the masque is the honoring of one's eccentricities despite conventional mores. To fashion the self for others (the cracks inside the mirror) leads to guilt, indecision, and madness. "True and False Unicorn" is a fascinating anticipation of themes dominating Broughton's work two decades later, when he devotes his cinematic and literary talents to raising the consciousness of gays and lesbians. Anticipated also are later periods of friendship with Alan Watts and Zen as translated by Watts into palatable forms for American counter-culture consumption.

Whistling Down the Labyrinth

Of the three concluding sections of *A Long Undressing*, "Whistling in the Labyrinth" has the most invention and style. This is a tripartite mix of playful and serious lyrics (and narratives): in a Blakean "Sermon of the Holy Infant" the child advises the "wintry children" of the modern "Age of Fire" in which the raging, destructive rhinoceros (Reason, a.k.a. Blake's Urizen) is enthroned lord of the world, to turn to the holy infant's "Love." If they don't, the "Hell-flood cloud of Cain" will descend, and sinners will

> kneel in praise where a Harpy's claw
> dandles the shriveling idiot babe
> who announces your hope of the world.

In "The Ape, The Lamb," Broughton confronts his physical and spiritual selves via the "ape in his ribcage" and the lamb of his spirit. Two playful birthday poems, one written for Broughton himself, another for a child, have a celebratory elan. Here is the conclusion of "Standing in the Need":

> Already
>   ark ! ark !
> my puppy dog barks
>   in the basement
> hearing far off
>   a key.
> Then
> when I open the door of the
>   sweet common place
> will a child leap forth
>   with a toy?

In a visionary parable, "The White Stag," a speaker shipwrecked and washed up on a beach, apparently dying, is visited in his despair by a magical white stag who circles him, three times paws the wet stones against his face, and kneels beside his "fatal wound," placing "his crown" in the dying man's hands. The hortatory "A Liturgy for Poets" is a slack mix of sacrilege (viz.,"The Three

Trinities" of "The Beast to be Loved") and forced religious exclamations laced with puns that don't work. This joking, pun-filled stanza is intended, one gathers, to tweak Christians:

> And with high spirit.
> Orpheus be with thee.
> Let us array.

A set of seven poems, "Visitations," shows Broughton at his best, and are in a dream literature tradition. There are gentle nods to "Sir Gawain and the Green Knight" (in "Gavin and the Green Uncle"), to Dante (Broughton, too, finds himself mid-life astray in a dark wood, in "a snowy despond"), to the Visits from Satan genre (in "Feathers or Lead?" a scary Boschian poem), and to pop culture (he meets "a nose bifocaled" Sophia in Heaven "lullabyeing a polyphonic Rockabye of Ages"). Tones range from the serious to the humorous. None of these visions is entirely resolved. In "The Night Watch of the Magdalene," a figure resembling a wandering Jesus enters an unfinished cathedral to find Mary M. cooking a stew. Jesus samples the salty broth and accepts the Magdalene's invitation to swing on a "Great Roundabout" nearby: "Hop aboard, my boy, we'll get things moving." Soon he is riding "a dangling swivel-seat built for two," climbing in an ascending arc. Other riders are female "figureheads, and maiden-hoods, goddesses, martyrs, and washerwomen." The Magdalene's laughter shoots towards him through a megaphone. She says not to worry, that Fathers and Sons swing on the other side of the great Wheel; all will come round. "Where...is this / wheel of misfortune going?" he shouts, as Mary's lamp dies, the wind rises, and tears run. He, a "miniature dial on that enormously numberless clock," rises "higher around the night."

"Gavin and the Green Uncle" turns on magical mayhem. The uncle emerges from a city basement apartment carrying an axe, anxious to collect a mysterious "debt" from his "sluggish" godson. With a single stroke he whacks off the godson's head. The godson crawls after it over the carpet, and returns it to his shoulders, and, with an "old scout hatchet," dents the uncle's "hoary green wound," returns the "shrunken" magic girdle given him at his birth, and decides to live on his own freed of the uncle's mystical green power.

"Feathers or Lead?" is a nightmarish excursion into illness and extremity. The Devil is disguised as a doctor who clamps his "stethescope claw" to the speaker's belly and pricks his liver "with his beak." The ill man is supposed to say whether the pain feels like feathers or like lead. Either answer is wrong. The remedy must hurt: "If you don't feel it yet," Satan ominously observes, "I can come much closer." Satan rises naked with a pair of hairy heads and a scalp between his legs:

> Feathers or Lead?
> Feathers or Lead?
>   and he rattled his teeth in my pelvis.
> Lead lead leaden as the jokes of Hell!
> For the curse thumped down inside me where
> feathers lack bones to fly them.
> O Doctor my Doctor!
>   I groveled at his hammer-toed feet.

The Devil prepares an even stronger dose of medicine:

> And he clamped my nose and forced my chin
>   with his cold wet rubber paws.
> Now you must eat the regurgitated loaf,
> now you must drink the excremental wine.
> Here is your mother's befouled placenta!
>   And he thrust her corpse down my throat.

The descent towards death terminates when the sick man rejects the Devil, kicks his black bag full of maggots aside, rips open his own guts and spills "filth upon him." At that point, Satan "the dungheap" cackles and slithers under the door. The visitation has proved nearly fatal; the speaker triumphs as much over soul disease as over physical malaise.

The remaining sections of Selected Poems lack the coherence of "Visitations"; yet, each contains original work. The parables flirt with the obvious and are too readily homiletic. In a set of jottings, "Soundings from the Shore," Broughton converses with the sea. After he declares that he wishes to "cope" with his life by imitating the sea's strength, he places a morning glory on the beach, as a gift. He's tired of the world's chirping "roaratorio / of meaningless questions / and wrong answers." Only in a hurricane's eye, the sea informs him, is there peace. The sea responds homiletically: If you accept whatever comes, including the buffetings, you'll succeed. Moreover, the sea reports, the tides are her ebbings and flowings: "Nothing goes forward / without first going / back."

Another poem, "The Sick Bone," cryptic and original, recalls Yeats. Only by being swallowed by the sea and returned "to the marrow dung of Time" will the weary bone (symbol of the poet's dessicated spirit?) achieve immortality, its "second birthright":

Take me in, take me deep, melt me in your mouth,
dissolve my brittle armor and my dried up heart!

Quick fusions of contraries appear as the poet holds a seashell, listens to
throbbing angels crying hymns, dying galaxies, and the "resounding well" of
"humanity" resolving "the crashing war of choices." The loudest of all songs is
"the quiet call / of Yes and No singing together."

The lengthy "Neptune's Anchorite: A Stinson Beach Journal" is a series of
verse jottings on controlling private demons. Though there is humor: "My baby
has been drowned in the bath / before I could throw it out," the central drift is
serious. Sick of "Either Ors," the poet maneuvers his shaky metaphysical boat,
boasting meanwhile of his own "particular tree" planted upside down, which he
intends to climb. Once again, he asks the sea for instruction: "So far I have failed
every lesson. / Is the whole course over my head?" The animals and eft-things
living nearby—the voles, frogs, raccoons, moths, spiders, snakes, rabbits, quail,
skunk, and bats—all are more at "ease" than he. An absurd sight, a seagull flying,
carrying a sardine can, momentarily diverts him. He craves to be a boatman on
a Bangkok river washing himself. The river of his ablutions is the same river he
daily "offers / his spit, shit, and urine" to, scrubs clothes in, and drinks from.
Though the speaker is too driven to enjoy much of the mystical calm he craves,
he stubbornly exclaims that he is "closer to Infinity than to any grain of sand."
He invents a few koan-like conundrums: Why do old trails tend to be traps?
Where did the canary go that he (the poet) thrust down the toilet? He desires that
an Angel of Life let "the death begin." Once dead, he may fly with gods, crawl
with worms, may be at last "merely human." His gift from the sea is a rare stone,
a stone, he says, which is a philosopher. The world lies ravished by the sun:

I rollick upon lucidity.
My skin exhilarantly sheds.
Is that my crutch washing out to sea?

A Long Undressing concludes with some sixty "High Kukus" (1969) and a
series of Zen poems ("'Into Every Life a Little Zen Must Fall'"). The "Kukus"
reveal Broughton again improvising on a received poetic form. There is a
marvellous kookiness and a crisp individuality. Here are some examples:

They keep cutting me off,
said the Whisker,
but that will never stop me.

* * *

Of course I'm infinite,
said the Grain of Sand,
but what's the rest of this beach doing here?

***

I may be infecting the whole body,
said the Head,
but they'll never amputate me.

***

There's practically nothing,
said the Eraser,
that ever comes out perfectly.

A Long Undressing is unique. Its satires, parodies, and loving refurbishings of traditional verse forms reveal a caring, first-rate sensibility. While Broughton may refer to his efforts as "small surprises," or "little poems," their impact is otherwise.

GAB POETRY, OR DUCK VS. NIGHTINGALE MUSIC:
CHARLES BUKOWSKI

I once witnessed a Charles Bukowski *first:* the debut of the great raunchy poet as actor. The vehicle, "The Tenant," was a two character drama written by Linda King. Bukowski contributed lines of his own, better developing his own image in the play. This line was his addition, as delivered by Miss King: "You may be the greatest poet of the century, but you sure can't fuck." In a lively way "The Tenant" turns upon the problem of whether a super-poet should move in with his girlfriend, who would then, one would suppose, buy him his beer, give him bj's, and let him abuse her. The event was choice. An actor scheduled to read the Bukowski role was unable to show, so Buk took over.

There were twenty people in the well of the Pasadena Museum—sad, alas, because of the significance of the event. Bukowski, script in hand, trod the boards. The props were a telephone—used with nearly as much frequency as Barbara Stanwyck's in "Sorry, Wrong Number"; a mattress upon which King and Bukowski, scripts in hand, fell to enact their erotic comings after dismal separations. The performance, pixie-ish, included a tender moment where Bukowski acted as W. C. Fields towards a child who had a brief moment of stage glory. Needless to say, the small audience chuckled, particularly over Bukowski's Bogart-like delivery. Ms. King, with various stunning Bridget Bardot-esqueries nicely foiled the poet.

"The Tenant" gave Bukowski a chance, under the guise of art and aesthetic distance, to extol his stature as a poet. Buk has never been known for his reticence, and his being utterly ignored hitherto by the literary establishment hasn't affected him in the least.

I remember how zapped I was when I first read him: I was teaching at the University of California at Riverside and had been given *Crucifix in a Deathhand.* I carried the book to a string quartet concert, began reading it before the concert, experienced chills, elevations, charismatic flashes, barber pole exaltations, and fevers in the groin. I had not read such poems since discovering Dylan Thomas in the fifties. Here was something awe-thentic at last! I nudged my companion who thought I was crazy. Bukowski was unafraid of life's terror meat-slabs, and he made the angels sing.

I began to ask others if they had heard of Bukowski. Yes, he was living in a Hollywood dump, they said, dismissing him as a charlatan steeped in booze, flop-gutted, and rancid-breathed. I gave up trying to explain his impact on me. Moreover, I didn't care whether he rolled in his own puke, or swallowed pints of maiden juice. He was a super poet. His example loosened my own writing. Lowell, Snodgrass, Wilbur, Ashbery, and Olson were dilettantes.

One afternoon, carrying a six-pack of Coors, I beat my way to Buk's door, four or five days before Christmas. He and his daughter were trimming a tree. There weren't many ornaments—half a dozen on the low branches. Bukowski asked me in. I found a man of charm—nothing of the horrible-retchable I had been led to expect. I have been a fan ever since. He, though, remembers the visit otherwise, and wrote about it in his collection *Beneath the Fortinaria*.

The appearance of *Burning in Water Drowning in Flame: Selected Poems 1955-1973* invites me to describe what I found so telling in his work and to point up what I find are unfortunate recent drifts. My remarks should dissolve some of the celebrity aura threatening his reputation. *It Catches My Heart in Its Hands* (1963) and *Crucifix in a Deathhand* (1965), two Loujon Press books, are among the dozen most beautifully printed and designed books of poetry ever. Since they are out of print, and rare, it is great to have those reprinted.

"The tragedy of the leaves" propels us into Bukowski's world: hangover, desertion by his woman, the screaming landlady, and a world that's failed him utterly. Set up for the big blubbery whine of self-pity? No! He transmutes all raunchy conditions through unusual images: "I awakened to dryness and the ferns were dead, / the potted plants yellow as corn...." How well *dryness* echoes *awakened;* the latter implies a grappling with the world, moving toward insight. Compression follows:

> my woman was gone
> and the empty bottles like bled corpses
> surrounded me with their uselessness....

The long vowel sounds are well-spaced, and Bukowski, sensing the positive, remarks on the sunlight brightening the landlady's note in its "fine and / undemanding yellowness." The occasion, he observes, demands "a good come-dian, ancient style, a jester / with jokes upon absurd pain." There's wisdom here: "pain is absurd / because it exists, nothing more." He believes that as a poet he is stagnant: "that's the tragedy of the dead plants." In this concluding passage note the effective slant rhymes *more* and *razor,* and the repeated *dead, dead, dark,* and *stood* accompanying some monosyllabic tough nouns, *Execrating, waving,* and *screaming,* mesh, as *hall, final, hell,* and *failed* weave subtle echoes. Here he manages to be tender towards a harsh landlady:

> and I walked into a dark hall
> where the landlady stood
> execrating and final,
> sending me to hell,
> waving her fat, sweaty arms
> and screaming
> screaming for rent
> because the world had failed us
> both.

Empathy is present in other poems. "For marilyn m." avoids sentimentality through a diction suited to the fey person Monroe was:

> ... and we will forget you, somewhat
> and it is not kind
> but real bodies are nearer
> and as the worms pant for your bones,
> I would so like to tell you
> that this happens to bears and elephants
> to tyrants and heroes and ants
> and frogs,
> still, you brought us something,
> some type of small victory,
> and for this I say: good
> and let us grieve no more....

"The life of Borodin," grandly empathetic, is effective reportage on the miserable composer's life. Wife-hounded, he slept by placing a dark cloth over his eyes. His wife lined cat boxes and covered jars of sour milk with his compositions. Nothing is overstated in this taut free-verse poem. The parallels between Bukowski's life and Borodin's are implicit.

"The twins" evokes another tremulous situation, one that a lesser poet might easily have wrecked. Here Bukowski confronts his hatred of his father, immediately after the father's death: "A father is always your master even when he's gone." To cope, the poet moves through the house stunned, then proceeds outside where he picks an orange and peels it. Common day noises of dogs and neighbors bespeak sanity. Back inside, the poet dons one of his father's suits:

> I try on a light blue suit
> much better than anything I have ever worn
> and I flap the arms like a scarecrow in the wind
> but it's no good;
> I can't keep him alive
> no matter how much we hated each other.
>
> we looked exactly alike, we could have been twins
> the old man and I: that's what they
> said. he had his bulbs on the screen
> ready for planting
> while I was lying with a whore from 3rd street.
>
> very well. grant us this moment: standing before a mirror
> in my dead father's suit
> waiting also
> to die.

The event is stark. To wear another person's clothes is, in a sense, to become that person. Bukowski's mimicry of death as scarecrow is macabre. Despite the hate, the survivor can't bring the dead man back to life.

"Old poet" treats Bukowski's distaste for aging (forty-two at the time) without a public to love his work. Finding his sexual energies diminished, he's reduced to pawing dirty pictures. He's had too much beer and has heard too much Shostakovitch. He swats "a razzing fly" and "ho, I fall heavy as thunder..." The downstairs tenants will assume "he's either drunk or dying." Despite his depression, every morning he packs off envelopes of poems, hoping to place them in magazines. Rejection slips annoy him briefly; but soon he's back at his typewriter:

> the editors wish to thank you for
> submitting but
> regret. . .
> down
>   down
>   down

> the dark hall
>
> into a womanless hall
> to peel a last egg
> and sit down to the keys:
> click click a click,
> over the television sounds
> over the sounds of springs,
> click click a clack:
> another old poet
> going off.

"View from the screen" might easily have dissolved into narcissism; it has all the accoutrements. It shouldn't work, but it does. The death-whispers of the heron and the bone-thoughts of sea creatures dominate his universe as the poet crosses the room:

> to the last wall
> the last window
> the last pink sun
> with its arms around the world
> with its arms around me....

The sun is benign. Its pinkness produces the pig-image, an unusual trope and one that eschews turning maudlin. The Platonic cave motif is obvious:

> I hear the death-whisper of the heron
> the bone-thoughts of sea-things
> that are almost rock;
> this screen caved like a soul
> and scrawled with flies,
> my tensions and damnations
> are those of a pig,
> pink sun pink sun
> I hate your holiness
> crawling your gilded cross of life
> as my fingers and feet and face
> come down to this....

Writing, for Bukowski, is for getting "feelings down." Now, that may sound like warmed-over Shelley. Bukowski's urge to write, prompted by a mix of sardonicism and angst, is as natural as defecation. An image allows him to translate pain into a testimony for his spirit, one fraught with "madness and terror" along "agony way." There's a time-bomb inside his chest, and if it doesn't go off as a poem it will explode in drunkenness, despair, vomiting, or rage. As long as he writes he leashes terror. "Beans with garlic" is about this. A terrific idea—beans as lovers! Beans as your words! Stirring them is like writing poems:

> but now
> there's a ticking under your shirt
> and you whirl the beans with a spoon,
> one love dead, one love departed
> another love . . .
> ah ! as many loves as beans
> yes, count them now
> sad, sad
> your feelings boiling over flame,
> get this down.

"A nice day" deals with a knife the speaker carries inside him. Bukowski can't feel doom, so he goes outside "to absolutely nothing / a square round of orange zero." A woman says good morning, thereby twisting the knife:

> I do notice though the sun is shining
> that the flowers are pulled up on
> their strings
> and I on mine:
> belly, bellybutton, buttocks, bukowski
> waving walking
> teeth of ice with the taste of tar
> tear ducts propagandized
> shoes acting like shoes
> I arrive on time
> in the blazing midday
> of mourning.

The concluding pun is effective, and the lines are original. Bukowski produces (invents) his rhetoric, and this sometimes betrays him. Often, his latest voice, in the gab barfly manner, sounds like imitation Bukowski. His best poems discharge energy. We are touched by a vital creative mind prizing the creative act. Nothing, not even bad booze, can diminish it. Call this *originality;* for, to paraphrase T. S. Eliot on Tennyson, Bukowski has originality in abundance.

In *At Terror Street and Agony Way* (1968) there is evidence of deterioration. Bukowski's paranoia intensifies. He's nastier than he's hitherto been. His sympathies are with outrageous, destructive folks: the guy who emasculates himself with a tin can; "the nice guy" who cuts up a woman and sends the parts to people. Bukowski senses that a sycophantic public expects outrageous cartwheels and titillations, and he obliges. There is a discernible drifting off from the earlier tender humanity. And there is a troublesome loquaciousness; the honed work of the early manner is usurped by rambling, grotty passages of prose masquerading (chopped into lengths) as poetry. And he is vicious to other poets, as he is in a parody of Michael McClure and in a tasteless piece on Jack Hirschman as narcissist Victor Vania.

"Sunday before noon," though it concludes with a funny piece of hysteria, reflects Bukowski' s current narcissism:

> going down
> are the clocks cocks roosters?
> the roosters stand on the fence
> the roosters are peanutbutter crowing,
> the FLAME will be high, the flame will be big,
> kiss kiss kiss
> everything away,
> I hope it rains today, I hope
> the jets die, I hope
> the kitten finds a mouse, I hope
> I don't see it, I hope
> it rains, I hope
> anything away from here,
> I hope a bridge, a fish, a cactus somewhere
> strutting whiskers to the noon,
> I dream flowers and horses
> the branches break the birds fall the buildings
> burn, my whore walks across the room and
> smiles at me.

There's evidence of the old originality here in the juxtaposition of peanut butter and roosters, and in the branches and birds, and in the buildings that open the poem and close it. But the stance, the narcissism of "going down," the wish to be wiped out, and to wipe out, is dull. There isn't much in life now (petulance) worth grappling for. There's a nagging tone as Bukowski slips towards the next binge:

> and I got out of bed and yawned and scratched my belly
> and knew that soon   very soon   I would have to get
> very drunk again.

Isolating *soon* and *again* with extra spaces emphasizes the sterility of the writing. Ditto for the repetition of *very*.

Bukowski now cracks wise with editors who reject his poems. He becomes a rhino-skinned poet s. o. b.:

> when a chicken
> catches its worm
> the chicken gets through
> and when the worm
> catches you
> (dead or alive)
> I'd have to say,
> ...that it enjoys
> it.
>
> it's like when you
> send this poem
> back
> I'll figure
> it just didn't get
> through.
>
> either there were
> fatter worms or the chicken
> couldn't see.
>
> the next time
> I break an egg
> I'll think of
> you.
> scramble with
> fork
>
> and then turn up
> the flame
> if I
> have
> one.

This poem has an attractive petulance, and the motif of chicken, worm, egg, is original. Also the minimalist lines work well. Yet, Bukowski drifts into cuteness; the starch in the initial images is smothered under narcissism.

Particularly off-putting is Bukowski's obsession with fame. In "The difference between a bad poet and a good one is luck," he regales us with his life in Philadelphia when he was broke, trying to write, and waiting for the ultimate handout to enable him to sit around "drinking wine on credit and watching the hot pigeons suffer and fuck." He hops a train to Texas, and busted for vagrancy, is dumped off in the next town where he meets a woman who gives him so many teeth marks he thinks he'll get cancer. In prime macho fashion, he greets a bunch of his mistress' cowboy friends:

> I had on a pair of old bluejeans, and they said
> oh, you're a writer, eh?
> and I said: well, some think so.
> and some still think so...
> others, of course, haven't wised up yet.
> two weeks later they
> ran me out
> of town.

He seems wistfully amused that trash men busy about their work don't know that he, Great Poet, is alive—a thought held, I would guess, by all great men who snicker in their martinis: "Oh, if they only knew how near to greatness they are banging those trash cans down there..." In "Lost" Bukowski waxes philosophical in the manner of a hip-Merwin. The Big Conclusion? "We can't win it." Who's surprised? "Just for awhile," folks, "we thought we could." This Life Significance Statement serves up duck-music as distinct from nightingale music. The loquaciousness is typical of his recent poetry. I call it *gab poetry*. The gab poem is related to Chaucer's fabliaux. Obscenities are sexual: a husband shoves a hot iron rod up his wife's lover's anus whilst the lover is taking a crap out her boudoir window; an old husband's young wife is being swyved in a tree just out of eyeshot of the old fart, standing amidst the flowers.

"Hot" is a good example of *gab poetry*. The speaker's been working at the post office, see, on a night pickup run. He knows Miriam the delicious whore is at home waiting for him, deadline 8 p. m. At the last pickup the truck stalls. Miriam is waiting. Speaker arrives late to find Miriam gone. She's left a note propped against his pillow, addressed to "son of bitch." The note is held in place by a purple teddy bear. Speaker gives the bear (heh heh) a drink and has one himself, the poem is prose cut up into boozy breath-groups. Nothing much poetically catches the ear—this is in a sense a one-shot (as in bourbon) piece.

Some poems, like "Burn and burn and burn," set in bars, exude an easy cynicism. Petulance accompanies the "vomiting into plugged toilets / in rented rooms full of roaches and mice":

> well, I suppose the days were made
> to be wasted
> the years and the loves were made
> to be wasted

Instead of the Victorian Ernest Dowson's roses and lilies of rapture (and vice), vomit and plugged toilets cram Buk's wasted days.

Perhaps, if we persist, we'll find the secret of life tucked inside a plastic envelope inside a box of Bukowski Creepy-Crawly, Vomit, Crunch Cereal. Jesus Christ, says Buk, "should have laughed on the cross." There's a secret here somewhere. When Bukowski equates himself with Christ, he's maudlin:

> out of the arms of one love
> and into the arms of another
>> I have been saved from dying on the cross
>> by a lady who smokes pot
>> writes songs and stories.
>> and is much kinder than the last,
>> much much kinder,
>> and the sex is just as good or better.
> it isn't pleasant to be put on the cross and left there,
> it is much more pleasant to forget a love which didn't
> work
> as all love
> finally
> doesn't work....

Beautiful people, says Bukowski, "don't make it...they die in flame...they commit suicide..." They "are found at the edge of a room / crumpled into spiders and needles and silence." They "die young / and leave the ugly to their ugly lives..."

One superb new poem, "the catch," is as good as any Bukowski has written. Guesses are that a strange fish is a Hollow-Back June whale, a Billow-Wind sand-groper, or a Fandango Espadrille with stripes. Folks don't agree. They examine the creature; it's "grey and covered with hair / and fat." It stinks like "old socks." Joyously, the creature promenades along the pier chomping hot dogs, riding the merry-go-round, and hopping a pony. It falls into the dust. "Grop, grop," it goes. Followed by a crowd, it returns to the pier where it falls backwards and thrashes about. Somebody pours beer over its head. "Grop, grop." It dies, and people roll it into the ocean and argue further over its name.

Charles Bukowski is an easy poet to love, fear, and hate. He develops personal legends as dude, boozer, and womanizer. And he can be winsome, almost childlike. By stressing his personality I perhaps short change his poetry. It shouldn't matter that he vomits a lot, gets laid less often than he'd like, that seventy-seven new poems appeared in little magazines this year, or that he's Black Sparrow's leading commodity. Many readers prefer his fiction to his verse. The latter, I think, even with the flaws, remains a more durable art than his prose.

PAUL CHRISTENSEN'S SELECTED POEMS

Since most of this book (*Weights and Measures*, University Editions, 1985) is printed in double columns there is far more poetry than one might suppose. There is range: many poems deal with childhood recollections and relationships with parents. Others deal with love, much of it recollected. There is a fascination with sleep, with loved ones in a dream state, and with the speaker himself relating and interpreting dreams. Violence salts several poems, with an emphasis on domestic violence. Many poems are either excursions into other voices, or reveal the poet's responses to other personas keenly felt, viz., the strange, tragic girl who loses a marathon; the speaker's mother; and a superb section set in "East Africa, 1952: A Dream Sequence."

Christensen's style is traditional. His preferred line is formally iambic (either pentameter or tetrameter). In those poems which seem less controlled ("The Prince," "A Final Parting," and "Blue Decisions") his master seems to be William Carlos Williams. Indeed, both the form and subject of one of his finest short pieces, "Lunch," echos Williams' famous poems on plums in the refrigerator:

> The joy is simple and perfect;
> to have a single nectarine
> cut in four on a plate on a table.
> The afternoon like a wall
> thrust up to heaven, shining
> and clear. Nothing
> in the soft, scented dark
> but the plate, the fork
> the hands at rest silently.

Christensen takes risks. The opening abstractions dissolve into the image of a sliced nectarine. The next abstraction, the afternoon as a wall, turns beautifully precise. There are many such moments in the book. Christensen's penchant for traditional modes is clear in his fondness for the adjectival phrase with a literary touch: "sudden wilderness," "Her nude moon-luminous body," "the small white focus of her face," and "the muffled knock of knuckles." The alliterative tintings, though quiet, contribute to the literary turn, as part of the mode. Christensen works, then, within received stylistic norms. Occasionally, there are echoes of Hardy, Yeats, and Roethke.

In the brilliant, "Lake Nyasa," the iambs are partially concealed in a loose, almost prose cadence, possibly inspired by Joseph Conrad, particularly the mandarin prose of "The Heart of Darkness." These lines describe the debris of civilization seen from a passing steamer:

>   The hulks of old
>   abandoned crafts upturned and dizzy in rust,
>   on blocks, under the winch chains stilled
>   forever. The disrepair of age, the past, the
>   corroding memory of the old Marine department's
>   transport yard, now a scrapper's plot, boneyard.

When I characterize Christensen's devices as literary I am being descriptive, not censorious. When he is most original, he is *painterly*, perhaps a better word than *literary*. Most of his poems have passages another poet (this poet for one) would envy. Here a distressed mother harmonizes with a difficult husband. The "onion air" of the kitchen sets the atmosphere, and the crisp detail of the mother turning her hands in a towel is uncanny:

>   Mother
>   lingered
>   in the onion air, her wet hands
>   turning in a towel, dinner warming on the stove.

Or this:

>   I felt starlight cross
>   my back like tiny knives, razoring
>   me to strips to feed to all the souls below me.
>   Here Maria Esterantz loses a marathon:
>   Her coached career crumbled to its end,
>   the shoes hung up without regret
>   as if they were two instruments of pain.
>   Elsewhere he inspects a childhood photograph of a now-dead brother:
>   As I inspect the enormous terror of
>   this photograph, I sense the leaden

weight of his body, as it pins him
there, immobilizes him, makes him
sluggish and dreamy....

Christensen is always in control. In "Emotional History in America," a rebellious son has a vicious contretempts with a father. When the boy realizes that his mother can't protect him, he runs

Up the backyard hill, across the
road, then out and round again
behind the house, swung further out
into this dazzling summer world
where each old sagging bush rose
up in flames, where sky turned
infinitely blue and the grass
we mowed now shined, like a pool
deep in the woods.

Most original is the incredible play, almost a commemoration, of the dazzling summer light—the "infinitely blue" sky, and the shiny grass—with the harrowing narrative itself. Surely, if the father catches the son a vicious beating will ensue. Does the son's sense of his own liberation, via his rebellion, produce a special high, which finds its lyrical equivalent in the nature he races through? The poem winds towards escape, with a resolution almost mythical—finding release by reaching the eye/ center/ deep dark hollow of the protecting forest. And the final ambivalence of the road twisting innumerable times is chilling: we seem to know, as the boy does, that he will seek to elude his father throughout his life. He is in fact, by writing this poem, repeating that time, reliving it. Here are the closing lines:

in this sudden wilderness, we
could no longer run, but
crawled among the gathering pines,
where I lost him, having gained
the one road out which twists around
a hundred, maybe a thousand times.

The best of the personal poems, and the longest, is "The Nap." Christensen as a boy sits listening to his mother sleep, and drifts fast into a mood that seems rehearsed: "I could feel the walls / turning into flesh," he says. Details suggest the child's view of the world: delivery men and their trucks appear as they do in story books. Inside, a momentary fear wells, as he imagines a burglar's "fox eyes." As he sits waiting, the whole house given over to "napping" ("nothing troubled the standstill of time"), the appearance of a neighbor shaking a mop lures him back to reality.

He contemplates "sonship, the filial role." He was the third child, at birth "asthmatic and chinless." And that birth (during WW II) he describes with humor: he's shot forth from his mother's womb

> a mortar pumped from her own
> chute into a swaddle propped in the
> old Plymouth, dipping in the city's ruts
> homeward to his sooty first day
> on the job. A warm tit erect and
> rubbery on his unwilling lip,
> squeezing the thin suety milk until
> his belly drummed. Tantrums
> in the yellow kitchen, the tomb-
> shaped darkness of unlit rooms....

There's always a flow: the mother's breathing rising "silkily" from her lungs, "weaving the darkness around." His own ties to that mother are much subtler than apron strings. The streamers ride through his memory back to infancy and boyhood. He recalls sexual stirrings. In this brisk passage he commemorates an early erection:

> I knead
> the cold knot in my lap until it stretches
> numbly on my leg, the forbidden
> lump
> knocking upward in its tent of
> corduroy,
> the chicken neck that's always left
> on someone's plate, erect, uneaten
> boney arc standing up now between
> tense legs, as if I charmed a snake.
> No sap—too diluted in my roots;
> I fear it, feel relief as it gives in,
> goes flat, cold nub again.

During four poignant moments of direct address to the mother (he pleads with her to rise up and "kick out these stops to life," not to die), his own fears burgeon, and streamers of time blow forward. Via the poems and dream/ memory, the mother finally wakens to that "fallen world we sojourn in." She climbs out of the "coils" of sleep, her eyes half-shut. She puts on tea, dresses, makes up her face to greet the father returning from the factory. The child scrutinizes her, assessing his own worth as vigil-keeper of her descent:

> Her hair hangs limp
> from all the love she hunted for;
> the drained emotions from shadows
> on her lips. I kept vigil
> during her descent, a child-soldier
> guarding his empty gate, while a
> father returns to claim his bed,
> my weapons turning into
> bones and hair.

The theme of the impressive long second section of *Weights and Measures*, "East Africa, 1952: A Dream Sequence," is the Conradian / Rousselian one of a questing soul traversing rivers, lakes, and jungles. Everywhere western civilization is in decay, both in the lives of wasted white men, and in abandoned, rusting machinery.

Among the dispossessed and displaced are a half-Hamite gardener at a college who postpones returning to his old Banyoro wife and recalls the bitter day of his marriage oath. An English Colonel lies dying in a stifling room at Djibouti, attended by a nurse who bathes him in lemon water and tries to cool his "red, blistered head." Soon a drifter goes to Toten ("Death") Island, populated only by rats. Here, in fever and delirium, a "stringy mound of / flesh, so white under the white-boned / sliver of moon" he descends into a hell he seems strangely to crave:

> The rats were everywhere; none came
> closer than the edge of sand where I tented,
> standing up to look at me.
> Their eyes in firelight like jewels,
> the diamonds of abandoned wrists,
> as
> if a ghostly dance swayed round me,
> those eyes like running water

> sparkling at midnight under the moon....
> I heard the dead cry out;
> the wind carried their agony out to sea
> and left it there. The path at the
> beach
> led into hell, and ghosts crowded
> into the high salt grass. They came
> for me.

"Lake Nyasa," the longest of these poems, runs to well over 500 lines, and is a fascinating narrative written in supple blank verse. The story is clear: the protagonist, an old Scottish ferry-boat captain, serves the communities scattered along the Nyasa. En route he receives intimations and a note from one McNudo who has sought the Captain out for vengeance: years before the Captain had enticed McNudo's wife away.

They first fight at Chinteche, an isolated place on the coast. Apparently, when the Captain loses, McNudo leaves him for dead. He revives, wires further up river to an old German acquaintance who arranges for a duel with daggers. The outcome again disfavors the Captain, who, badly slashed in face and chest, falls forward, McNudo turns, thinking the German has called for an interval, and the Captain drives in a fatal stab. He's arrested, and, found guilty, is doomed to wander "all Africa" as a "ghost."

The story reads like a lurid tale in a Murder-in-Exotic-Lands genre that Somerset Maugham might have written. And the Captain is brother to Conrad's Kurtz, though he lacks the latter's obsessions with power and death. Our Captain has premonitions early (in the subtle erotic scenes with his mistress) and shows fear as he waits for his "double." Conrad's "Secret Sharer"? This energetic moment is from the culminating scene:

> McNudo struck again, across the chest,
> an inch long purse of blood unzippering
> the Colonel's breath, which made him fall
> forward awkwardly as McNudo looked back
> to see the German call for time, but the German
> merely stared and the colonel's steel found
> passage in McNudo's back, safe harbor
> to the in-land shape of heart, cut through the coast's
> entanglements, still the rebellion, until
> McNudo dissolved in flurry of nervous breaths
> to his puddle of disaster on the floor,
> his mouth moving in a breathless whisper

full of blood, his fingers touching the boot toe
of the colonel.

In Part III, Christensen returns to the same motifs he explored in the opening section: mother, childhood, women he has observed and loved. Violence now is intensified. In "Whorls" a rape occurs, a playing out of Satanic lust (in fact, in the woman's mind the man slithers away as a snake). Surely Eden has gone wrong; "there is no God / swan slackening his loins." Eve wrenches in his "grip and bite":

> the jerky spasms of
> his legs against her, pushing,
> penetrating, his fingers
> dug deep into the tender flesh
> of her shoulder and neck.

"A Final Parting" turns for effect on the opening vision of a superbly detailed view of a woman's wrist, as observed by a former husband who now sees her (and himself, one assumes) aged. Love is affirmed, however, in "Looking for a Pulse," in the images of breasts "stiff as peaches, the / pitted tips."

Perhaps the most important poem is "The Far Relations," where observations of his son evoke his own boyhood. The lad, he writes, "is made of steel: / his veins are wires telephoning to his mother's heart," though the mother is absent "in the cold / mountains of her own life." With deep affection, Christensen observes the boy take off for school: "His shoes / are large, cumbersome gravestones / of his youth, which he drags half- / heartedly with him." There's much left unsaid between father and son—a smarting fact conveyed by Christensen in an aside, is an image of toys "stuffed with truths / they have never spoken."

These African poems demonstrate, as do Christensen's poems which inhabit psyches other than his own, that he has several strings to his lyre. *Weights and Measures* should not go unnoticed in the poetry world.

ROBERT CREELEY'S
FOR LOVE REVISITED

Robert Creeley's *For Love* (1962) contains poems written between 1950 and 1960. In its influence on younger writers it ranks with Ginsberg's *Howl* and Olson's *Maximus Poems*. I still recall the excitement I felt on first reading the book. I was working on my *Songs for a Son* (W. W. Norton, 1967), and had not yet read the Black Mountain Poets. Since my poems commemorated a deceased son, I wanted to give the illusion that a child could understand the poems; in other words, my diction was to be pure and comprehensible. I had no idea that poets were writing a style of the kind I required. *For Love* was there when I needed it. I am pleased to find its impact undiminished. In this reassessment I shall describe some of the seminal features; I shall not pretend to say everything that needs saying. My discussion is organized around these topics: Grace, Emptiness, Play, Is/It, Kids, and Thomas Hardy.

Grace

In "Le Fou," dedicated to Charles Olson, when Creeley describes Olson's breath-group poems as vehicles of *grace*, he reveals as much about his own work as about Olson's; and his treatment of the breath group, projective verse style is a better introduction to that style than any prose essay I have read on the subject. Grace, Creeley says, in keeping with the slow rhythms of the breath, "comes slowly"; a length of breath determines the *beat* of the lines. Grace implies a form so effortless we are unaware of the poet's struggle with resistant materials. Obviously, the notion that the artist maintains a tension between the grace he creates and the resistances of subject matter and language is central to aesthetic systems, particularly of classical ones. And here is a bone: in an odd way both Creeley and Olson are classical writers.

In "Le Fou" Creeley's hesitancies suggest a voice getting the beat exactly right. An examination of masculine in relation to feminine feet, and of monosyllabic to polysyllabic words, produces a descriptive log of the poem's flow. Creeley's line-spacings, too, allow the individual breath-groups sinuosity. Interestingly, this is the purest formally Olsonesque poem in the book; Creeley (at least here) prefers the more traditional stanza form to the explosive breath groups arranged in varying positions on the page. Always, whether he is writing in an unabashed projective manner or in a more traditional one, Creeley senses that kinetics must be transmitted (the *energy,* to use Olson's word) from the charged first syllable all the way, line by line, through the living body of the poem.

"Le Fou" resembles a charged, sinuous dance. As it moves within its form, we move out from it, to new earscapes, eyescapes, tonguescapes. The poem evokes a gracefully waving plant, a moving dancer. Yeatsian? Yes. The question: is the poem the dance, or is the poem the dancer? Some of each condition seems appropriate. The idea teases.

Emptiness

For Love doesn't whine or snivel over a "universal emptiness." Poems float easily between the poet and the void. Wallace Stevens would have approved. Yet we must set the ground. It's as if each poet/artist has his scrap of desert to display his works on. The desert blooms with canvases, posters, books—all affixed to stakes driven into resistant soil. To create art, says Creeley, "is the courage necessary." Only then is the poet free from debilitating, consuming sterilities of place and time. Defiance, or, rather, indifference, is the appropriate stance, symbolized for Creeley in the act of the mailman who steals and burns letters. Creeley doesn't care; let the mailman destroy; he can't harm you. Meaningless-ness, hence, assumes meaning.

"The End," a funny improvisation on loneliness, turns a famous passage from Walt Whitman to its advantage. In order better to touch the world by being entertaining and distinctive, Creeley's poet buys a new hat. But he bombs, is ignored, and is left with "a feeling like being choked." He can't absorb the rejection. His new gray hat sickens him, and he has, he reports, "no purpose no longer distinguishable." Paradoxically, Creeley imposes that ego on the world, which he deciphers on its terms. Perhaps this is why his triumphs are often incomplete: his ego blinds him to what the world's demands.

In "The Innocence" he fumbles to re-see, to re-teach himself. The brutalities of a competitive society derive from church, family, and state. Symbolically, he must relearn that fire burns and water drowns. "The Innocence" opens with obvious, child-like definitions: the sea is a "line / of unbroken mountains" as the waves freeze into visual patterns. The sky "is the sky." The ground "is the ground." Our life-line is here, on that ground—a fact requiring reaffirmations. On the earth-line we experience the mystical. Mist shrouds shapes in strangeness. Considering the amorphous shapes, we sense "another quiet," the mystic energies of the universe. Slowly, the speaker grows aware of leaves, rock, and other parts of the visible landscape he has hitherto not seen. His vision, his own, remains imperfect. This is in a sense his triumph: for only through haze does an existential sterility produce beauty.

Play

Fun/play is a most attractive feature of *For Love.* Sophisticated allusions to medieval love lyrics appear. In "Chanson" a warm intelligence informs the refrains—one refrain is archaically playful, the other stark and contemporary. *Lady* and *madame,* wife and mistress, are polarities. The gentleness (perhaps I should say *gentilesse*) of looking backwards is conveyed by this line: "one hoists up a window shut many years." Why? To allow a lark (remnant of an older poetic convention) to appear. The image of the bird is subtle, gentle, tender.

The most playful of these poems, and perhaps the most famous, treats the disruption of a marriage in which the woman is a crude, contemptuous, emasculating beast and the man a sensitive, feminine, courtly creature. Shades of Jungian animus and anima. Here are some of the trappings: "things went on right merrily," "little cheer," violets in the spring, heavenly mercy shining down on the lovers, the lady aloof and remote from the blandishments of her lover, the lady vengeful. Rhymes, joyously wielded, turn gross:

> Oh come home soon, I write to her.
> Go screw yourself, is her answer.
> Now what is that, for Christian word?
> I hope she feeds on dried goose turd.

The poem is not, however, a putdown of the medieval genre from which it derives. It celebrates the form as a device for exposing a modern domestic conflict. The concluding section is a tour de force evoking the earlier genre.

Creeley delights in fractured tenses—another facet of his humor. We skip while he laughs, daring us to catch him as he romps through his verse fields. "Don't sign anything" begins:

> Riding the horse as was my wont,
> There was a bunch of cows in a field.

Bad grammar, yes. Anti-Romantic, yes. The anti-Romanticism is the primary fun: the first line could launch a medieval poem. But Creeley kicks the traces. And his range matters: to bring off his contrast is no small triumph. He's a playful, obstreperous child. The mirror always looks backwards and forwards simultaneously. Grotesqueries of language, illiteracies of feeling and speech, displace the enamelled past. Creeley forces us to see how far we have come, or how far we have fallen, from tradition. His horse decides to chase the cows, and the speaker in the saddle must follow as "uneasy accompanist." In other poems also, Creeley produces blisters of grossness: "a greasy hand, lover's nuts"; "the trees, goddamn them"—W. Wordsworth turns in his grave; 'I have to take a piss"; "tits raised high / in the sky," etc.

Is / It

These are two of Creeley's favorite words. *Is* is staunchly and simply *being*, clipped and vigorously assertive. It is the object pointed to before being named, the abstraction (riddle) stated before the finger-poet-god-Adam points naming the object. *It is*, together, are signposts in the desert, the created thing delimiting Existential space.

"The Riddle" is a skillful plosive feast. *Grace* in the hesitancies, philosophy in the tone. *It* and its echoes are almost always accentuated, providing small stress-peaks for playing less-clipped rolling sounds. The rhythm/sound patterns are subtle, to be heard with the outer ear, with the inner ear, feasting: wealth— a pickup of rushing and meaning threading quickly over from one line to the next, an excitement rare in poetry. The "question," as I read it, is the eternal enigma of the male-female connection: Creeley's speaker, maddeningly hesitant, gives the impression he'd be really boring in bed. The woman is commanding, "imperative," while the man is "lost in stern/thought."

Kids

Reading Creeley is to re-experience our minds as children, when nonsense and fantasy were as real as stubbing toes. A story then was never a lie. Cracks in the pavement were magic crevices—if you stepped on the wrong one you might disappear forever. In Creeley's "The Cracks," a children's game becomes a rendition of a nasty adult relationship. "Jack's Blues" depends upon our fantasies working to a logical truth. Exaggeration:

> I'm going to roll up
> a monkey and smoke it, put
> an elephant in the pot. I'm going out
> and never come back.

So, Jack eludes his troubles by playing child. When you want to berate him he won't be there.

Other poems, particularly some of the love poems, employ fantasy to contrast the speaker's dissatisfaction with the real world of his flesh and blood female. In "The Whip" the speaker lies in bed with his woman who is sleeping, "very white / and quiet." A fantasy-woman appears on the roof. At this point, the real woman utters an entirely unromantic "ugh" and puts her hand on the speaker's back. The touch restores him. The fantasy-woman dissolves. He feels guilt that he betrayed his wife. And he turns to her for love.

Thomas Hardy

Part 3 of *For Love* reveals affinities of tone, diction, and manner with Thomas Hardy's poetry. Creeley has absorbed the older poet well. My feeling is that Hardy has been most influential on later poets. But critics remain myopic. In Creeley's "Song," the agents, like Hardy's, are elemental forces: rivers, land, sea, wind, trees...these are the backdrop for the poet's feelings. The quatrains provide an illusion of concreteness, and are forms loved by Hardy; the elemental wind is curiously specific. Whether the setting is Dorset or New Mexico doesn't matter. The sudden personal, philosophical stress is also reminiscent of Hardy, as are the hesitancies behind the questions and the direct simple rhymes:

> And me, why me
> on any day might be
> favored with kind prosperity
> or sunk in wretched misery.

The form is beautifully simple: dimeter, trimeter, followed by two tetrameters; the simple rhymes—two plain monosyllables set against two polysyllabic rhymes; the use of old-fashioned phrases—"kind prosperity," "wretched misery." And what could be simpler than the response to the question "why me?" An apothegm: "be natural, while alive." Once dead we "go on another/course, I hope." Creeley's whisper reflects a tone common to Hardy.

"Kore," also, deals with simple, elemental acts. The first stanza risks the inversions Hardy favored. Here is Creeley:

> As I was walking
> I came upon chance, walking
> the same road upon.

Even the casual reader of Hardy is aware of chance as a prime mover. In "Kore" chance produces a vision in a light green wood of a lady led by goat men, moving to a flute. "The Rain," as in Hardy's poems about rain, is the occasion for self-reflection and an uneasiness about that self, implicitly religious, implicitly romantic. Love, like rain, enables the poet to escape fatuousness, fatigue, and indifference. The problem is to soften the ego's edge—finding one's self at last "wet / with a decent happiness." For both Hardy and Creeley time is a unity. The present is for questioning one's destiny. Past and future, as parts of the present, yield comfort in that they are cut from the same die. The questioning never ends. Hardy's "Ah no, the years, oh," the refrain of "During Wind and Rain," his finest lyric, is echoed in Creeley's "The Plan":

> the way, the way
> it was yesterday, will
> be also today
> and tomorrow.

Hardy called himself a meliorist, which means that while things are bad they are getting better. Creeley puts the idea thus (in "The Immoral Proposition"): he writes for the "unsure egoist" who knows that "God knows / nothing is competent nothing is / all there is." One's salvation and strength, it seems, reside in one's ego. Says Creeley, the healthy egoist must be sure; the "unsure egoist is not good for himself."

SHARON DOUBIAGO'S EPIC:
HARD COUNTRY

Venus rules show business."—Sharon Doubiago

Hard Country has nearly 10,000 lines. An orchestration of modes and themes in the Whitman and Projective verse manners, lavish with explorations of American history (the struggle for the West, the American Civil War, Viet Nam), primitive myths, personal and family histories, restless wanderings after archetypal lost lovers, the subterranean connections of male and female, and these counter-culture preoccupations: pop celebrities, literary figures, ecology, and drugs. One poem, "Sitting Bull," will introduce Doubiago.

Like most of Doubiago's poems, "Bull" employs an expansive free verse line, and is divided into sections, each a modulating movement. The theme, the plight of the American Indian, occupies much of *Hard Country*. On her mother's side Doubiago inherited Seminole, Choctaw, Cherokee, Shoshoni, Shawnee, and Irish blood. Her father was English, from colonists arriving just after the Mayflower. She is never sentimental or flabbily outraged, nor does she write what I have called Ugh Poetry, where a well-intentioned WASP poet makes natives speak like primitive retards. Doubiago is tough, empathetic, and inspired in her interweaving of history and myth, often merging her own psyche with figures from the past and those of her imagination. A quasi-mystical hero, Ramon, serves as a lodestar. No later lover ever equals the idealized, lost Ramon. He appears with Doubiago (she's 14, he's 15) on the book's cover, in a photo snapped in front of "Eden's Heavenly Hamburgers," Ramona, California, where Doubiago worked.

Sitting Bull, the only son of Hunkpapa warrior "Returns Again." Himself a "mystic," Returns Again shook his barbed tail at the Taurus "on the opposite side of the universe" and then named his son after this largest of the constellations. Astrology, popular in the 1970's, helps explain Sitting Bull, the hero of Little Big Horn. Doubiago has fun with the colloquialisms "bullheaded," "plow ahead," and with the easy rhyme "tail / gale":

> His people observed he was like a buffalo,
> headstrong and fearless, opinionated,

incapable of surrender. In short, bullheaded.
In a winter blizzard buffalo never turn tail.
They face the gale and plow ahead.

Though not handsome, like any good Taurus, Sitting Bull was "courteous and gentle," a lover "known for endurance and fertility," who married nine wives. His first human "victim" was a Crow woman, thought by the Hunkpapas to be a whore, Venusian. She was lashed to a pine, heaped with brush, and set afire. Venus, Doubiago conjectures, must have prompted Bull to save the woman, for singing a "song of Mercy," he shot an arrow, terminating an agonizing death by fire.

Like all good lovers in *Hard Country* Bull is sensuous and spirited. He learns to read and write; his signature is a man's head holding a line in his mouth that runs to a buffalo floating in the air. When he meets with U.S. Senators, he is both assertive and humble. He is "Father Sitting Sacredly," for *sitting* assumes many states: "IOYOTAKA means *sitting sacredly*. Bull in Lakota means *Father*."

Doubiago underplays the carnage of Little Big Horn, glossing by speculating on the nature of Taureans who "are slow to anger." Once they are angered though, beware. The battle of Big Horn itself is casually recorded in a brief stanza that reads as if it were written by a child taking notes in a history class:

The Battle of the Little Big Horn
was a rare day
when Sitting Bull got mad.

Since "Venus loves show business," Big Horn is a diversion for the gods. The Venus Show trivializes Sitting Bull by sending him to Europe with Buffalo Bill's Wild West Company. In a Comic Book tone evocative of the death of grandeur, the hero declares: "It is not good for my people / for me to be parading around like this." He returns to lead his tribe to Canada and freedom. Shortly, a she-buffalo tells him to go once again to the land of his ancestors; the whites will "soon be bewitched" and dead natives will be reborn as light/wisdom streaming into space, brightening the darkened earth. A meadowlark warns Sitting Bull that a Sioux will kill him ("Many Taureans are murdered / by someone they love.") His death does indeed occur, an event Doubiago treats with candor. The omission of definite articles suggests an Indian speaking:

In white man's world Taurus rules money.
His old friend Buffalo Bill

> wanted to cash-in on the publicity
> of his death. In white man's world
> more Taureans are in prison than any other sign.
> Sitting Bull was killed by the Sioux police
> called Metal Breasts because they wore
> the badge of the dollar sign.
> Or was it only the initials US
> overlapped one on the other?

When Sitting Bull is pulled from his cabin to be shot, his death is a transcendent "return" to his father *Returns-Again*. There's a Biblical roll to Doubiago's style, a simplicity, and an elevating passion:

> the sun eclipsed and the earth opened
> and in a great landwave slid over him
> and the tall stems of prairie grass
> at Grand River where he was born,
> to which he returns again,
> brushed against his eyes
> and he saw what he will see
> so long as the grass may grow
> though the plains turn to a bowl of dust
> a pale sickly child named Europa
> swept-away on the back
> of a sacred White Cow.
>   *   *   *

Doubiago' s hard country is indeed hard, in the sense of endurance. Like Ginsberg in *Poem For These States,* Doubiago peregrinates throughout America. When she writes of Los Angeles, Mendocino, or Tennessee, those particular locales determine both her exterior and her interior lives—experiences, recollections, and meditations. Like Thomas Wolfe, one of her mentors, to whom it was gruelingly apparent that while you can't go home again, you keep looking "homeward," hoping that an angel will assist you to a whole self-vision. While Doubiago quests for America she hungers for a nation rid of pollution, nuclear power, and for an alternative life style (even if it means living out of your car, displaced). One of her "Plainsongs" goes this way: "Oh, let me occupy space / without filling it."

Her strategy is, in a sense, to allow "story" to occupy poetry without actually filling that space with narrative devices, an insistent chronology, and the padding indigenous to most fictions. In a letter to me (October 1, 1986), Doubiago writes: "I know the story is not 'obvious.' I didn't want to write a novel (though goodness I wondered why not a million times; it would have been so much easier!) I wanted to tell the story from inside out rather than the traditional outside in. This is my 'language poetry / semiology' orientation. My Charles Olson. My feminism. My female voice, etc. My Indian." This story line, which Doubiago says no reviewer has so far seen, matters in the same sense that "story" matters in an epic poem, viz., those by Homer, Virgil, and Milton.

Doubiago's "story" opens with the threnodic, eleven-part "Visions of A Daughter of Albion." The husband of a young woman whose marriage sours brings lovers home, to make her happy, so he thinks. She falls in love with one, a man whose mother drowned herself, and she becomes a hard-pressed female who like Persephone seeks her underworld. After the love affair concludes, fulfilling a vow, she visits the Tennessee lake where the mother died.

When her husband abandons her, "drowned," she goes West to find him. Her peregrinations take her through Washington, south through Oregon and then through Idaho, Utah, Wyoming, South Dakota, and on to Michigan. On the next leg she visits Ohio, Kentucky, Tennessee, and Louisiana. Eventually she accompanies another lover west, where they split up at the Colorado River. The heroine's parents retrieve her and drive her to Los Angeles.

Doubiago's mix of lyrical with narrative and expository writing prevent monotony. Her poems breathe, and when she writes of Psyche as the archetypal female, Psyche may live in a tacky stucco house in Pasadena, or she may be the Spanish/Indian Ramona questing for her dead Indian lover Ramon, or she may be Marilyn Monroe on a mythic sex-jaunt with Jack Kerouac at Kalaloch the northernmost Washington State beach reachable by car, or she may be the soft-porn heroine Emanuelle, or she may be the Indian Sacajawea leading Lewis and Clark along the Oregon trail, or she may be Doubiago's grandmother, mother, or a lover's suicidal mother-in-law. Doubiago has an immense gallery of interchangeable female figures.

Stunning passages are numerous. Here she's back-packing along the Oregon trail. Night. She turns towards her sleeping lover:

> I hear you
> like the breathing of horses
> heard a mile away in deep winter.

This potent one-liner is rife with hints of a dismal teen-age destiny: "Three boys on bikes race toward Idaho's oldest jail." Here the dual meanings of "damned" river are effective, i.e., the river, literally damned, is in Hell: "Night like a river that's damned." This passage has an aching sexual wisdom: "the spirit's desertion of the flesh / after sex." And, "war is about our sex, war is the hatred / of the body, like / napalm, the fleshfire / that can't be put out." This moment, erotic, reveals an uncanny empathy with the male:

> The sweet flesh of his chest
> beneath the unbuttoned shirt
> aches untouched.

She celebrates fellatio:

> ... when I kneel to you
> and for the first time take you in my mouth
> I feel the fish beating for the cold pulling
> of a distant sea.

Here, energetic alliterations excite her:

> the world
> goes on without you, canebreak, cabin creeks,
> covered bridge, it doesn't matter
> walking into these woods, your genes
> winding through all this funk,
> gullywasher, rusted
> mobilehome down in hollarslide, scattered parts
> of cars parts, hanged black men
> across the Cumberland.

Elsewhere she envisions a "roaring surf" of immense silver bears "subdividing, / turning upright on hindlegs / filling the sky with the living pounding sea." She evokes a cramped lower middle class living room:

> We keep our legs folded beneath the plastic couch
> so the family can get by.

As a child she attends her grandmother's funeral:

> The piano cried.
> Your hair was sprayed blue, controlled

with nets.
Someone had made a dumb painting of you
on your face.

*   *   *

To suggest that Doubiago is a poet of jewelled parts is to demean her vision. None of her topics is so perceptively treated and wide-ranging as Woman—her sexuality, her relation to men, and her writing. In "Letter to Luke Breit In Point Arena" she spends an entire night writing. The act is pioneering for a woman caught in the "middle of this doomed and damned continent," in a world of "sullen men." Anxious for self-identity, she swells with much to say:

> I've always felt
> as Billy Budd, my life at stake on the words
> that won't come, mute before the obvious.

All through the night she works, using pen rather than typewriter so as not to disturb her family:

> reading through the dozen books, wading through stories and flesh,
> and dislocation and death, searching for the key
> to this overstuffed country, stories and people and land
> I have pulled to myself, like sperm to the egg:
> the American soul, hard, isolate, stoic, and as Lawrence said:
> a killer.

She slips on her boots and goes outside. To the east a shaft of light splits the dark. A comet "spraying gold," drops "behind the rising sun..." a great unbroken tongue telling a story of two women: a pioneer meets an Indian squaw. They display their babies. Again in her own kitchen, Doubiago fixes breakfast. As her children leave for school, their bus "gearing down the ridge," she craves for the time when she will not have to fix kiddie breakfasts. Dismayed, she reaches for Breit's letter:

> And I understood, Luke, that you are the poem, the passage
> I had sought all night, the love with which you begin
> and the love with which you make
> poems for the people, and your faith that there is
> a place in each of us that can't sell out, yes, even though
> *the heart as prisoner.*

In "Insomnia: Somewhere The Four Corners of the Sioux" she lies with her sleeping husband on a floor and is distressed: he plans to leave her. She conveys her fears through a "blazing man":

> Miles to the north a blazing man
> whose rainbow colored flesh fills the yellow clouds
> pulls me from our daughter's bed
> through the window
> in the direction of the storm.

Poetry can't assuage Doubiago's pain. When her husband departs, she travels west searching for him. He eludes her. On her journey, though in misery, she manages to create poems:

> I wake and do not know who sleeps,
> his back to me,
> or in what black night I'm birthing
> the child. I hold my elongated hands
> beneath the foreign bulge
> as I emerge from the Pacific.
> *Red, yellow, white, black,* together
> is brown, the color
> of the fifth race.

She assumes the role of *Amazon,* the legendary female warrior, a necessary posture in a male-dominated universe:

> the mythic California woman
> who removes her breast
> to more precisely
> aim the bow.

Her brown chest is a warrior's. She bends towards male poets sleeping (or dead) on the ground, then passes, leaving them behind to "play" their "bonegames." Men are the death principle manifest. Doubiago, subscribing to male values, once vowed never to be a poet. The "law and order of poetry" excluded women. A woman's words, she believed, were "almost worthless." Moreover, Art must exclude such themes as genocide and murder. The "dead in Earth" cried out. Poems are not Nazified museum pieces:

Where words are molded like human skin to shade the light
like special collections
of goldfilled teeth.

Reading Akhmatova transformed her life:

[Akhmatova was] the poet who saw everything,
her husband at the firing squad,
her people, lovers and poets,
her whole generation destroyed,
her son in prison for the poetry
which she burned, after committing
to heart every word

Poetry is Orphic:

You must make it living
for the Dead who do not forget the living

but livable

for the four infants found alive at Wounded Knee
wrapped in the shawls of their frozen mothers.

For women poetry is a transcendence of the "inward meanness" of men. Writing stills Doubiago's hunger; for its purest forms are neither male nor female. They wear rather a broadly "human ego."

In another dream poem, "Crazy Horse," the Indian brave approaches her "naked on his horse," surrounded by whites trying to kill him. Doubiago's revolver "blooms into red-hot and yellow flames," useless. When he, "dark and lean," shows her how to shoot, she holds off the murderous whites, saving his life:

He is not like any man I have known.
He takes me all the way into the male world.
There is no separation as with other men with women.
Our survival depends on each other.
We are deep sexual mates in the physical eternity.
He is the one I have waited for, my strange,
familiar Oglala.

Through her poetry she perpetuates his "life":

> He lies in me long, searching quietly, as with a free
> hand, a deep and great place.
> I stir on him slowly, rising upwards, as through a flood.
> He becomes a part of what is there, a hard, gold depth.
> Behind his face the small red-hawk flies, making his killy-
> > killy crying. Without quickening his pace, moving deeply,
> > deliberately,
> he waits as I come to save his life. Only I can take death from him,
> this violet-dark son who has been killed and shines no more.
> My crazy Oglala, my strange animal.

What emerges so profoundly from *Hard Country* is the brutal awareness that sex falls dismally short of its promises. Ramon the mythic lover remains a vital part of Doubiago / Romona's psyche, a norm, like Crazy Horse, for judging all subsequent lovers, most of whom fail. As Doubiago pursues the white male, she refuses to blur distinctions between the Isis / Psyche / Emanuelle / Ramona / Loretta / Sharon force and the Sitting Bull / Ramon / Crazy Horse / Breit force. This culture remains male-dominated.

In "Song of Songs: The Lady In The Lake," the mother we've already seen drowns herself, wearing a Sunday dress, "the one she married in," a white hat, and gloves. "I'll see you in heaven," says her note:

> [She] then steps in, slipping down through the last miraculous air
> in her Sunday clothes, entering veiled, in prayer, the hushed
> sanctuary, the green cold, her earthly dress now
> dragging her the long terrible path down
> through holiness and voices, through faces
> lit in darkness, the terrible wrath gone over her
> as her navel, at last, *O Jesus to thy bosom*, oozes her out
> into the beautiful waters her sons swim in,
> floating her mother's farm in golden light, in songs of the planets
> the jubilant weeds of the glory land enfolding her, a fish now
> going down under the world

This vision is mature, the empathy profound. Doubiago's struggle to rid herself of the societal pressures on a sensitive, doomed sister to Psyche, Isis, and Proserpine, allows her to evoke the tragedy with a power that transcends sexuality. Doubiago's voice is a positive life-expression countering the male's boneyard of death, sex, and war.

LATTER-DAY PRE-RAPHAELITE:

ROBERT DUNCAN,

OR, WHERE THE BEE SUCKS

1.

Those of us who admire Robert Duncan's poetry will welcome *Scales of the Marvelous* (ed. by Robert J. Bertholf and Ian W. Reed), for it presents useful information about Duncan, assembling much hitherto scattered, and provides commentaries on his work. Most of the contributions are sufficiently conjectural to leave us free to create our own Master-of-Rime.

My personal image of Duncan the poet is of a Lady in a medieval tower who has withdrawn her bridge, forcing us to admire from afar. Occasionally, some perceptive soul will throw down his own bridge and dash madly into the castle, overcome the retainers, and proceed up those stone stairs to the tower where the Lady waits in all her brocades, wearing a chaplet of roses, ready to bestow her favors. Around her are mounds of arcane books, a complete set of first editions of *Oz*, and piles of the Lady's manuscripts. There is also a picture of Alice lifting her skirts—Alice B. Toklas, not Alice in Wonderland.

When I view this Lady who inspires poet-critic knights to untold feats of verbal courage, I do not confuse her with Tennyson's Lady of Shalott, a kindred soul who, as a pure art-for-art's sake creator, has shut herself off from all direct experiences with life. Duncan's Lady, wiser, knows much about the ravenous outside world and the encyclopedic lore underpinning that world. She's not about to stare at a flesh-and-blood knight and die; she'll devour him in her own way. She stirs up hungers in our blood for the long-gone courtly days when poets sang and cantered for their Muse/Lady, who was herself free of syphilis, impetigo, bed-lice, and armpit odors. By contrast with her ancient Greek counterparts, the Muses, our Lady is splendidly clothed: she's a figure for tapestries. Her wrist and exposed throat are probably far more erotic than her entire body would be standing naked before a court full of jongleurs and crazy poets dressed in silver.

This image of Poet-as-Lady is not as misguided as it may seem. Look at all the references to ladies, medieval settings, magicians, courtly love business, and mixed sexualities in Duncan's work. No American poet since Pound is so versed in a poetic tradition originating with Provençal and earlier poets. For Duncan poetry is a rarefied, aristocratic act transpiring outside the vicissitudes of on-going political strife and change. He uses the images of the jongleur, the Master-of-Rime, and the Lady to produce the ambience of this ancient tradition; this is his way of insisting that poetry transcends history and human pettiness. The Lady, then, as Inspirator of Poetry is to Duncan what Duncan becomes to contemporary poets influenced by him.

The metaphor of the medieval conveys Duncan's sense of Poetry's exalted role—as does his language, consciously archaic as it often is. And, if he invokes the ancient jongleurs, can Dante be far behind? We see Dante, with his big nose (to be reincarnated later on George Eliot's face), wearing his funny cap with the earflaps, his thumb in a book he wishes Duncan to read, waiting to take Duncan with him through the Infernal on the way to Paradise. Bridging as he does the medieval and the Renaissance worlds (as did Chaucer, another of Duncan's mentors), Dante symbolizes Art as Religious Event, as Visionary World.

I stress this (and I am not simply delaying a discussion of *Scales of the Marvelous*) because somehow this primary connection between Duncan and the bygone world, largely prettified and sanitized and enameled though it is, is crucial for understanding Duncan's poetry. It is barely touched on in this book. Duncan strikes me as something of a latter-day pre-Raphaelite, a projective verse Dante Gabriel Rosetti—a poet who was himself a translator of Dante, Blake enthusiast, student of the arcane and the mystical, practitioner of the different arts.

The essays in *Scales of the Marvelous* fall roughly into three groups: reminiscences, overall considerations of Duncan's work and analyses of individual books and groups of poems. The reminiscences are the least valuable of the contributions: too brief, they are sentimental and unctuous about Duncan and his private life. Joanna and Michael McClure explain that Duncan's workshop in San Francisco during the 1950s "was a divine milieu." Helen Adam's adulation is most disappointing: Her own gifted work is intimately tied to Duncan's (they are Rosicrucian soulmates), and we might hope for more than an extolling of his "genius." In a valuable reminiscence, Hamilton and Mary Tyler recount their friendship during the forties, when Duncan was writing *The Years as Catches*. R. B. Kitaj's "Etching of Robert Duncan" positions Kitaj in that world of the fifties, with Jonathan Williams, Creeley, and Duncan. Lou Harrison's "Note" on music remains disappointingly just that. Since the title of this anthology includes the word *scales* (I assume that the reference is to music, and not to fish or those over our eyes), there remains a need for a fuller treatment of Duncan and music.

Other contributions are more ambitious. Before making extended comments on four of them—Denise Levertov's, Jayne Walker's, Ian Reid's, and Michael Davidson's—I will briefly mention each of the others.

Don Byrd charts some of the thorny connections between Pound, Olson, and Duncan—a valuable piece. Eric Mottram examines metaphors in *Roots and Branches* in a rather stultified academic tone. Thom Gunn writes on the homosexual motif in Duncan, and demonstrates what I have sensed throughout Duncan's work—that he largely eschews the overtly autobiographical, preferring layered meanings reaching through several levels of time and space. Nathaniel Mackey's description of the "Uroboric impulse" is somewhat overwhelmed by quoted matter, and he is basically a pretty wooden writer (viz., his gargoyle term "Uroboric" means that Duncan's work reflects "a need or desire to root his experience, artistic or otherwise, in an assurance of precedent provided by those who have gone before"). By contrast, Gerrit Lansing says as much in two pages as Mackey says in sixteen. Sean V. Golden's "Duncan's Celtic Mode" is an informed romp through the arcane; one learns something here. The final essay, by Mark Johnson and Robert de Mott, explores connections between Duncan and Whitman—a fertile "field" indeed—but fails to deliver much beyond a few general observations.

Denise Levertov's lengthy "memoir and critical tribute" nicely bridges the reminiscences and the critical pieces. Levertov details the intense sharing, largely via letters, that transpired between her and Duncan over more than twenty years. She quotes from his letters, and we see the shaping of an important poetic between them. Being younger, Levertov saw herself as Duncan's pupil. His poems formed for her, she says, "a kind of trans-Atlantic stepping-stone." She was grateful to find "that old, incantatory tradition" in Duncan; for as a young English poet she had sought an alternative to the "dull and constipated attempts at a poetry of wit and intellect" characterizing British poetry right after World War II. Duncan, she found, seemed to make her own impending emigration to America "more possible, more real." Yet the roles they played for and with one another were not always easy. As her own aesthetics formed, she grew through conflicts with Duncan rather than through submissions to him. "A mentor," Levertov observes, "is not necessarily an absolute authority, and though Duncan's erudition, his being older than I, his often authoritative manner, and an element of awe in my affection for him combined to make me take, much of the time, a pupil role, he was all the more mentor when my own convictions were clarified for me by some conflict with his." Her perceptions of Duncan as man and artist are chillingly apt—his aesthetics of the object, "the presented thing," as he called it, come clear. She was somewhat in awe of his sophistication, the "almost encyclopedic range of his knowledge," and his living in "a literary and sexual ambience I didn't even know existed." Their first contact in the early fifties was "almost a disaster," she says, and she objectively describes the occasion. Throughout the friendship, Levertov seems to have been overly serious: She suspected Duncan was critical of her when he was really being playful, and she often felt inferior when confronted by his intellect. Her account of the cooling or falling-off of their friendship in the early seventies, when she involved herself with the anti-war movement is poignant.

Writing in a more technical vein, Michael Davidson discusses Duncan's multi-layered responses to Olson's open field theories of composition. He writes easily and perceptively about these complex issues: the hermeneutic as a means for Duncan to grasp the origins of language; Duncan's sense of the poem as an *enactment* rather than *a reflection* of cosmic and natural orders; and Duncan's fondness for Dante, Blake, and Whitman, all of whom seemed willing to allow the poem to *command* them, rather than the other way around. Davidson is incisive in presenting Duncan as a *receiver* of the poem, to whom the poem dictates, discovering its own necessary language and fields of relevance. Duncan emerges as a Romantic who employs language "as a series of transparent signs" leading towards lost Edenic or Atlantean civilizations. He desires "a new prosody," one undetermined before the actual writing of the poem. Through the almost alchemical changes, transpiring between the poet's brain, the objects he observes, and the mystical and hermeneutic abstractions, the poem's shape or form is determined. The poet invents persons to assist him: the "Master of Rime," a parallel of Nietzsche's Zarathustra, a woman "who resembles the sentence," a Lion who is the creative imagination. Poems become "language-events"; *feeling*, in Whitehead's sense, lures the poet along towards a "hurt and healing" love. "A Poem Beginning With a Line By Pindar" is central to Duncan's poetic and cosmology, and Davidson is brilliant on it, demonstrating how the poem circles around "those old stories" until it locates the "scene" of the writing.

Jayne L. Walker's tracing of Gertrude Stein's influence is one of those essays where a couple of summarizing sentences might have said most of it. For the specialist reader, though, Walker usefully details the history of Duncan's interest in Stein and his fascination with her incoherent language. Walker concludes (rightly, I think) that Duncan's imitations of Stein are consciously experimental: "He was never completely converted to her theoretical and epistemological premises." When he imitates Stein by employing words that "explode into multiplicity"—words loaded with historical meaning and with their prior uses in literary tradition—he operates "in opposition to her theoretical premises." A problem with Walker's paper is that she gives Duncan credit for too much originality; I don't see where Duncan's "assault on the structure and functions of language" is all that "radical." More radical than Stein's? Joyce's? And what of e. e. cummings? (The latter is never mentioned—and yet it seems to me that the Lady of cummings's Mystical Verbiological Mythicizing-Poeticizing was as radical, if not more so, than Duncan's.) And one can argue that a collage technique, no matter how imaginatively employed or how brilliant its contents, is still an easy way of avoiding the kinds of connections and transitions the poet has to make in lengthy traditional poems. The defense for open-field poetry is that an undercurrent of themes suffices as a structure; also, that initiates on their knees before the Lady of Myth and Verse in her Tower will understand without having the connections clarified (only the humdrum worry about such matters).

As his contribution toward de-mystifying Duncan, Ian W. Reid develops the idea of "plural texts." He decides that we are "co-poets" with Duncan, in a "collaborative response." Once again, we are told of Duncan's obsession with ritual and verse, with music and dance, with our "tribal" sense of hearth and home, and with "communal consciousness." It seems to be this latter phenomenon that allows us to *co-poet* (if there is such a verb). According to Reid, Duncan as myth-maker is primarily a "retrospective one" who seeks a return "to first things." (Can you think of any myth-makers who aren't retrospective?) Reid does present some insights about the war poems Duncan wrote during the sixties: he points out that they are not "anti-war poems but war poems, studies in struggle," in which the Vietnam War is present, "a ganglion of pain," a current manifestation of war, that "abiding social and spiritual reality which brings to poetry a mythic dimension." But, finally, Reid is trapped by Duncan's intellectuality into an even more prodigious display of learning: the poet and critic dance together on opposite sides of the room, furiously twirling their Loie Fuller drapes and spinning through brain-fields of the arcane. Fortunately, when I return to Duncan's poetry I find that his energy, zest, and passion are still intact.

There are pitfalls to writing projective verse, obviously—pitfalls that no one in this volume says much about. These critics assume that Duncan is a major (which he is) and nearly faultless (which he is not) poet: his Lady's skirts are never rent, her maquillage never runs, and she never mistakenly mouths a word askew. It seems to me that any poet who thinks that he becomes a transcriber for his poem rather than a direct shaper of it may be in big trouble. According to this belief, the poem underway determines its own "field," and the poet—almost as if he were an automatic writer—must pursue. If the bunny is excitable, the "poem" will take many jumps and bumblings through the gorse, furze, and blackberry shrubs. If the bunny is simply out there sniffing the air, hoping for another bunny in heat and relishing life, obviously his "field" won't be as pulsating and disturbed and helter-skelter. By this standard, every shape and direction a poem assumes must be good because the poet received and transmitted it. I'm afraid, folks, it ain't necessarily so.

Another pitfall is erudition. Duncan, one senses, has mastered much that his followers have not, and any trivial, esoteric bit of information they may possess about pygmies, skuas, the diets of seers in ancient Egypt, the positions of planets during the burning of Rome, etc., becomes instant expertise. And even Duncan, as masterful as he is, can at times write preciously; strange orts crumble from the Lady's ruby lips. The collage method at times lacks cement (and I find this true of moments in the highly-praised Pindar poem). Even Homer nodded, as they say.

My fussings about some of *Scales of the Marvelous* should not dissuade readers from buying and reading it; it has strengths. It is the second volume in a series published by New Directions called "Insights: Working Papers in Contemporary Criticism" (the first was on John Hawkes). "Working Papers" nicely reflects the spirit of the Duncan volume. Obviously, I would have liked the weaker pieces omitted and the reminiscences strengthened. I would like to have seen more of an objective assessment of Duncan, less adulation. The editors seem to view their book as part of an on-going exploration of Duncan's writing. The statements made here by the contributors, then, are not to be seen as final. My guess is that the Lady in her Tower will be delighted with these courtiers. In *Scales of the Marvelous* there are several fine breachings of her moat.

2. *Where The Bee Sucks: A Meditation on Duncan's "Night Scenes"*

As Roland Barthes said, the need to say "I love you" is a lack. In Robert Duncan's trio of "Night Scenes" that lack drives a young poet into New York's glaring neon streets where he wanders the homosexual world of quest, pursuit, and connection. He is fear-ridden—there are cruising police cars everywhere. The time seems to be the mid or late fifties—before minority protest movements, when gays were routinely bashed by fag-haters and entrapped by the police. In this courageous poem Duncan creates Whitmanic music; each of the three movements is a strategic improvisation on a young homosexual's coming of age.

Confrontation
An "up-riding" moon attached to a line flows from a lion's mane—created by traffic lights. Ascension: an image of stunning visual beauty tied to earth moves

through the sky. Street lights symbolize "sexual avenues" of threat and motion. These avenues, "whaleshark dark," push up blunt noses of loneliness. They seem subterranean, at psychological levels below the lions of the street with their brilliant lighted manes. In neon-glow nests and shadows the young man moves. Neither lion surfaces nor whale-shark depths swallow him. Consummating his cravings for other males releases Eros—his guilt recedes. The warm male hand going to his throat says No; the vigorous male hand caressing his groin says *Yes*. God's face, he knows, has rarely blessed the homosexual. The "divine" glimmers accusingly from the windows of cruising police cars. Protect society! Procreate more soldiers, police, fathers!

Duncan, the first poet in America to publish "cocksucker" in a poem, is the courageous poet of the Barthesian letter Z, that letter of deviant, reactive energy. Homosexual drives demand lightning dashes through streets rife with police and gangs of queer-beaters. A pull of incredible forces: a straight line sails to the moon; a zigzag of denial and fear jolts its way through the streets.

Celebration

The penis is a sperm fountain-stamen. Duncan's celebration is a collage-music of lover/lovers in a "grand chorale" of sexual being. A marvelous panegyric, improvisational, on the bliss of male sex. The hero's life-line no longer zigzags—it becomes a direct Whitmanic current "forth-flowing" from "green lovers" in "a fearful happiness." The hitherto inexperienced youth sees in the eyes of his lover a resolute mystical eye. Opposites spring forth, twined, as a "light toward the knotted tides of dark." The lovers inspire the "Prince of Morning" to open "a door of Eros." Filled with sperm, sated with bliss, the Prince "falls" into wisdom. From the Beast (copulation) emerges Beauty.

Duncan's turn to a lyric mode (to a modified aubade) is a celebration. "Maiden hours" dance, "circling" to slow the lovers' ecstasy. Archaic, semi-medieval allusions borrowed from Provençal love-poetry and from Shakespeare's *The Tempest* suggest timelessness. Morning "steales upon the night." Darkness dissolves. The lovers' "rising sences / Begin to chace the ignorant fumes that mantle / Their cleerer reason." Homosexual love, transcendent, sweeps ignorance and guilt away. Loving another man releases a total sexuality, a fresh music developed from "the first melody" of the first movement of "Night Scenes." And yet, another paradox: the very core of sexual ecstasy is female. A Shakespearean innocence blesses the lovers—the Cowslip and the Sucking Bee. Duncan's youthful lover enters the flower—"Where the Bee sucks there suck I." Semen-honey sweeps up the stamen, primal, as "the mothertides of the first magic," Adamic, when Adam, as yet alone, discovered masturbation, and flowers, and the mystery of generation.

We are all, in a sense, Adam in our penis-wisdom—a lover's mouth is far superior to our own hand. The lover knows "I am not I"; I am, rather, a texture of sexual identities. As I suck, my lover's penis "lifts lifewards." The "spirit of the hour" descends. And it doesn't matter that my lover is anonymous. There's no lessening of intensity, of becoming. All longing and incompletion dissolve as I shape my throat around my lover's "single up-fountain of a/single note...." The resultant "grand chorale" of identities is fugal, not frugal.

Transcendence

A professor, said Barthes, completes his sentences. I assume then that a poet may *not* complete his, preferring elipses, smoke-hints, fumings at the mystical gates, collage effects arranged from other poets (medieval lyricists, Shakespeare, André Breton). The beaker bubbles over. Brain zephyrs waft bubbles along the moon's track towards the golden harpstrings of the sun.

Part Three of "Night Scenes" is just such an evocation of the *overheard* rather than the *heard* joys of maleness. Food and labor ("circulations of food and rays") illuminate "the torsos of men and trucks in their own light, steaming." A gargantuan celebration, one Whitman would have loved. The poem *is* a male body. The sinuous lines of flexed sweating muscles straining in fields and warehouses create sexual cathedrals for the mind. If Part Two of "Night Scenes" is a resolving of our female selves, this part, since the female/male elements are now synchronized, reflects a new male freedom—to love men without guilt and recrimination. The rosy slit of the penis symbolizing the heart's meat-dream, is an "opening in Paradise."

Duncan's youth rejects his earlier dreaming and is no longer closeted. The males he enjoys now are not the males of fantasy disguised by the artifice of his imagination—he doesn't require medieval or Shakespearean escape motifs. The poet Breton provides clues. The image of his *parvis*, or forecourt, of the poet's imagination / temple, stimulates a fresh vision of potent males. The mystical Byzantine Queen of art is now sterile: penises are no longer glowing tapers, nor are the gorgeous flanks of strong men lion-flanks. One's sexual cravings are not diluted into mystical feelings and imagery. Thoroughly open treatments of homosexuality in art are possible now, without disguises. The Queen, therefore, becomes the Zolaesque queen of the belly of Paris—a "temple of produce" is her palace "of transport and litanies." In her Outer Court, half nude men are seen "mounting and dismounting" trucks (and one another). The Queen savors that primal beauty (music) engendered by the loins of men loving men. In these modern environs the poet is at home, free. His heart "smokes." His fumbling through the zigzag streets have reached the moon. What an incredible interweaving of allusion, fantasy, realism and art! "Night Scenes" is a pioneering poem, merely one of an impressive gathering of his works on sexual themes.

CHARLIE CHAPLIN BETWEEN THE ON-SALE SHEETS
AT MACY'S:
LAWRENCE FERLINGHETTI'S SELECTED POEMS

"there is some s. I will not eat"
— e. e. cummings, from "i sing of Olaf glad and big"

Light-Headed Dandelions Float Over the Landscape

In his "Populist Manifesto" (1976), Lawrence Ferlinghetti delineates what poetry should be and do. Poetry, he says, is "the common carrier" that transports the public "to higher places / than other wheels can carry it." Like drifting leaves, dandelions, butterflies, moths, angels, and fallout, poetry continues to tumble into our "still open" streets. Implicit is the idea that while the streets are closing, poetry continues to appear quietly, even where it's unwelcome.

Ferlinghetti is optimistic. The world, so hostile, so various, so wracked with hypocrisy and upheaval, is still peopled with "lovely men & women" (Whitman's "wild children") who need poets to lead them again into "open air." The esoteric nihilist and the effete poet must return to a populist mainstream.

His "Adieu à Charlot," from his "Second Populist Manifesto" (1979), is both an elegy for Charles Chaplin, one of his favorite self-images, and for the death of *duende* in contemporary poetry. The stark didacticism here is made palatable by Ferlinghetti's freshness, humor, and intelligence. The "blood duende" flows throughout the works of Poe, Lorca, Rimbaud, D. H. Lawrence, Kenneth Patchen, and Ginsberg—"Sons of Whitman," Ferlinghetti calls them. *Duende*, the life force so prized by Lorca, is the potent *subjective*we have lost. And that explains Ferlinghetti's recent assertion: "Modern Poetry is Prose (But It is Saying Plenty)." Furthermore, contemporary poets are isolated in their "separate lonesome visions." Within some writers, these "Whitmans of another breath," the *duende* lies dormant as the blood-song of a "dark singing." It waits amidst chrome, steel, and glass, between "the tickings of civilization," and is heard in the "silences" between the cars we drive "like weapons" over the freeways. Somewhere up the road, poets will reclaim the land and the vast subjective sea; then, in time, *duende* will assist poetry to eschew the prose voice it has assumed.

I am moved by Ferlinghetti's call for poets to reawaken and prevail over the "short-haired hyenas" of politics and religion dominating the world. Poets must drift through the fields, streets, and suburbs with the ease of "light-headed dandelions" borne along on sweet duende-zephyrs. The dream is archetypal, primordial. And who orchestrates this dream? The poet.

An Unidentified "Asshole"

In "Eight People on A Golf Course and One Bird of Freedom Flying Over," Ferlinghetti satirizes a sick culture through images of seven power-mad fascists and one "little Woman" who, in good anti-ERA fashion, goes along with the men who exploit her. The seven males are: the President of the Earth, the King of the Car, the Head of Religion, the Military General, the Media Czar, the Multinational Banker, and the Chief of All Police (who carries the clubs). As they assemble on the golf course, they are disturbed by "some dumb bird," who flies past their radar screen. The Police Chief complains that every time he shoots the bird down it rises again—that "one / unidentified asshole" keeps on escaping. Yes, folks, that indestructible bird is the poet who like the ancient phoenix rises from its ashes.

"Director of Alienation" is a more ambitious treatment of the theme. As he so often does, Ferlinghetti invites us into his poem via populist images, in settings familiar and commonplace. Here we ride the escalators at Macy's and regard ourselves in the classy mirrors. This is a horrid conformist world, machine-tooled, and plastic, amid which the alienated poet seeks his angel (his *duende?*). Once again, the estranged poet is a reincarnation of Charlie Chaplin. When a store teletector scans him he turns paranoid. As the floor-dicks approach, afraid the rascal will throw some new underwear on his filthy body, Chaplin returns to the escalators where he's not so visible. Full-length mirrors seem arranged to make him look his worst, so that he'll buy (or steal) new clothes. He decides to play the game, so shucks his "grungy threads." He slides down the escalators naked and climbs in between the on-sale sheets on the on-sale bed. He uses the new flush toilet, showers in the portable shower, and leaves the bath wearing "something" sexy. Keystone store cops chase him. To escape, he grabs an Eva Gabor wig and freezes. He has time now to meditate on decadence—current culture is a "wrack" (clothes rack?); and he imagines the seven floors of the store as equivalents for Dante's Circles of Hell.

Faced with a dead American Bicentennial year, the only way to belong is to rush to Macy's basement and work your way up through all seven stages, or *bowges* [the levels of Hell in Dante's *Divine Comedy*]. At the top you'll reach the Credit Department where you are "consumed." Amid "this alien corn" (in the sense both of Keats and of "corny") the comedy turns bittersweet; for the alienated anarchist comic-poet-man turns suicidal and jumps off, waving his "plastic jewels and genitals." The poem is a brilliant homily—energetic, funny, accessible—almost. It's when we review the suicide that we grow unsure. Ferlinghetti, when he's enraged, never plays the injured butterfly withdrawing to mend his damaged wings, weep, and pursue private obsessions. He's never the aesthete, although he knows a lot about the aesthetic experience. When he feels anger, he subverts it via humor (see the marvellous Neruda-like "Underwear"). His victims never quite know whether he's laughing at them or with them.

In "Baseball Canto," Ferlinghetti attends a game. Somewhat ironically, he poses as a plain bloke who, like all good red-blooded Americans, loves baseball. But he is hardly a plain bloke, for as he awaits the first pitch, he reads Ezra Pound, probably the only soul among the thousands there so occupied. During the playing of the "National Anthem," he's amused by the white umpires wearing their black suits and "little black caps" held over their hearts, like Irish cops at a funeral for "a blarney bartender." There are numerous literary allusions, where the alienated poet enjoys his role as recalcitrant angel, an "asshole" unidentified, lost in the conformist mass. Whenever he is of the devil's party, Ferlinghetti knows it.

Body of Being

One of the most cryptic and effective poems on a socio-political theme is "White on White" where Ferlinghetti employs Chagall-like images of a railway station platform, a riderless white horse in flight from "a torn village," and an angel who appears as the platform crowds up with people fleeing a fiery holocaust. The poem is an exercise in *white*.

Suddenly, Ferlinghetti zooms in on the railway platform jammed with people who are met by placards: "No pasaran / Go Back Wrong Way." Behind them, white searchlights sweep the skies. Gun turrets loom over old city walls. Fascist-politicos, we guess, have ravished the earth—no passage is safe without "white documents." Then we see the angel, who seems a figure of hope as he waits on the platform to carry "the body of being" away from the chaos. This body, I gather, is that precious *duende* seen earlier—the blood-body of sanity, beauty, hope, and mystery. As the angel waits, moving its fragile wings, "white phoenixes arise." Who are these phoenixes prompted by these celestial pinions? Possibly the spirits of anarchist poets ascending from the ashes of the present towards a rebirth, one still mysterious in its shape, known only by the "white sphinx of chance" who, like all good sphinxes, remains silent about those future "desert roads."

Despite my simplistic review, "White on White" invites several readings, and even then the poem never wholly resolves itself. It remains cryptic without ever flagging in quality. Ferlinghetti's imaginative and conceptual energies are high.

Up-Town Qualities / Dick and Jane Riffs

Jazz, e. e. cummings, Dick and Jane primers, and comic-book language are important influences on Ferlinghetti's style. In a culture where people no longer read, traffic signs have to be printed in large capitals, and directions must be repeated ad nauseum. Insipid dialogue and the language of comic books (and soap operas) suit our sense of *writing*. In "Home Home Home" (the title itself is a lip-strumming babble) is written this way, as a devastating satire on commuter culture:

> home to the nest
> home to the warm caves
> in the hidden hills & valleys
> home to daddy home to mama
> home to the little wonders
> home to the pot plants
> behind the garage....

Ferlinghetti wields this writing with immense skill—baby nursery lines for commuter-class kid-adults ridden with dope, sex, psychological, and real estate hang-ups. Here, a ninety-seven pound housewife, driving "two tons of chrome and steel," goes three blocks to the supermarket to buy diaper pins for baby. Daddy's a-hunting in the city, working as a salesman on a big deal plastic job. On his way home, he drives oblivious past "wet-backs" laboring in Salinas Valley vegetable fields. All he anticipates is being safe and smug in his tract house surrounded by his appliances.

While Ferlinghetti's repetitions and the funky end-rhymes may suggest the Campbell Soup cans and Brillo pads popular in paintings of the '60s, they really aren't like Warhol's series on Marilyn Monroe and the auto wreck. Ferlinghetti's primer-talk is exactly that—babies talking to babies—spoiled Ken and Barbie doll-people who've never grown up. In Warhol's pictures, slight changes occur as the frames change; the central figures of Monroe and the wreck remain static throughout. In contrast, Ferlinghetti never repeats the same detail, making mere minor changes in color and shape. His repetitions relate more to jazz, to "up-town sound," as he calls it, than to painting.

Ferlinghetti, of course, was of the Bay Area jazz-poetry scene of the '50s, one initiated by Kenneth Rexroth well before the Beats in their lurid carapaces descended upon San Francisco. Ferlinghetti was also a seminal devotee of poetry as oral performance, of word-riffs rendered in jazz modes.

"In a Time of Revolution" assumes a combo in the background as the poet declaims his lines. At the outset, he adopts the voice and tongue of a drag-queen fond of adverbs (*very* and *gently*), which he employs lavishly to describe some "very beautiful" and "very fucked-up people" in a restaurant. "Very" cool, he soon abandons the soft-toned adverbs and the drag-queen manner. His line-breaks allow delays for interweaving combo-sounds, as people zonked on booze or dope drift back into little peaks of awareness before retreating to blissful passive states.

One of Ferlinghetti's best poems in a jazz style is "Salute." Employing repetitions, he gives various folk the finger—and he does it well, much better than most authors of the serial poem. Serial poems are usually boring; the repetitions resemble ancient Chinese water tortures. In defense, one reads only the right sides of line (right brain / left brain) where things change. Ferlinghetti knows that a good jazz-set has to keep the cats awake; so he rings changes on the abused serial form and employs some expected figures—police with dogs, rednecks with sawed-off shotguns, hunters in pickup trucks—all socially-approved killers of man and beast. But he has surprises: he roasts a state trooper; and he sees poets and prophets as killer-fascists: to "every prophet or poet with gun or shiv and any enforcer / of spiritual enlightenment with force and any

> enforcer of the power of any state
> with Power
> And to any and all who kill & kill
> & kill & kill for Peace
> I raise my middle finger
> in the only proper salute.

My Sweet Old Etcetera / Aunt Lucy

The influence of e. e. cummings on Ferlinghetti seems considerable, and deserves a fuller treatment than I am able to provide here. Most of Ferlinghetti's poems, to some degree, evoke the shade of e.e.c.—the satiric thrusts; the knack for offending fascists, conformists, and misguided poets; the lively language—much wordplay, punning, pop rhymes, lower-case writing; the echoes of older poets, (Ferlinghetti likes Keats, Whitman, Yeats, Eliot, Pound, and Dylan Thomas); the reduction of humans to doll-states—cummings would have loved Ken and Barbie dolls; the political-social dimensions—cummings was here the very model of a modern anarchist general; the kinky sexuality—surrogate whores, doll-women, weird dildoes, and assorted promiscuities; a ruthless, often funny, self-scrutiny—cummings looks into a mirror and sees "a clown's smirk in the skull of a baboon" and a "shape who merely eats and turds...ere with the dirt death shall him vastly gird"; and the consciously tacky endrhymes, rendered in a music-hall manner. cummings, never officious, eschewed the pompous and the sententious for a humorous and healthy perspective on himself. If, as he believed, we live in *lower-case times,* there is no need for a self-aggrandizement symbolized by the capital I. His humor wins because, like Ferlinghetti's, it transpires here with us—no *ex cathedra* deliveries from some windy pulpit, podium, or Tamalpais eminence.

The elegy Ferlinghetti wrote on the murders of George Moscone and Harvey Milk by twinkies-freak Dan White, "An Elegy to Dispel Gloom," employs cummings-like language, line-breaks, understatement, and allusions to lines from older poets: Here is Ferlinghetti on blood and sacrifice:

> It is pure vanity
> to think that all humanity
> be bathed in red
> because one young mad man
> one so bad man
> lost his head.
> The force that through the red fuse
> drove the bullet....

The effect, though seemingly playful, is serious—a dramatic irony similar to that found in cummings—or, in Gertrude Stein, whose shade seems to hover over lines 4-6 above.

Ken Barbie look-alikes appear full-blown in "Two Scavengers in a Truck, Two Beautiful People in a Mercedes." A garbage rig pulls up beside an elegant convertible, revealing a young man in a "hip three-piece linen suit," wearing sunglasses and shoulder-length blonde hair. He's with a young, blonde, casually-coiffed female in a short skirt. A red light pairs this unlikely foursome. The future, Ferlinghetti implies, belongs to the men in the truck, not to the mannikins in the

Mercedes. In "Lost Parents," "throwaway children" keep searching for their disposable dads and moms who are racing down the freeways pursuing sexual and encounter group assignations, in a contemporary movie gone amok. The children never succeed in their Jungian quest for lost parents.

I began this essay with some trepidation. Like so many other poets I had merely accepted Ferlinghetti's presence the way one accepts the daily smell of journalists (or of socks and shoes, or of Ray Bradbury's poems—they are always there). I read Ferlinghetti, cummings,and Dylan Thomas much in the 'seventies. Ferlinghetti's best book, I believed, was *A Coney Island of the Mind*—not much of interest seemed to happen after that. How wrong I was! He has grown impressively. His faith in an "endless life" is contagious without being sentimental; and his saturnine iconoclasm and technical skills are brilliant. The world may be full of plastic hearts, plastic politicians, and plastic poets. As long, however, as Ferlinghetti and canine trot freely through the world there's hope. It may take some time yet for the *duende* he longs for to resurface full-throttled. Until then, reading him will show us how to avoid some of the shit the world expects us to eat.

References
Readers may wish to recall a couple of moments in e.e.cummings, relevant to the "Aunt Lucy" section above: Cf. cummings' "little girl / with the good teeth and small important breasts"; little Effie "whose brains are made of gingerbread" and the "little bride and groom" made of candy standing atop a wedding cake, being admired by the little bride and groom being married. See cummings's "Ever-Ever Land" addressed to "sweet morons" who may or may not see that "sameness is normal"; "Jehovah buried Satan dead," where cummings declares that "this world is all aleak" and we are caught without life preservers; "kumrads die because they're told" and the famous "i sing of Olaf glad and big," one of the great anti-militarist poems in the language.

WIDE-AWAKE BUTTERFLY: TESS GALLAGHER

Of the poems on family matters in Tess Gallagher's *Willingly*, the last is the most complex and passionate. Here she accompanies her younger brother Morris and his ten-year-old daughter Leslie to cut wood. Morris was not their father's favorite son; in fact, he was so often and severely whipped that Gallagher looking back says that today the man would be jailed. The father recently died of cancer. Morris resolves the father's distaste by becoming uncannily like him; though he does not beat his child, he chain-smokes Camels and loves the woods. He's even given his daughter Leslie his father's name. Morris loves cutting trees—he boasts of a pile "of logs / high as a house he's thinned from the timber."

There were childhood tensions between Tess and Morris. When the father shamed Morris by taking Tess fishing and leaving him home, Morris drew pictures of his sister "all over the chicken house," armless sinking below the waves. They share other memories: their dad felling a tree; the logging horse Old Dick; the skeletons of hounds shot because they were superfluous "arches of bones leaping with beetles and / crawlers into the barkrich earth"; Morris lost on a hunting trip, distressing the father.

Much now is resolved—Morris can boast to Tess of his daughter's prowess/virility: "Sonofagun, I wouldn't trade four boys for her." When Gallagher explains to him that tree cells are like human blood cells, and that trees are the earth's oldest organisms, he's only mildly impressed, "has his own way of thinking about trees."

Gallagher's drift is towards what will unify experience by merging it with larger concepts, viz., time, aging, death, memory, and panoramic natural forms (particularly mountains). Morris is the pragmatist and doer, with his mind on the particular tree he is felling. He's sensitive to the despoilation of the Washington forests, and if he means to exist as a logger must move to Alaska "where the trees are." As an archetypal loner he feels increasingly displaced, even betrayed by the wastage of the forests. The gnawing paradox for Morris, as for any sensitive logger, is that for his livelihood he contributes to the diminishing of the forests he loves.

On the return home, Leslie falls asleep between Morris and Tess in the cab of their ancient truck. Morris wryly observes the sleeping daughter, wakes her briefly: "She must be part butterfly, just look at those eyes," he says, as she falls asleep again. Once home, he carries her from the car, then, seeing that she's awake, puts her down and tells her to walk for herself: "Wide awake. Butterfly." The image is most appropriate for Gallagher herself: all of her poems are marked with intense seeing, of objects observed with the clarity of a large lidless-eye.

Most of her poems begin blindly, denotatively, almost as though they are journal entries, or moments in letters to friends or relatives, of seemingly unobtrusive life-events. Some starts are mundane: "We are three women eating out," "I was coming down the wide, painted steps," "When I get up he has been long at work," "A women is reading a poem on the street."

Gallagher uniquely forges these experiental poems into things of rare lyrical beauty. A poem on descending "wide, painted steps" devolves into a profound love poem: a lover is leaving, apparently for good, and the speaker is anxious to accompany him. Perhaps her independence has driven him off. Has she been too subservient? Now, she declares, she would go submissively, like a farmer following a horse "to keep the rows straight." She invites him to see her in her own way:

> Think of me as one who lives things quickly,
> cruelly as a car could live it.
> Think of me as one who stands in the streets,
> speeding past with the stopped wheel
> in my hands, and the radio, its small heart
> flickering along the trees ahead.

Her trio of dining women love flirting with a young waiter. As Jerry serves them crepes flambeaux he blushes, "like a young russet girl." The lips of the women, "good-looking and older," are "red with fire and juice." Gallagher weaves a subtle motif of the swift nature of happiness—Jerry has pleased the women and senses the ephemerality of joy, which dies at the very moment the women themselves are in full glow.

Other poems begin cryptically, drawing us immediately into drama. Here is the opening of "Some With Wings, Some With Manes": "Over the stone wall her hand comes, / each knuckle enlarged to a miniature / skull." Immediately, Gallagher's uncanny empathy for others, lavished throughout this book, appears: the arthritic woman (the image of knuckles as skulls is splendid) pushes her walker up to the wall separating her yard from the one Gallagher rents. "Effort," to the old woman (her name is "Dolly") "is nobility." The woman means to be helpful, tells Gallagher that her peach tree will, if pruned, be heavy with peaches—but Gallagher won't be there; she'll have moved away.

Dolly insists that because she keeps moving she will live longer than a sister, victim of the same disease: "She / sat down with it and that was the end of / her." The woman's stark "reluctance" conjures an image of a long-forgotten, favorite kite strung up in a peartree. After days of battering, the kite disappears ("the tree caressed it / into flight, one day I wasn't looking"). The image is complex. Does the arthritic woman, hanging on, resemble the kite caught in the tree, maintaining visibility though crippled? Will death soon make her invisible? Once the tree loses the kite it becomes any other tree. After her death, will Dolly's yard be like all the other neighborhood yards? Or is Gallagher, as the old woman chatters on, lost in private memory, the image of the kite, then, being utterly personal? Both possibilities are true, I think, and the image is characteristic of Gallagher's complexities. Like the best poetry, much here is elusive, viz., in this passage where the precise nature of "ecstasy" evades us. Is a defiance of disease/death conducive to ecstasy? Is the tattered, tree-trapped kite a living image of the child's joy when the kite actually flew?

> Somehow we knew in our child-hearts
> when a thing is ruined, not to meddle
> with ecstasy by setting it free. We left it,
> though it ruffles the mind yet.

And there's more: Gallagher enters the old woman's house, and is shown an "elaborate coverlet" stitched and pieced with great pain by those arthritic skull-fingers. To see the quilt the old woman leads Gallagher down a "grassy corridor / to a room sleeping like a princess." The image of room / princess has reverberations: death is the prince who will appear. And the quilt pattern itself evokes the mystical: "'Cathedral Windows,' she says, / and the razed light of her hands / falls over me." How tempting it is to over-stress the symbolism: windows to Eternity. What makes this image effective is its mix of reality and the transcendental. At the same time, Gallagher's pragmatism matters; this is a literal quilt fashioned by the crippled fingers of a real woman with literal designs of cathedral windows. The kite trapped in a tree was an actual childhood kite remembered. Veracity is paramount, as it is to all writers of reportage—to Thoreau, Whitman, Melville, Frost, or Wakoski. One counts the bean rows, determines the measurements of harpooned whales, observes the scary eyes peeking forth as so many firkins from the New Hampshire woods.

Her several gifts Gallagher often seasons with humor. In "Linoleum" she's fresh, sceptical, and bemused. She's been thinking of the Jains, the Indian sect that avoids killing any living creature. And here she is, washing her car with a rotating brush, in an orgy of anti-Jainism. Those dead bugs gush off "into a soup / of grit and foam...." The Jains atone for her "neglect"; for, she says, if we all behaved as Jains there'd be no one "heartless enough to plow the spuds," for fear of slicing a worm in two. She recalls the considerable list of Jain virtues, and their short list of vices: anger, pride, greed, and illusion. She drives to the supermarket, hears the radio news (most of it violent) and feels "a longing / for religion, for doctrine swift / as a broom to keep the path clear." Later, alone in her kitchen, she re-reads the Jain lists, takes up her broom, and begins where she stands, cleaning the linoleum.

"You Talk On Your Telephone; I Talk On Mine" blends humor and seriousness. During a lengthy phone call, she walks to a window, telling the caller that he/she is unaware she has done so. Identities ebb and shift: if she were to hang up and call back would they pick up where they left off? "It would still be us, right?" Much of the poem records the off-the-wall notions she entertains as the call transpires: "Who can depend on coincidences anymore to give / significance." The Africa "of our childhoods, tigers chasing their tails / around the butter-tree." Running out to a phone booth near an all-night gas station would be like phoning from a "glass coffin" standing on end. A remarkable image, that last one.

Original observations grace nearly every poem. Here Gallagher describes elk shot by her father and brothers: "The elk hung / their golden heads in the dirt / of the shed. A long suddenness had / closed their eyes open." A father dies:

> Like a cut rose
> on the fifth day, you bowed
> into yourself and we watched the shell-
> shaped petals drop in clumps, then,
> like wine, deepen into the white cloth.
> Later, remembering the father will be like having seen him in a dream:
> So does
> a bird dismiss one tree for another
> and carries each time the flight between
> like a thing never done.

Reading the Japanese poet Mutso Takahashi, "even in translation," is "to stroke open the eyes / of a dove." She and a stranger hug so "truly" and "tenderly" they "stop having arms." And this is like a koan: "A tree is bending / but the bird doesn't land."

While humor and special flashes of insight are devices for distancing serious themes, so too is Gallagher's fashioning of tightly chiselled cadences to convey stark material. In "Each Bird Walking," a son must bathe his invalid mother—something each of us fears we may be called upon to do. Simply seeing a parent naked carries a Biblical taboo—the drunken, nude Noah revealing himself to his sons. I would assume that for a son to bathe a nude mother is more difficult than to cleanse a father; sons tend to revere their mothers more than their fathers. Gallagher presents totemic fears.

Enjambment and alternating pentameter and tetrameter lines heighten the drama. A series of present participles thread through softening the stark beat. The mother assists the son who is bathing her:

>   ...moving
>
>   the little she could, lifting so he could
>   wipe under her arms, a dipping motion
>   in the hollow. Then working up from
>   the feet, around the ankles, over the
>   knees. And this last, opening
>   her thighs and running the rag firmly
>   and with the cleaning touch
>   up through her crotch, between the lips,
>   over the V of thin hairs

The poem next takes an amazing turn—the new theme is the "end of our loving," a declaration by the lover which prompts Gallagher to look "to see what was left of us / with our sex taken away." The style varies now; lengthy adverbial phrases, in Whitman's manner, are the primary sound clusters. Single, interrupting words dropped in hasten the stanzaic flow:

>   On our lips that morning, the tart juice
>   of the mothers, so strong in remembrance, no
>   asking, no giving, and what you said, this
>   being the end of our loving, so as not to hurt
>   the closer one to you, made me look
>   to see what was left of us
>   with our sex taken away. "Tell me," I said,
>   "something I can't forget. " Then the story of
>   your mother, and when you finished
>   I said, "that's good, that's enough."

This wind-off might strike one as worthy of a female Ernest Hemingway—the absence of self-pity, the simplified delivery of a momentous resolution (here of love), the implicit toughness—all of which raises the issue of Gallagher's view of herself as a woman.

In "Conversation With A Fireman From Brooklyn," the male/female polarity is rendered with clarity and humor. Gallagher meets a fireman in an airport bar. The dude "doesn't mind / women firefighters, but what / they look like / *after* fighting a fire, well they lose all respect." He doesn't like his women "sweaty and stinking." Oh, the stereotypes!

In "The Shirts," Gallagher displays a collection she owns, all (green, blue, flannel) from different men. Her favorite shirt belongs to the man who's loved her best:

> Man with the passion to burn his love out
> in me, nightly, daily, the white-hot
> tongs of love. He wears it to breakfast.
> Wants pure maple syrup. He likes the pitcher
> full. He can stand the sweetness.

In "Bird-Window-Flying," she's been gathering armloads of green alder, and remembers a lover, the memory sharpened by a stunning image of a bird flailing against a window. Once the creature exhausts itself, she cups it in her hands ("warm over the heartwings") and recalls the lover, released—as she now releases the bird. She enters her house, builds a fire, glories in her woman's passion, potent, ready to deliver:

> All
> all the walls, all the
> wings of my house burning. The flames
> of me, the long hair unbraiding.

A long poem, "Boat Ride," commemorates an episode from her Washington girlhood, an early morning fishing trip for salmon, with her father and a male friend. As usual, the details recollected years later in memory are most vivid: the preparations, reaching the water, catching loathsome dogfish rather than salmon, the father's lack of faith in the survivability of either spirit or body, and the play of her own imagination (the boat's chugging motor suggests *pigtails* and *cello*). Her role as female is complex: she must see to it that her friend, a visiting New Yorker, catches fish; she must humor the father, providing an affectionate gentleness (this is her last fishing trip with him); anticipating the father's approaching death from cancer—he asks for his billfold, as if "even his belongings might be pulled into / the vortex of what would come."

Later, after the father dies, Gallagher's mother brings out her dad's old silk vest and cleans it, in "Black Silk." Women as survivors. They spread the garment on the kitchen table, smooth it out, examine it, the mother declaring: "'That's one thing I never / wanted to be...a man.'" Gallagher goes to the bathroom to see how she looks wearing the vest in its "sheen and sadness." Sounds of wind chimes and the mother crying. Gallagher makes a choice against returning immediately to comfort the mother; she must be self-reliant, a woman acting unsentimentally:

> Time
> to go to her, I thought, with that
> other mind, and stood still.

Gallagher never abandons basic male/female polarities. A woman must be loved for her "sweetness," which in no sense means subservience, an issue Gallagher resolves in "Painted Steps."

There is more to be written of Gallagher's fascination with horses and with birds, seminal metaphors, yet further evidence of her rare pragmatism; her sensitivity to the psyches of others; her maturity as lover, sister, and daughter; her celebrations of life especially when it is harrowing and difficult; her immersions in nature; her eschewing of the sentimental and the facile; her flexible verse music; and her always surprising imagination.

In my own southern California backyard a butterfly settles and rises and settles again as it wafts over a lavish spread of multicolored nasturtiums. It has an uncanny sense of where it means to go—its eyes are indeed wide open, a "wide awake butterfly."

*   *   *

Note: In a recent letter to me, Gallagher explains what she meant to say about the mother-son taboo. "I think it's maybe also more than the nakedness that is feared, but also that intimacy with the primal energy of the mother which Freud has warned sons of with the term 'Oedipus Complex.' Sexual desire for the mother is taboo as part of that primal energy. My poem is an attack on the mother aversion mechanism of Freud's theory—the idea of mothers as eaters of sons....I wasn't satisfied with just presenting the washing ritual, but...moved the poem into the giving up of the love between narrator and son so this plays back as ending over the ending of the mother, and adds a fresh layer of pain that is somehow also beauty for me. But the ultimate action of the poem seems to cleanse even the lovers and the perception of the reader, I hope, who receives the story that can't be forgotten. The poem is 'memory alive'—to use E. Dickinson's words from 'Remorse—is memory alive.' I'm not interested much in remorse, but memory is really that amazing gift I want to serve in all its inflections." [May 20, 1986].

FUNKY POETRY:

GINSBERG'S *THE FALL OF AMERICA*

Funky poetry is my invention for a genre of poem best executed by Allen Ginsberg. Poetry in Salvation Army clothes hung with rusted medals and pendants culled from the trash heaps of America and from the head shops of eastern mysticism. Poetry in Whitman's easiest colloquial, cataloguing, suspiring manner, of the Whitman clad in frayed and soiled Big Mac overalls just in from the barn of the universe, that Vedantaesque-pseudo Blakean-Kerouacian stables. The poet is to locate nuggets in the animal-magical ordure of this life—these states.

Yes, a tatty form, a diarrhea (frequently) of phrases and projective verse breath group clusters, a telegraphic mode intended to speed (no pun intended) the reader along towards enlightenment, and at its best evoking Gary Snyder's sufi-zenism by scaling the nearest ponderosa pine towards nirvana, drunk on manzanita tea and the memory of friends' anuses. In an issue of *Camels Coming Newsletter* (3) Ginsberg produces this cover-page definition of literary pollution:

> What's literary pollution? Immediate association,
> first thought, is plethora of books mimeo mags
> papers arriving in mail & more in bookstores
> wherein's reprinted every body & soul's amateur
> celestial ravings & scribblings. More than eye can read.
> Over-load of poetic information. A million
> authors can't be read, even by most well-meaning scholar.
> Space age proliferation of written paper &
> conspicuous consumption of raw language.
> Towers of Babel ! So I shut up and meditate
> an hour a day, silence.

An hour a day suffices for meditation! That leaves twenty-three hours for verse! There are few poets (male and American) more prolific than Allen Ginsberg! And it is his glory and his pain that he publishes the faintest of his tape-recorded eructations along with powerful, energetic poem-statements-feelings. His presence on the American (world) literary scene as liberating poet-figure— great baggy-kneed, balding courage-poet who redirected poetry in the 1950's and served to direct, as everybody knows, the way of living through rock and dope then—all this has been sufficiently noted. He is so popular that people who never open a book flock to his readings—a true culture love-hero.

So, understandably, whatever he chooses to see in print is automatically of some interest, simply because of his position as King not only of May but of every month. His poems fly into the world like hailstones—or perhaps they drift like feathers and leaves to the mouths of caves.

What interests me is what works in Ginsberg's art and what doesn't. I can't obviously say everything here, but shall merely describe one quality, *Funk*. My grapes are sweet, and should fall merrily to the ground as loving and sharing. I shall focus on *The Fall Of America: Poems of These States 1965-1975*.

I realize that when I complain about Ginsberg's poetry I trample on the skirts of motherhood, apple pie, and the flag, not to mention Whitman, W. C. Williams, various Indian gurus, Blake, Snyder, Bob Dylan, and Robert Creeley. I mean to be helpful, I think.

Funk damages Ginsberg's poetry and at its worst is literary pollution of the very sort he decries in *Camels Coming*. When the mode succeeds however, there is a feisty humorous quality, one charged with energy and a melancholy poignancy. Then the elegiac tone works well.

In *The Fall of America* telegraphically presented information is prolix. Yes, I admit that prolixity is crucial if one hopes to achieve a journalistic sense of a journey across around, through and over "these States." But after the fifteenth poem mentioning sites like Oroville, Nespelem, Dry Falls, Lincoln Airforce Base, Riverside, Ruby, and US 80 near Big Blue River, you feel the juices of AAA strip maps in your veins. There have to be Refreshment Gasoline Spirit and Bladder-Relief Stations along the way.

Authenticity. Yes. That's needed. A sense of the literal locates one's peregrinations (or meandering) towards transcendental consciousness. What makes this device *funky* is that the peregrinations seldom go anywhere far, or *far out*, remaining dull places on the map. True, sometimes there are cows, road signs, goats pissing, nameless persons, colors, and towns. And sometimes the poetry is compressed, visually provocative, and symbolically alive—viz.:

At Dry Falls 40 Niagaras stand silent & invisible,
    tiny horses graze on the rusty canyon's mesquite floor.

I like that. This next passage, though, I don't like: its attempt to elevate the commonplace is strained. And the disporting of the final line as three staggered phrases moving across the sky is facile. The cannon image is forced:

> Moss Landing Power Plant
> > shooting its cannon smoke
> > > across the highway. Red taillight
> > > speeding the white line & a mile away
> Orion's muzzle
> > > raised up
> > > > to the center of Heaven.

The example, ecologically relevant, is essentially static. We've been there before. Seldom in these new poems does Ginsberg transmute the funky, smog-ridden, garbage-strewn, junked landscape of the present into the rage of *Howl* and *Kaddish* and *Planet News*.

Also, at its worst, Ginsberg's Western Union man style is monotonous. Slabs (globs) of phrase-subjects parallel each other without syllabic variation. See "Continuation of a Long Poem of these States" and "Reflection in Sleepy Eye," dedicated to Robert Bly, with its "much land, new folk." When the method works, Ginsberg develops objects in a landscape:

> At the end of a long chain, Billy makes
> > a circle in grass
> by the fence, I approach
> > he stands still with long red stick
> > > stretched throbbing between hind legs
> Spurts water a minute, turns his head down
> > to look & lick his thin pee squirt —
> > > That's why he smells goat like.

Ginsberg's personages are for the most part funky counter-culture figures: Bob Dylan, Timothy Leary, Buffy St. Marie, Barry McGuire, The Rolling Stones, Jack Ruby (this one puzzles me). And he's often sentimental. A passage of pure *funk* leads from field grasses called "timothy" to (You've guessed it!) Timothy Leary:

> Timothy turned brown, covered with
> > new spread manure
> sweet smelt in strong breeze,

it'll be covered in snow couple
months.
& Leary covered in snow in San Luis Obispo jail?
On the other hand, this moment from "Memory Gardens," on Kerouac's burial, is a fine use of the telegram style:

...Jack drank
rot gut & made haikus of birds
tweetling on his porch rail at dawn—
Fell down and saw Death's golden lite
in Florida garden a decade ago.
Now taken utterly, soul upward,
& body down in wood coffin
& c on rete slab -box.
I threw a kissed handful of damp earth
down on the stone lid
& sighed....

Another device central to *funky* poetry is the omission of articles: "in Florida garden a decade ago"; "bending his knuckle to Cinema machine." There is an analogy here between moth holes in the fabric of your Salvation Army cast-offs and the fabric of your verse. Tattered Whitman too. Each missing article is a moth-hole, each dangling phrase another spray of clay beads or South American ritual seedpods attached to your sleeve.

Language at times takes the form of *Zap Comix* language, tatty, transparently untutored, unconventionally lettered, hokey:

Kesey's in Oregon writing novel language
family farm alone

The first line above tosses out key words creating a little Kesey world where the speaker maintains his breath and provides latch points in a miasmatic fog-consciousness. Here we don't need connectives: "Man, it's like, well, you know, man, outasight, it's like words ain't that needed, like, just get what needs said laid out, each word a slap of paste slapp'd down with a trowel. Know what I mean?" This writing, I suggest, is *speed-writing*, equivalent to *speed-reading*. Perhaps these poems should be read down the middle of the page.

Too frequently Ginsberg can't allow an easy idea to drift off after a breath or two; the motif becomes a series of funky gulps. Here, in Riverside, California, he ruminates on an automobile graveyard: "Palmtrees on valley floor / stick up toothpick hairheads." This metaphor points up the inadequacy of language at competing with paintings. Ginsberg's metaphor is a weak attempt at haiku. To opt for the easy effect is a camp act. Note how *hanging* becomes the latch for what follows:

> Toy automobiles piled crushed and mangled
> topped by a hanging crane,
> The planet hanging,
> the air hanging,
> Trees hang their branches,
> A dirt truck hanging on the
> highway —

"Hanging crane" is interesting; a crane "hangs" the crushed automobiles. A big leap to "planet hanging," then down to the pallid "air hanging," losing the death-doom and pathos of the car image (following the news of Ginsberg's uncle's death); then to a Robert Louis Stevensonian "trees hang their branches." And, is the dirt truck "hanging" around waiting to haul dirt? Is it hanging suspended? The motif conglomerates: a hanging-word stew boiled up in a Maxwell House coffee can over a vagrant's fire. Yeah! Walt's open road! Let's free-associate, much as the undisciplined mind associates, cultivating the obvious, hoping that in the refuse (garbage) filling the corner where we lie ecstasy may blast us towards transcendental Blakean cock spaces, towards Neo-K(C)untian Nirvana-Consciousness.

G-d knows, I'm not one to demand that poems be well scrubbed! I like gross, wild, expectorative, glandular, spuming poems. I insist however that the writer's mind engage me; let him sort through his dirty linen on his own. Poems, I'm saying, should reveal the small fraction of the iceberg above the water; keep the rest of it, its bulk, beneath, hidden from view. To present the complete bare-assed truth is a campy prostitution of the long-poem. To imply epic dimensions, as *The Fall Of America* does, assumes freshness, inventiveness, and originality. There is not enough mica in the rock; or to wrench the image, the poet's jockstrap is tattered.

After Gary Snyder, Ginsberg better than any other American poet (except, perhaps, for Philip Whalen) has earned his brownie points and badges for the sincerity of his quest after truth. His peregrinations through South America and the Far East are well-documented, as are his prostrations before the seats of various gurus and visionaries dead and alive. One senses in *The Fall Of America* a vast mellowing out. The overwhelming Hebraic-Jeremiah tones so searing in *Howl* have devolved into:

> Louder wind! there'll be electric to play the
>> Beatles!

> O wind ! spin the generator wheel, make
>> Power Juice
> To run the New Exquisite Noise Recorder, &
>> I'll sing
>> praise of your tree music.

> Sir Spirit, an' I drift alone:
>> O deep sign.

> Cigarettes burned my tastebuds' youth,
> I smelled my lover's behind.

In fairness, I should say that shreds of the old anger occur in his poems on Viet Nam, once he moves past sentimental Dos Passos-type camera eye passages. "Returning North of Vortex" and "War Profit Litany" are good examples.

Yet, what finally fails is Ginsberg's power to transform the wisdom of the east into a fresh vision for the west. Perhaps I expect too much; since, in general, gurus depend for their success on pointing towards grand abstractions without very many specifics. Hypnotic fire in the eyes, a sense of presence imagined as trembling in the trees within a mile or so of the guru's cell—these do not invite precise definition. Ginsberg's handling of the meditational chant invites the funky responses of a doped religion freak who ignores the role of intense discipline as essential to faith. Here are some examples. The first is refreshingly camp. Ginsberg is lying in the grass on Independence day:

> Independence Day! the Cow's deep moo's an Aum!

In "Guru Om" he presents his own discomfort over "boys and girls in jail for their bodies poems and bitter thoughts." He interlards *Oms* and *Gurus*: "Guru Guru Guru Guru Guru Guru Guru Citaram Omkar Das Thakur...." His own physical discomfort contrasts with his metaphysical discomfort as *Guru*: "Guru is equal to the Om of the Seeker." There are references to Dehorahava Baba and Nityananda and Babaji and Blake. To the initiate these would mean something. Perhaps the names are meant to be Cabbalistic. You chant a name and talismanic power ensues. And the metaphysical surrender almost works. That it remains statement, though, finally intrudes.

In its third part, the poem moves into an hysterical collage, with allusions to Leary, Errol Flynn, the stock exchange, Hilton hotel faucets, gasoline fumes smothering trees in Ganeshpuri. The world of rubber, glass, neon, and aluminum have cheapened Maya, Samsara, and Illusion. Thoughts of his mother move Ginsberg back to his body where "all beings" are "at war."

In general, Ginsberg's mysticism flickers through his mind with little more impact than the funky news of the day flashed over the radio, scenes out the window of his volkswagen, or memories of persons. Hindu motifs are patchouli moments, aromatic trappings of a hippie or flower child way of life in which the *Urantia* is displayed and not read, in which Hesse's novels are carried around unread, in which thonged medallions are hung with bells around necks and waists, in which ubiquitous canines of no immediately definable breed romp freely among the smog-infested trees, and in which almost every devotee can maintain with ease the lotus position for an hour, particularly after a few tokes.

I hunger in *The Fall of America* for more. The elegies on Neal Cassady are the best parts of the book. And "Please Master" is a brilliant incantatory homosexual poem. "Bixby Canyon Ocean Path Word Breeze" is a stunning as a *funky* poem that transcends its methods. It is beautifully imaged (the butterfly, lupine field, and morning glory), tender in its celebration of a benign nature, clean in its formed short line, and quietly passionate. It closes with one of the happiest of Ginsberg's inspirations from Walt Whitman: the image of the sea as "grandmother." Also in the earlier "Bixby Canyon" the lines improvising on Cassady's body as a sea plant are of a high order.

Funky poetry explains only one feature of Ginsberg's style. Since Ginsberg is our most accomplished practitioner of this verse, it should help to define the genre. My attempt has been *towards* such a definition.

ALFRED STARR HAMILTON:
AN AMERICAN TREASURE

I was unaware of Alfred Starr Hamilton's poetry until a friend recommended that I obtain the Jargon Press edition of his poems. Jonathan Williams published the book in 1970 (it is still in print), edited by Geof Hewitt, one of David Ray's students. In the 1960's Ray was teaching at Cornell and editing *Epoch*. Hamilton sent cardboard cartons full of poems and stories to Ray (I've seen four or five of these stuffed boxes myself—all of unpublished manuscripts). Ray kept them, believed in what he saw, published a sampling in *Epoch*, and interested Hewitt in this eccentric man's work. Hewitt finally persuaded Williams to read the poems. The result was the Jargon Press edition, the only sizeable collection of Hamilton's work to date. As Williams says on the jacket: "We are living in the Badlands. Dorothy's ruby-slippers would get you across the Deadly Desert. So will these poems."

Hamilton was born in Montclair, New Jersey, in 1914, graduated from high school, and was a catch-as-catch-can worker from 1932-1940. He was drafted into the Army, went AWOL, and was Dishonorably Discharged. As Hewitt notes, Hamilton sometimes signs his name, adding *D. D.* as a private joke. When *The Poems* appeared, Hamilton was unemployed, living in a rented room on a thousand dollars a year, cooking frugal meals on a hotplate, and writing poems. Shortly after the Jargon edition, Jonathan Williams wrote to the *New York Times Book Review* about Hamilton. The result was a flurry of interest in Hamilton's welfare. Numerous people contributed cash to help him out.

Trying to characterize Hamilton's poetry is like trying to report the color of a chameleon just before he changes hues. Whatever one says of him seems *almost* true. He is an American Primitive, a Grandpa Moses of American poetry —let's start there. When we examine the poems though, we see that he is more sophisticated than a Grandpa Moses could ever be; he is far less detailed and enamored of objects. Further, his grammar is good; and he doesn't fit the image of your basic Sunday poet-farmer busy shovelling manure and pitching hay. While he doesn't use many literary allusions (among the rare ones are *Alice in Wonderland* and Thoreau), his allusions are sometimes literary—if that makes sense. Here, for example, in a simple poem, "Sphinx," he provides an unexpected conceptual, literary turn:

THE SPHINX

The sphinx said;
I wanted no hurt
I wanted no pain ever again
I wondered if that was all that was ever meant
And ever happened.

In "Sheets," he improvises on a mundane act, as a primitive poet might, without using literary models. Ironing becomes a metaphor for a moon fashioned in his own image. Have you ever thought, dear house-wife or house-husband, of ironing the moon? Hamilton produces a stunning visual image of fantasy and affection. He invites us to see the poem on its own terms, via his imagination, which evokes TV cartoons: quick dissolves of forms into other forms (the fox pursuing road-runner seques into a juggernaut), and a resultant hilarity, a tonic disruption of our sense of reality. Here is the poem:

SHEETS

How wonderfully the moon was to have been ironed last night
And carefully kept the moon in its place
And last night I ironed the moon
And lifted the daffodil back on top of the daisy
And folded the daffodil back on top of the moon
And carefully carried the moon upstairs
And kept the moon in the daffodil closet
Last time I ironed the moon.

One of several poems on angels (he seems to live with them as easily as old Emanuel Swedenborg did) is a good example of his irreverence for normal syntax. He opens with a conditional phrase and concludes the poem without ever completing it. The poem remains open-ended. The angel will understand—and since that's most important, Hamilton sees no need to appease inferior mortals who can't think like angels. He warns the angel that if he visits the city he'll be contaminated:

THAT HAS BEEN TO THE CITY

If you're an angel
that has been sent to the cleaners

More often than
a farmer has been sent to gather the harvests

but if you're an angel
that has been to the city to gather its dust

Well, if Hamilton is not a Grandpa Moses, perhaps he's a Munchkin Prince dropped to earth from Munchkin-land where he's been regaling Billie Burke with his verses. An informed Munchkin might write these childlike riddles, these non-sequiturs requiring an agile fantasy to decipher them. And there are many puns, juxtaposed objects radically evoking one another, and sudden jabs from a Rocky Horror Show. A golden sun evokes a housewife's golden dish washing suds: "golden sun's suds." Manpower "is M. P. H. faster than manurepower." "Thank your iron stars, bub" becomes "an iron sea bubble." In "Chinaware" broken dishes become the occasion for a *Beware* poem; for the broken pieces as they become broken angels are the pieces of our own broken lives:

CHINAWARE

But they are the fallen angels
That fell downstairs
I picked some of them up
    I left the pieces behind
Others were whole
But others were more like ourselves
I wanted these most of all
Some of the broken parts of our lives that are never
To be put back together again

Often, one of these Munchkin motifs is a playful sketch fraught with chilling overtones. The arrangement of the brief poem "White Mice" is not what we would expect—he's left out some lines; that's how it sounds. But has he? No. The first line sets a locale. The last two lines jump logically to an army of mice who don't seem to come from "in back of the stars" but rather from somewhere else in space. The event of the mice "invading the moon," excites Hamilton, and he dashes ahead, as a child might, anxious to express a vivid, off-the-wall image. The title here, as it happens in so many of Hamilton's poems, is actually the first line of the poem:

WHITE MICE

Somewhere in back of the stars,
But the white mice invading the moon tonight
Must have come from the Milky Way

Hamilton suits the role also of a Cole Porter, of a composer of popular songs, unembarrassed, improvising on the old cliches of *June, moon, spoon.* Hamilton is no Emily Dickinson listening to Protestant hymns, risking ear damage from the persistent rhymed tetrameter quatrains. When Hamilton uses popular music motifs (these relate also to his fondness for the pop-folk sayings), he stands them on their head, making them his own. "Swan in June" is an example of his wry use of pop-song motifs:

The moon is a swan in June
The moon can paddle and paddle
And be the moon all night long.

"June Silver" also owes something to pop music. But how refreshingly original Hamilton is: images of black and blue silver, and images of motion, result in a childlike spontaneity:

JUNE SILVER

I wanted you to know of
The black June bug
That buzzed silver

But I wanted you to know of
June silver, of blue silver
During the month of June

I wanted you to know
I rocked in a rocking chair
And all along the silvery vines

> I wanted you to know I knew
> Of a boy who rocked on top of a rocking horse
> And up and down the wiry plains
>
> I wanted you to know of
> Blue silver, of black silver
> During the month of June silver

In "Walden House," by evoking the spirit of Thoreau, he plays off his penchant for fantasy against reality. Here, at least, the latter wins out: Hamilton loves mom's apple pie and can tell you the variety of the apples she's used; but he also loves that fantastic, goo-piled pie in the Munchkin sky:

WALDEN HOUSE

> Are you a fierce nomad?
> Are you a friend of sword and disaster?
> Do you know of the only star in heaven?
> Do you know of only the sun's daily sword
> That pushed the scorched wagon wheels forward?
> Are you a goldhunter?
> Are you a Scythian mountebank?
> Are you a plainsman who fled the plains?
> Will you recross the deserted desert airways?
> Or are you a Walden traveler?
> Do you have your meals at the Walden House?
> Do you read your wanton heels to your shoemaker?
> Are you a city traveler?

The riddle form, so effective here, is one of Hamilton's primary forms. Anything is possible, depending upon the freedom of your imagination, and your willingness to risk that imagination. The lines themselves could easily be adapted for music by some nasal-voiced, Country-Western plucker.

If the composer of pop songs seems a useful parallel, an even better one is that great iconoclast-composer Charles Ives. Hamilton is the Charles Ives of American poetry. Ives' cacophonies resemble Hamilton's cacophonies of syntax, grammar, and imagery. And the latter's use of puns and blatantly frayed folk materials would have appealed to Ives, who in sophisticated ways took the prosaic and the mundane from small town American life and made them his own—the brass bands, the popular tunes, the patriotic songs. And, like Hamilton, Ives always remained indifferent to the large world that ignored him. Hamilton keeps himself entirely removed from the poetry Rat Race; he sends his work nowhere apparently, except to *Epoch* magazine.

One more parallel may help to fix our elusive butterfly, a parallel with Christopher Smart (1722-1771), the English poet who wrote from a madhouse. His *Jubilate Agno*, with its famous section "For I will consider my cat Jeoffry," has a marvelous fey spirit. His cat becomes a cherub: "For he is of the tribe of Tiger. / For the Cherub Cat is a term of the Angel Tiger." His angels resemble Hamilton's; and the latter's use of the serial style, the questions and refrains, and the wise-child, all suggest Smart. Nothing is too illogical or bizarre for either poet. Stellar washings outdistance readers who expect logical progressions. We follow Smart and Hamilton through the conch-like trammeling of their free-spirited brains; and if we fail to reach it's our fault. I don't think that Hamilton was consciously imitating Smart, or that he even knows Smart's work. I am saying that a tradition exists; and if we are to appreciate Hamilton's poetry, whatever we do to place him in a tradition may prevent us from dismissing him as a hopeless eccentric.

So far, I have focused on Hamilton's playful side. He also presents the tragic and the frustrating. Despite all the stars and the angels and the miracles of colors and forms changing before our amazed and startled eyes, he never pretends either that God's in his Heaven or that all's right with the world. In "Stalk" he says that he hopes to leave "a doubt in the mind of mankind."

And, in "A Crust of Bread," he wonders about his being a poet—he always wanted to be a bird. His concern is for the pains of birds, even for the despised starling—he cares "first of all" that they are fed. In "Travel Along," he warns us that our fantasies may lull us into believing we are doing more than just "rolling along" through life only half-awake. His pure iconoclasm and distaste for a hostile society erupts in "Rhododendron": "I could have written on the back of a parchment leaf / The story of our terrible municipal lives." The personal pain aroused by his dishonorable discharge appears in several poems. In one, "False Faces," he berates G. I. beer as a form of poison ivy:

> "Even Himmler who'd accused us of rape
> Gasped at ivy 3. 2. American poisoning"

In "Deign to Design," a chilling sense of lost hope accretes around the image of a steel pin, possibly from a grenade:

> If
> it's
> a
> steel pin
>
> It
> isn 't
> to
> dig your grave with
>
> If
> it's
> dug
> already

In these poems, personal bitterness is a vivid loathing; the Army has Hamilton fast by the buttons:

IT'S ARMY BALONEY

Is hatred baloney?
And getting one's teeth into it
And getting one's teeth out of it
And never forgiving any of them for any of it

HOLD FAST, ARMY BUTTONS

Ironically, those are brass buttons
that are made of holdfast iron

Dumbfounded, those are brass knuckles
to have been tied to just straitjackets

Those are a tyrant's muscles
to your best vest buttons

We may take our pick of several Alfred Starr Hamiltons—Grandpa Moses, the Prince of the Munchkins, Cole Porter, Charles Ives, or Christopher Smart. No single figure's work entirely reflects Hamilton's elusive originality. Like a good pixie (or leprechaun) he'll keep leaping aside once you think you've grabbed him. Perhaps though, that's how a true "gentleman of our darkness" is supposed to behave. In one of his best poems, "Guardian," he does stay still long enough to write a poem about the poet (himself) as a beautiful rooster, guardian of the dawn; Bo-Peep's pasture land is brought into tune and harmony, and the world, through the illusions of the poem, is temporarily secure:

GUARDIAN

Contrast Rooster's white feathers
With the greater surrounding darkness,
But he sings with all his blue might;
An iconoclast of old scoffs at the ghosts of the pastures,
Bespeaks of himself, stalks and struts in the
        eerie morning moonlight;
But he sings with all his white might,
Because truthfully he is our gentleman of the darkness,
And out in Bo Peeps pasture land, and morning miles away,
He is the savior, He is the guardian of the new dawn.

GALWAY KINNELL CLIMBS THE MT. MONODNOCK:
THE BOOK OF NIGHTMARES

Finding flaws in Galway Kinnell is like fussing about the Matterhorn, or Monodnock—a magnificent presence should be enough to satisfy any cantankerous soul. Few poets have been as well-dined and admired on the Poetry and Visiting Writer Circuits as Kinnell—the fact of his craggy presence and his memorized recitals of his work provide the chemistry for unforgettable appearances. One is carried away, as if in a Föhn wind. His books sell, and young poets, particularly those attached to prestigious writing programs display them, garnering Brownie points for perspicacity and generating the uncritical reverence one bestows on natural wonders.

My sense of Kinnell's work, after several years of reading it with admiration, is that it has become repetitious; his self-critical sense seems diminished. He overstates here, is sentimental there, and overuses certain tags. He sets off an easy Existentialism. (The fact that Kinnell apparently knew Albert Camus is not beside the point.) *The Book of Nightmares*, here under review, has been almost universally praised. I make my complaints realizing that there is still enough power and originality in Kinnell to nurture numerous lesser poets.

Nevertheless, Kinnell seems here to have exhausted much of his bag of tricks, presenting too many old devices. They don't explode as they once did. Consider his diction: certain words appear with the inevitability of sightings of Cher Bono's navel. Here are some navel-words: *darkness, light, bone/bones, haunted, existence, dying, graves, scars, rot*. The most cursory reading of *Nightmares* reveals these overworked tags. Consider *darkness*. Not only is the word sentimental, but it belies much precise meaning. A flag with *darkness* written on it goes up, and we are excused from any potent engagement. We experience a general gloom, a hissing bleakness. The poet spreads soft black butter (tar?) over our minds.

As a philosophical concept, of course, *darkness* had meaning in the forties and fifties when French Existentialism was in vogue. *Darkness* then was what *roses* were to the 1890's, and what *fuck* became in the 'seventies. There's no use rerunning the Sisyphean tape. Kinnell lays his black slabs out much as he laid them out in the earlier books.

Why should we expect a poet to change as he ages, to transmogrify his wisdom as the dregs of living accumulate around him, as barnacles to the sides of Moby Dick? Thomas Hardy held on to similar views all his life, and barely changed them. And Hardy was frequently bad—repetitious, obvious, self-pitying. Often, though, humor and irony made the gloom palatable.

Kinnell lacks Hardy's saving irony. His interior bleeding is exactly that—unadulterated interior bleeding. The ease of his thinking, and the predictability, evoke an addiction to slick philosophical concepts. His sufferings fail to communicate much pain. I begin now to squirm when Kinnell presents me with duplicated images of an Existential Ur-mensch facing me, holding his guts in his hands, his underwear sweat-fetid, seedy, his body scarred in various stages of healing, as he prepares to tuck his guts back into the cavity so as to free his hands for pushing that Sysyphean boulder back up Mt. Monodnock once more.

Perhaps Kinnell is tiring. Perhaps, famous, he merely repeats what delirious readers expect. I once believed his poems the nearest modern equivalents for those Oedipean moments in Greek tragedy. I still respect his early work—and his personal courage on his trips to the South with freedom riders. And there are memorable flashes in *Nightmares*. The central sections of "Under the Maud Moon" are powerful treatments of birth; the early portions of "The Hen Flower" exude brilliance; and "Dear Stranger" is inventive. Too often, however, Kinnell lacks what the nineteenth century poets called tact—that poetic sense allowing the poet to know when he has violated form by pushing emotion too far (sentimentality); or by settling for mannered, dull writing; or by his overwriting and straining.

To be more specific: Kinnell frequently echoes the periodicity of old-fashioned writing. This slab is reminiscent of the delays Matthew Arnold loved. Perhaps by using it Kinnell sought to add momentousness. Alas, however, he fails to edit out the excessive. Kinnell learns his "only song" during glimmerings of "the Maud Moon" when the Archer lay "sucking the icy beistings of the cosmos, / in his crib of stars." The poet creeps to riverbanks, with "their long rustle / of being and perishing," reaches the marshes and the oozing earth, and touches "the underglimmer" of the world's beginning.

Another of his devices is to employ prepositional phrases for portentousness; "he who crushed with his heel the brain out of the snake..." This is cheap William Morris. "In the Hotel of Lost Lights," periodicity winds down to a facile moment. *Post, postcards, posterity* is facile word-play. Using "this anguished alphabet of worms," he writes for *him* his final words, and posts for him "his final postcards to posterity."

More egregious than these brief lapses is the sentimentality. His poems to his children are much praised and they are effective whenever Kinnell recites them in public; and it is difficult to fault a man who writes sweetly of his kids. Usually, the fate of the siblings is his own. "Little Sleep's-Head Sprouting Hair in the Moonlight," with its mythic overtones (the name sounds like a papoose-name), coming fairly well on in the book, will illustrate. When the poet lifts the child from her bed during a nightmare he waxes sentimental. Kinnell hasn't earned his descent to pity. How does he know Maud feels lost? Isn't this the old pathetic fallacy where a poet imposes human gut-feelings on inanimate nature? A child, in a sense, especially a sleeping one, is an inanimate person (Wordsworth notwithstanding). It's as if Kinnell injects his child's veins with needles full of his own spleen. The image of "broken arms" doesn't work. He forces the image into the crushed shape of Existentialist suffering: Maud screams.Kinnell sleep-walks to her and holds her up to the moonlight.The child clings to him, hard "as if clinging could save us." He says that she thinks he "will never die." He seems to "exude" to her "the permanence of smoke or stars"—all the while his "broken arms" are healing themselves around her. In section 3, the clever "caca, caca" section, Kinnell moves through the cuteness of indulgent parenthood, comparing his eventual descent into oblivion as going with his daughter down "the path of vanished alphabets."

Imagine Dylan Thomas' ghost standing somewhere in the shade examining the contents of his nose, hardly a momentous sight; yet *Momentosity* is the word I invent for Kinnell's writing. I hope that his next work will reveal fresh turnings. A principle of art holds that the more you struggle for the momentous the less likely you are to achieve it. There's an ease to the rising of every biscuit (poem); there's a leavening of freshness lurking somewhere in most of our nightmares.

PEANUT BUTTER AND JAM:
GREG KUZMA'S *OF CHINA AND GREECE*

When there's peanut butter and jam for the home-made bread and bowls of soup full of garden vegetables, there's no real need, Kuzma says, for poetry. When you're in the woods with friends (who may even write verse), poking in muskrat holes, counting crows, inspecting homestead wells, dropping to your knees to grab alfalfa and sniff it, with your dogs whirling about you "like satellites," you don't need poetry. When you visit your folks you don't need poetry: your mother doesn't "retain language," and when you talk of writing she stares through your beard to your face. Your dad, "for whom life is / nuts and bolts" never mentions either "poetry or life"—he's anxious to get his beer and olives—he's "a man beer made," complete with huge belly exaggerated by a Banlon shirt. And so it goes. In a land, like ours, "of much to do," which fears reflection and meditation—the central stillness of art and beauty—poetry, turns itself back upon the poet, who is drawn solipsistically to verse. To borrow Matthew Arnold's terms, the poet remains a Hellenist in a world of Hebraists. The positioning is rough.

There's a sense throughout Kuzma's new volume that a poet never chooses his role; he is, rather, chosen—in the sense that ancient poets felt chosen. Poetry is a form of mania, Plato said. The modern poet's visions, like those of the ancient priests of Apollo, result from a driving, universal consciousness. The universe, Kuzma writes, "is wordless," particularly so in its grandest forms, viz., near Cedar Breaks, Utah, where Kuzma teaches. Poetry is never able to express "the extant." Poetry sets itself "in terms" of a real landscape, finds words where no words are. The physical universe is a "mirage / where half seeing is our full substantiation." In his swooping after subtle nectars, the poet is as incapable as the western hummingbird of imbibing "literal" surroundings. The bird, Kuzma writes,

climbed

and dived at incredible speeds—
swooping so near the ground
I thought he would bash his little head in—
bend his bill like a too-fine needle

> against dry leather—the wings
> a kind of mechanical blur—
> but softer—
> and all for a few flowers.
> We did not, of course, speak.
> And in the sky above us,
> what a blank yet inevitable parchment.

Kuzma's paradox is one that many poets must feel who after years of little recognition tire of the craft, who doubt, but who yet continue "that dull meditation." Kuzma even speculates that he is "finished as a poet," that the years since the 70s (when he was touted as a hope for American writing) were "lost years." The urge to write seems diminished: "Months have gone by and I have not had any urges."

From the vantage of a mid-career crisis, he meditates on his life. A neighbor's large tree has toppled into his yard, a tree with no marks of decay:

> All the years a tree was falling apparently
> I was teaching myself through poems
> what it was I thought and felt and ought to think
> or feel, how they were problems, what their falling
> had to do with me, the fallings (the lesser ones)
> of their leaves, the irony of the thick heavy trunk
> and the fragile delicate leaves, etc.,
> so now that I have been through all that so many times
> I can at last go out and stand next to the tree
> without self consciousness or anxiety of any sort....

Earlier, in "The Poet," Kuzma is more casual about his transformation. The need to *figure* his "condition" was immature. He complained and renamed too much. "Let's face it," he now writes:

> poetry is a lot of work,
> a lot of wishing.
> Poetry is, oh shit, we had better go off to the library /
> to go on talking like this.

Obviously, Kuzma hasn't quit writing—this book proves that. He's now more the *receiver* than the rambunctious eearlier self. Now, eschewing fame, he seeks "a grand impersonal stillness," which paradoxically remains "deeply personal." He waits

not wanting anything not knowing
what to do next or if anything will ever begin again
in terms of which we will be called upon to respond.
I think it is a condition of absolute health,
youth and vigor joined together with age and exhaustion,
where the foot dragging past and the nearly airborne future
come together in a quick click,
and the present spreads outward on and on forever
like the circle of wave set up by a pebble dropped
into the ocean. No
it is more motionless even than that, even than
that thin ridge of wave a thousand miles from the center.

If it appears that Kuzma (he has published twenty books) has settled into an easy descent via aging towards the eternal roll, or that he basks contentedly in Crete, Nebraska, quite the opposite is true. When *Of China and of Greece* appeared, huzzahs should have rung from the minarets, calling all devotees of verse to trek to Mecca (New York) instanter. Alas, the book has received little more attention than a stone dropped down a well in Crete, Greece. In "The Human Condition," Kuzma writes with self-humor of his move to the midwest, where he has lived for ten years

secure from the dangerous coasts.
Nothing could get to me.
Weather started elsewhere, and
gave fair warning.
The great events, the rises and falls,
occurred elsewhere. I sat
still and warm in my house—like dough—
rising gently into a round brown loaf.

In "The Night of January 12, 1978," where he commemorates the death of a brother in a car wreck, the mature origins of his verse are clear. In a sense, the poem was "received," beginning as many of Kuzma's poems do with a disarming casualness, as if he's talking to us quietly in a room. The beginning echoes one of Wordsworth's truisms, one no one would quarrel with: "Many beautiful things in the world" compete for our attention. There's no hint of a coming Sophoclean pain.

When beauty overwhelms us, we turn inward; too much beauty says that the world is a disarming place. Yet, a glimpse of a jay at a feeder occasions a "necessity like thirst" that leads to poetry. We shall never be "comfortable." If we are to write anything good, we must "be at odds" with life. Psyches must flow towards a "necessity like thirst." And for Kuzma it leads to brutality expressed in an anguished, tender language. Most effective is the ironic thrust of making the central agent parenthetical:

> Our deaths, after all, await us,
> casually in the future
> like so many newspapers left on porches,
> like car accidents, tragic yet
> compulsive (one just destroyed my previously
> invulnerable-seeming brother—twenty-five years
> old, who had fucked maybe only three or four
> women, and not all that well probably,
> who had written not one published poem—
> and who, in dying, has broken not only
> his mother's heart and his father's heart,
> which is somehow inevitable under the
> circumstances—but who has also destroyed
> my life, the one I've known these past 9 years.
> And I sit here my guts ripped out and
> my eyes run red in sorrow).
>
> Death, I assure you, resides in the
> very fiber of existence, the louse
> under the blue jay's wing, for instance, is there
> for the careful viewer.... We must
> not, therefore, stay too even with the world,
> failing thereby to see its essential
> lack of hospitality....

A poet must be "tested," must know that he may be rescued from the rim of the precipice; but it isn't likely. To embellish the point, Kuzma varies his orchestration, modulating from an intense minor key to a reflective interlude. These tonal shifts are frequent in Kuzma's work, and mitigate against egotism. Both poet and reader share in the undergoing—the latter's life may differ in details, but the jolting meshes both parties:

> This I can tell you
> is one of my fondest hopes
> indeed perhaps the only one

so do not laugh at me
if I seem clutching at straws
perhaps it is so
but would you want to be in my shoes
certainly not
and I would not want you there....
Sure, everyone has bad days, and
there is sadness everywhere.
The truly tragic is always just around
the corner....

The poem reflects on Kuzma's father, his own sensitive boyhood, and Jeff the brother who misjudged "a bit of distance." The casual key is shattered by an image of a 2x4: the brother's

                         dreams took shape
against the odds of his
birth and fortune.
This stops my tongue.
This strikes a 2x4 across my writing arm—
cracking the bone.
This pours blood into my mouth
and ice down my throat.
I sit here in the chair and squirm—
there is a blade cutting me—
and no matter where I move
it lacerates. Jeff, Jeff I call out . . .
then BANG—his car's hit,
his body is thrown violently forward
against the wheel
smashing the ribs,
the organs of the abdominal cavity
mangled by the shift lever
then the head goes forward
into the hard dashboard and glass—
face I have loved, shoulders...
and oh I am screaming now
God damn fuck son of a bitch
God damn God damn the
bastards into the phone.

Kuzma gazes at actual events as if he lacked eyelids. To avert one's gaze from the tragic (and from the beautiful) is to be less than human. When faced with traumas the normal impulse is to play possum. We must SEE what the physical universe perpetrates, Kuzma says, are we totally human.

Kuzma leavens his vision with humor. A hospital meal consists of "shrivelled peas, a laminated lump of meat, a jellied gravy, coffee bitterer than dust." He recalls the pale white flesh hanging below his grandmother's arms, "the flab" he jiggled as a child. To fill our hours, we "wave at growing carrots," admire well-manicured lawns, and observe a shirtless neighbor "hosing down a patch of / noisy weeds."

One of his most detailed poems, "The River," reflects his mode at its best. Written in cadenced lines (oscillating between pentameters, hexameters, and heptameters), the poem, like the river itself, meanders, recording flora and fauna, moving on to a swimming hole, from which one floats past an old mill with briars:

> To a certain extent the river seems less here, has
> less on its mind, as I suppose in an analogy our
> avid talkers, the ones who do the most among us,
> suggest less depth of feeling.

Another style, more reductive, dominates much of this book, and seems spoken by a survivor invented by Samuel Beckett, or by the cartoonist Abner Dean. At other times, lines read as if they come from a primer. And there are clear echoes of Kuzma's mentor Donald Justice: see his denotative, unpretentious lyrics on the pained child still resident in the man. And the elusive title poem, "China and Greece," is dedicated to Richard Eberhart, that maestro of the casual: "The groundhog slumbers in a heap / of dust."

What these parallels have in common is an ingenuous tone where a mature adult returns to innocence to re-examine a complex universe. The poet becomes a new Adam who wakens in a stupor to a world he needs to comprehend, if he is to survive. He writes Somnambulist Verse recited in a sleepwalk-dream state:

> Last night a terrible dream.
> I was here, as before.
>   I was where I am, and who
> I am. I was in the chair,
> and the chair where it is.
> There was the light, where it is,
> where it was,
> and I could not see the light.

I knew it was there,
but I could not turn.
The chair held me. ("The Room")

At its best, the mode assumes a verse mathematics. In this passage, allusions to syllogisms and redistributed terms are appropriate. Kuzma sets the terms, averaging amounts:

For years and years my wife was
unhappy and yet I was happy. For
years and years I worked to be
happy and I was happy, while all
the time my wife was unhappy. Now
that my brother is dead and I am
unhappy and cannot think of being happy,
she is happy and content with herself.
Probably the average amount
of happiness in our house
has not changed.

An important variation on the mode is the Serial Poem, made popular by Ginsberg and Waldman. Success here depends on the poet's agility to think up fresh illustrations for the undistributed primary term. "Sometimes" is a 70-1iner developed around "I am afraid" and variations thereon. We are grabbed at once: "I am afraid of being crushed in the pincers / of an enormous dog. I am afraid of / breathing into my lungs the gastric juices / of my own stomach. I fear that the semi-trailer truck / will suddenly blow a tire and come swerving into my own lane...." The mix is rich: threats from within the self, threats from the external world: accident, disease. Here is a grim moment, the details serving as talismans against his death:

I am afraid of having my skull crushed under the plate
of an enormous press which someone is lowering
a fraction of an inch at a time, of the skull cracking
first like a walnut shell, and the momentary relief
of the eyes growing milky and then popping out,
staring back up briefly upon the twisted face, the
teeth pinned against each other, the splintering,
the facial bones breaking through the skin like a
wrecked ship coming up from the placid bottom

where all these years its rigging was a place for fish
to swim through, and the blood of course and the
squirting brains.

In conclusion, Kuzma borrows from a chain-saw massacre movie:

I am afraid that my hands will be hacked off by a big man
wearing a lumberjack shirt, first the left hand
and then the right, and that I will be then asked
to walk all the way home, looking down at my arms
and out again at the world, the butterflies, the lawn sprinklers
spinning their little silver cornets.

"Maybe" is a longer excursion into the serial mode. The equation is clear:
X = mother and father; Y = their life together; X + Y = Disaster. This equation
is useful "in the windows of those many years she saw X and he saw Y." Kuzma
speculates on the reasons. Each possibility is never the whole, yet is part of the
whole:

Maybe it was bitterness up in the throat, of not
having clothes that fit, of not being told yes
even once in a while....
Maybe it was the two cultures bouncing off each other,
the west and the east, the dream of more
against the dream of less, or the dream of getting back
against the dream, of finding first.
Maybe it was the children, or the first child,
coming out of her, of sex leading to that, or the
penis throb, cunt throb, leading to that, to shit smell ....
Maybe it was how he snored all night, shaking the room,
or the way he left beside the bed his underpants.
Maybe it was she, maybe it was how she hung on the bathroom rod
her scrubbed out underpants, this hurting him,
this distracting him from his wrench and pliers.

The serial technique is like a pinwheel, the red stripes the serial phrases
spinning faster and faster until the talk / poetry returns to stasis having exhausted
the conditionals:

Maybe he was driving home one night
and in the road a deer was bleeding to death.

Maybe she would not have stopped.
Maybe he did not stop.
Maybe he is forever going back to that place.
And the snow swirling around them both.

The final poem "I Will Rub My Arm," equates the act of rubbing an arm with writing verse. Kuzma's aim always is to return to the world a full measure of his "engagement" with the world. He will be misread ("many will think me foolish or vain, / at best a failure"). A "few," however, will be moved. The act of writing, despite his quizzical attempts to eject poetry from his life, is his reason for being. His potent individualism, his almost celebratory sense of his need to endure a senseless, hostile world, all appear:

I will rub my arm.
I will rub through the first layer of dirt.
I will rub through the second layer.
I will sit in the tub and rub my arm with the cloth.
The steam will rise.
I will rub my arm down to the first layer of skin.
I will rub a red rose rush upon my arm.
I will rub until it goes away, the skin goes.
And then I will rub to the second layer.
I will rub my arm. No one will stop me.

In the final lines, the stoic resolution, the tough-minded, obstinate corrective for a world gone mad enhances and resolves private anguish and the obsessions of *Of China and of Greece*. Kuzma's ruthless honesty mirrors a life-view essential for the 'eighties. His readers should be legion. There's plenty of jam and peanut butter for his homemade bread.

LYN LIFSHIN:

THE ICE MADONA AS BOARDWALK TEASE

Most currently fashionable poetry evokes upper middle class cravings, achievements, and preoccupations. Proletarian poets like Charles Bukowski, Lawrence Ferlinghetti, Charles Plymell, Wilma Elizabeth McDaniel, William Joyce, Michelle Clinton, Harry Northup, Wanda Coleman, Fred Voss, Antler, Todd Moore, and Philip Levine consltitute a minority. Upper middle class writing is apt to be self-obsessed and written out of or around Writing Programs. University Presses publishing a token two to four books of poetry per year, and glossy conservative poetry journals, feature these writers. Among them I include John Ashbery, Mark Strand, Amy Clampitt, Carol Muske Dukes, Rita Dove, Dana Gioia, and William Matthews. My purpose is not to condemn specific poets or journals; I wish rather to examine how Lyn Lifshin reflects the conservative world of poets like those I've mentioned, who are roughly of her generation and who are middle-aged. The list is long.

On the surface, Lifshin would appear to share little with these poets. She has developed an anorexic poem, a form from which she seldom departs. She has a unique voice—it would be difficult not to spot a Lifshin poem at once. And nearly every literary journal publishes her. That she is known as the Queen Bee of the Little Mags has not always resulted in kind estimations of her work. Nor have her sexual obsessions. She appears self-absorbed to the point of creating a myth-Lifshin, complete with "crotch-sweat" (one of her phrases), and an array of estrogenic body-signals intended to excite men. And yet, once her uniqueness is acknowledged, she remains tenaciously upper middle class.

Almost singly obsessed with sex, Lifshin presents the raunchiest frustrations and fantasies of the bored suburbanite female. She smears herself with an estrogen compote other poets merely hint at as they sanitize their outpourings to suit conventional tastes. My examination of Lifshin's *Kiss the Skin Off* should stimulate a fairer appraisal of her work than it has so far had. She seems shamelessly autobiographical, which, of course, may be illusory. Let the reader be warned: my Lifshin may not be the real Lifshin!

My Lifshin has never had to think about money. She derives from fairly well-to-do parents—a withdrawn but successful father, a smothering mother who wished for a son rather than a daughter. The mother dominates Lifshin's life. Fearing her mother's death by cancer, Lifshin presses her "close, terrified / I'm losing what / I don't know." Lifshin delineates herself as a Jewish American Princess posturing at age 40 as a sex-object.

In "Mammogram" she is "wrapped in white like / a bride or corpse." She exudes the "smell" of roses. The bit of gruesome fun (contrasting bride and corpse) may be unintentional. I prefer to think Lifshin is not taken in by her solipsism. Snow White symbolizes the depraved / deprived suburban woman. To accept at face value the information she supplies, we perceive Lifshin as a perfect daughter. For years she was a virgin, earned A's in school, "passed her Italian," and always did "what was expected." She cleaned carpets "with ivory snow." She stood "straight as a live oak," as her family wished. She was Snow White asleep in a "bell jar," ill-equipped for the prince (husband) who eventually awakened her from her "daze." Illiterate sexually, she feared that men were dirty-minded dwarves, "all anxious to prove their / virility as shorter / men often do."

She sees her ideal self as "Raven," a sort of Theda Bara or Vampira. Perpetually "starved," she chain-smokes, greedy for the sexual life she lacks and fears. Safe on her couch, almost in a masturbatory reverie, she imagines her eyes glowing like coals in a grate. She applies patchouli, drinks wine in "oversize glasses," and sees her steaming "nights" as "rich" lasagna. She remains "starved," still fighting her adolescent battle with her weight, craving to be skinny. She's always checking herself in mirrors—is she really fat? Only in "late / afternoon shadows" do her plump thighs look thin. She wears her hair long to appear thinner than she is and she diets until she passes out. The hair, she hopes, will allow her to transcend her despised self to a "new self."

When she walks the Cape Cod dunes she is a girl again. Men whistle and still dream of her in her "old fashioned white dress" with its belt of "plum velvet." Her fantasies don't change—and when she is an old woman she'll "hug the same moon." She likes pearls, those gems so appropriate for sorority and debutante types. Pearls keep her safe, "not wild not interesting." Eventually, she craves for more, to be a poet hiding in trees, throwing up bad wine in toilet bowls. She throws her pearls into a drawer (why not in the trash? Will she want them later on?) and flings a hippie's iron pendant around her neck.

"Atlantic City" renders the perpetual teenager, mother-dominated, who promenades the boardwalk at Atlantic City. She's brought far too many clothes, obsessed as she is with stimulating males. She requires her mother's approval for all she does, and sends mixed signals. Mom, who wishes for an alluring daughter, thwarts Lyn's relationships with men.

For six hours, Lifshin, on the boardwalk, teases with her "hips and eyes," safe since Mother hovers in the background. A second "Atlantic City" is even more specific: Lifshin wears a dress "as tight as / a hooker's stagger," six-inch spikes, and frizzy hair. Sailors

> rub
> their eyes from
> my maybelline cats
> eyes to my
> slick tanned
> legs.

She's safe; but there's tension. She dreads remaining a virgin until she marries—such women miss a lot.

The frankest, most devastating, of all the mother obsession poems is "Photographs Of Mothers and Daughters":

> you can almost always
> see the mother's hands
>
> the daughter usually
> nests in a curve of
> the mother's hair or
> neck like it was a cave
>
> the way cats do the
> night it starts to snow.
>
> some seem to suck
> on the mother's breath
> you might think the
> mother had eyes
> in her fingers
> often her hands
> are on the daughter's
> shoulders pulling
> her close as if
>
> she wanted to press
> her back inside.

Her omnipresent mother defends her always. Daughter *doesn't* punch the boy next door. She *doesn't* kick the Girl Scout leader. She *doesn't* jump into the open grave. Mom boasts that her daughter, "beautiful," does brilliant "science projects," and is splendid in anything she wears. The reason she's never invited to dances is because she's too "smart" for the men. Mom even rationalizes her daughter's poems: "take out / the dirty words and // you'd love" them. Daughter "can do anything."

Daughter, however, rarely experiences sexual fulfillment, and fails even at kinky sex, with the males, not Lifshin, as the wierdos. Why does Lifshin attract such losers? Does her image of herself as night-blooming Cereus serve instead as a Venus fly-trap? Does she still persist in adolescent guilt, needing to convince her mother that she's a virgin? Is attracting crippled sex partners a way of maintaining that prized virginity?

Lifshin takes clues from beaver mags devoured by males: *Playboy* and *Penthouse*. One of her fantasies is that wearing no underwear, she stands in her kitchen displaying her "beautiful bush" through a hole in the floor, right over the lusting gaze of workmen in the cellar. Once again, she is an inaccessible turn-on, the ice-virgin tease, securing her "purity" via a play on "crack": the workmen are down there "to fix a crack / and of course do." In the turn-on mags, she finds, no woman has "a period or hair / where it shouldn't be." Penises throbbing are always nine inches long. Women's "tits point to the / ceiling." All is fantasized; there are no lawyer's briefs, poems, or highly caloric food. Blonde-haired women, like vampires, rip open men's jeans and give blow-jobs. Like the sex-starved housewife, Lifshin's women

> dive through
> leather with their
> own crotch hairs
> always dripping
> like a porpoise.

Lifshin visits an old dude in Syracuse. Subconsciously turned on by him (she's "intrigued" by his cane), she wears a panty girdle. When he pulls her to his bed (she pretends he wants merely to see her poems) she refuses. He snarls, gives her orange juice, and says that

> if nothing happens
> come back and lie near
> me in bed.

Of course, she boasts, she never went back.

In "I Didn't Want To," a mouse scoops out a hole inside Lifshin. As a potential lover he fouls up, badly. If he'd be quieter, less demanding, she'd let him live behind her desk. His ego is enormous—he leaves pieces of himself lying about, "to flaunt the / territory he'd taken." Lifshin kills the mouse.

At first, her males resemble kittens. Soon, however, they turn into pissing toms, soiling her couch. The worst of the toms is a husband, in a marriage that languishes unconsummated for ten months. Did her own powers of attraction-repulsion generate the husband's impotence? Was mother too omnipresent? The only things that "grew" during the marriage, Lifshin sardonically reports, were her cats. Her mother loathed the man and nagged Lyn, accusing her of being a sado-masochist (see "Smother Mother").

The husband eventually departs, ironically taking up with another woman (he's potent with her). Then, disillusioned with his freedom, he returns to plague Lifshin, his "ice madonna." He's utterly self-obsessed, talks of suicide and dying, hates her poems (they deprive him of attention), and pours "ice on the stairs." Later, at 3 a.m., he phones, with this advice:

> Listen
> put a cactus in
> your honey place
> another in your
> heart hang up
> the phone

"I Should Have Known When He Ate The One Provolone Sandwich" arraigns the obsessive, greedy, violent husband. Always the taker, he "sulked if no one gave him books / or tickets or meat." Friends called the police:

> Because he loved me so he
> called me selfish pushy Jew
> and broke into my bedroom
> bit the wires then tried to
> steal the cat and feed it
> stolen mice and glassy wires.

He insists that Lifshin attend a Buffy St. Marie concert with him. She refuses, he breaks the door:

> In the tangle
> of torn phones bruises ripped
> cotton a few days later:
> those tickets rose like
> an oil slick stamped
> with some singer's name I
> never heard of, good only
> for

So much for this husband. What of other men? The men Lifshin desires are often images of the father who never said she was either pretty or sexy, who was obsessed with business, and who never touched her: he would have disinherited his kids without a qualm. An artist reminds Lifshin of her dad. They are about to screw when the artist's wife appears. A new dream of her father occurs during a visit to Notre Dame in Paris. Dad rubs against her. Years later, like a bored suburban female, Lifshin returns to the "what-ifs." In a starved life, unfilled fantasies from the past require completion. Lifshin seems enamored of the executive type, again, possibly, an image of her father. A man stands before some stained glass (art), with a waxed mustache, wearing a three-piece suit. He drives a BMW and has a "place in the Berkshires." He's the perfect Eastern rich suburbanite.

One of her longest pieces, "The Librarian," contains her major themes: the castrating female, the impotent professional male, the upper-middle class cultural values—good books, Pavarotti and opera (she's never quite at ease writing of Elvis Presley), and good wine. She's wonderfully sardonic about this male. Remove the *is* from *penis* and you are left with *pen*. The librarian is a frustrated poet; his pen / penis, alas, "runs out of ink":

> he edits his wife out of
> the house, presses his
> balls up against the dust of
> dark card catalogues, burns to ram
> the world with what's in his head
> He wishes he was bigger, hides
> behind an enormous desk. When
> it comes to women he's
> fast to revise....

Here Lifshin is in control. Her puns are delicious: "presses," "head," "bigger." The librarian suffers, apparently, from having a minuscule penis. To recompense, he "revises" Lifshin:

> So he gives her the feather
> stuffs her on an untouched
> shelf, says she hasn't
> any spine. He seals her lips
> with library paste. If he
> were to touch her breast it
> would be with a memo
> saying quiet this is not the
> place to visit or talk. He's
> afraid of using himself up ....

After trying all of Lifshin's "holes," unable to "get it in," he "kicks" her out with the books:

> he tried to stuff
> himself inside me as if
> some of my words would ooze
> thru the tip of where
> he should have been
> more sensitive and he
> couldn't get it in...

Finally alone, his penchant for "cutting up women," as for scrapbooks or library files, he masturbates:

> His pen is
> like a penis made
> of fluff he twists and
> sweats rubs his head
> between his hands

While other men excite her, they remain fantasies. The pain of having her teeth worked on by a dentist, overtly sexual, leads to this rumination:

> if I could just
> pad myself with enough
> men they'd be a moat
> bandage to keep from
> feeling what was
> jabbing me

A physician tells her that if his wife wrote Lifshin's dirty poems he'd never let her leave the house. When he actually hears this line: "he poured chocolate in my cunt," he departs, offended. Lifshin's sister reassures her: "some people / like their chocolate in a cup."

For the maturing Lifshin, poetry appears to be an extension of her girlish boardwalk parades. She craves to be a sex-machine. The damp aroma of her poems resembles that of Erica Jong's work. Lifshin has been called the female Bukowski—but Bukowski is rarely a myth. Lifshin is always one. Her portrait on *Kiss The Skin Off* is glamorous: brunette hair partially conceals a creamy face. She wears a casual sweater with a necklace, not of pearls, but of beer can tabs. She is probably more beautiful now than when she paraded Atlantic City.

Paradoxical attitudes toward men and sex parallel her sense of poet-self. Her writing both advertises that self and shows that she is a virginal, even transcendental, poet. In "Losing Connection" she is again with her mother, feeling sweaty and stupid. She goes to a liquor store with a fat man she hates. She's losing things—people's phone numbers, her pocket book. The butcher leers at her, winks, and says something "sexy." She shouts that she's a poet, as if that will restore the connection she's lost. She's on the phone. The phone "screams back" that she's exhausted her allotted time.

"After A Day We Stay In Bed Till The Sun Is Close To Setting" equates her vaginal and face lips. She's spent the night with a man after giving a poetry reading and confuses her need for sexual identity with her need to write—pagan vs. profane loves:

> My mouth is dry I
> need to have his
> poem where my clove
> nipples press into his
> blue striped cotton
> smelling of sun
> and wind in the pine
> trees a mirror that
> will reflect my dark
> eyes I need this as
> much as he needs to
> invent me to
> become himself

In "Too Many Readings Too Many Men" she is honest about the sexual dimensions of her public appearances:

> performing is like
> becoming wet after 17
> orgasms in one
> afternoon with nearly
> half that many men
> you're out of breath
> from the showers
> pulling on clean
> nylon see thru
> black bikini v's
> so they can imagine
> you in the way
> they want to and
> you smile and
> say what you've
> said for the 100th
> time in a way that's
> freshly deceptive
> drawing them in
> like a glistening
> pink slit not letting
> them see what was
> once there isn't
> as they drown in
> what is in
> their heads

Part of her tease-act is to absolve herself of any guilt; men create their fantasies. Like the female spider (the image appears in a pair of poems) she's not responsible for the male who visits her web. One poetry fan is so turned on she becomes his centerfold:

> Poetry's too easy
> he said he was light
> but dark on the
> inside asked me to read
> a sexy poem and would
> I mind if he came on
> the phone imagining
> my he was sorry it wasn't
> a taller body.

Here Lifshin has it how she likes it—the telephone sanitizes the sex act transpiring on the end of the line.

At her readings, while her poet's role enshrouds her like a cocoon, she projects an image of a kinky figure. In a panegyric to her lips (both sets) she is revealing:

> lips full as thighs
> lips that juicy
> lips that bite on
> themselves like
> guilt. Her vaginal lips are
> "silent as the lips of
> stone in the garden
> filling with icicles."

Her attitudes towards other poets is so harsh one senses that she abides no other poet on her turf. The belly-dance of words transpires for her carnival alone. "Poetry Reading Benefit" reveals a horrid view of other writers. One busily steals lines by copying them on his boots. Women in the audience are so sex-starved (especially "the older ones"—is Lifshin an agist?) you can hear their ribs crack as they clutch themselves with their arms. Macho poets read, chop wood, and watch breath hover over mountain streams. A stripped bodybuilder declares that audiences prefer wrestling matches to verse.

While I love Lifshin's sardonic bite, I am bothered by her ego. Rarely does she empathize with us. While a poem on Martha Graham shows affection for the dancer, it tries too hard to justify Lifshin's barrenness. Her poems are her children. In "Army Brat" poems

> write them
> selves in the
> dark when you
> hadn't planned them.

While verses for Alberta Hunter and Muriel Rukeyser read like jottings, these are excellent: "The Old Hunchback In The Chicken House," "Jeanne Marie Plouffe," and "Getting The Goods." In the latter, murdered Thai infants are stuffed with heroin and transported to Malaysia. Plouffe is a French-Canadian servant girl brutalized by the upper-class families she works for.

The skinny poem is indigenous to Lifshin, as are peculiar, often messy enjambments. The poems sound alike, and the enjambments seem arbitrary. Here for example, confusion is rampant:

> black hair snakes the
> child gurgles then
> doesn't a plastic rattle
> bobs on the water like a
> head . . .

To transfer action from hair snaking the child to the child gurgling doesn't work. And the reader simply does not know until thinking back that "doesn't" means that the child has just died, and has nothing to do with "plastic rattle." This passage is messy:

> it was hard to
> throw my arms a
> round to bubble and
> kiss and not just...

Accompanying such flawed poems are others superb in form and theme. One of these is "Reading Those Poems Because I Can't Get Started Thinking Of The Phone Call That Came, That You Might." Note the interweaving of *weed, flower, deer,* and *decay.*

> before i get to the
> end of the line my
> head's milkweed
> something in me
> drifts out into the
> trees thru the
> stained glass my
> black seeds flying
> out to where you
> say we'll find
> columbine they
> get hung up in the
> leaves words sinking
> in where they can't
> grow like what
> was starting to
> in the shot deer

        left in the
        snow all winter

    Such a poem reveals a vision lacking in her poems of adolescence. Lifshin has always spoken with a unique voice, and is often on target. To mix metaphors, the good news is that today her lyre has more than three strings.

PAUL MARIAH: RECIDIVIST OF VERSE:
SELECTED POEMS: THIS LIGHT WILL SPREAD

For male poets, Zeus types, poems spring full-blown from their brains. Other poets, Neptunes, engender poems from the froth and spume of creative ejaculations. Both sorts feel responsible for their progeny. They must see to it that they are well-placed (published) in the world. Each poem, including those already published (generally in obscure places), remain a worrisome responsibility. The life of a book of poems is brief; to go out-of-print is a form of death. And those little waifs who never find a slot in the world must twist rancorously inside the poet's brain. The occasion of a Selected Poems allows a poet to resuscitate poems out-of-print, and to launch hitherto unpublished pieces. A good poet needs to know which of his waifs deserve new life, and which like Kaspar Hauser should be kept in a cellar on bread and water.

The occasion for these musings is Paul Mariah's *This Light Will Spread,* a gathering of poems written over fifteen years (1960-1975). About half of them are appearing for the first time. This collection has been ignored by reviewers and the poetry world in general. My guess is that the arbiters of taste don't really know how to treat it—Mariah is not a safe, palliative, comfort-inducing poet. He writes out of a searing life: three years spent in an Illinois state prison where he was incarcerated for sexual deviation; a decade of activist causes, political and sexual—during the late fifties and sixties he participated in protests against war and for gay rights in San Francisco and Berkeley; secretary to both Kay Boyle and Robert Duncan, and an interviewer for the Kinsey Institute; twenty years of immersion in gay San Francisco, and twelve years as a counsellor at various half-way houses; and, finally, a dozen years as a publisher of a courageous literary magazine *ManRoot* and of ManRoot Books. He has featured Jean Genet, James Broughton, Jack Spicer, Amnesia Glasscock [a.k.a. John Steinbeck), David Fisher, Cocteau, and Cavafy, among others. He has also published numerous lesbian and gay writers who had had few quality outlets. In short, he was a vibrant force in our ongoing cultural life. His progeny are numerous, and they come in various guises, hues, and tones. The name Mariah, incidentally, is a pseudonym, and is a wry comment on police and their paddy-wagons, as well as on social *pariah*.

Let's scrutinize some of his poetry. The opening prison sequence, even without the much-printed *Persona non Grata* (its exclusion is a mistake, I think), is most valuable and moving. These derive from Mariah's prison life when he taught himself to write and served as a librarian and tutor to illiterate inmates. Experience in itself does not make good verse—craftsmanship, intelligence, and compassion are needed; and Mariah has these qualities in abundance. His lyric voice is assured, poignant, and playful. He moves beneath skins; we *feel* his Genet-world as prisoners make love, endure shake-downs, marry one another with rings made of cafeteria spoons, suffer solitary confinement, and develop scars over wounds that never heal. Like Genet, Mariah transforms this maiming world into an existentialist metaphor for decency and loving in the face of injustice, brutality, and terror. "Shakedown and More," in almost painfully cramped, projective-verse lines and rhythms, evokes both fear and love:

> Silver is missing
> From the messhall;
> All
>
> Prisoners suspect.
> Cells torn open
> Like wounds
>
> Setting out
> In search of
> The germ,
>
> The spoon stolen,
> Each frisked
> As he returns
>
> To his cell.
> Shakedown for
> Contraband.
>
> All known hands
> Are checked
> For shivs.
>
> One lives in

Terror that it's
Not marked

For him. Still
It may be found
As a ring on

Newly wedded hand
Or as a worse attack
A knife in the back.

Here is a portion of a moving panegyric "Muse Elektrique" written for a
Puerto Rican prisoner Mariah taught and loved. He writes in the man's idiom:

The wife is dead. You live yr life in rivers
That flow thru yr veins. My senses, name-givers.

The parent living has not told you there embedded in rock
Living Fossil, that yr father is dead. In Puerto Ric

O bottle slashed him in too-drunken quarrel.
You've sensed Absence: the father, the wife, the teacher. I often glanced

At you studying under my teacherguise while the class
Workt assignments, and the guards pit-pattered ass

From room to room, cell to cell, no matter where I look always
I find you lockd in the closet mind that plays

Teacher. What delight we found in that lockd closet!
I aftercelebrated you in a series of Christmas Sonnets

The closest thing to giving I could give. Penniless.
You played Handball on cloistered days. We, with finesse, splayed

Each other in the shower when we could. Now we are older,
Growing together: you there, I here. In slower, so much slower

Tones I am giving up my life to live
Among my bones. You, Isolate, do not know that I've

Written these lines for you. My letters seized,
My poems contraband. I write this in silence....

This prison sequence should be read with Mariah's *Persona non Grata*, still in print after numerous editions.

Several poems written to an Army Deserter relate to the prison group, and reveal another aspect of Mariah as social outcast, as a lover of another social outcast. As love poems, executed in letters and poems, these are tender and moving:

My hands are invisible now
Around you
Around your shoulders
As you look thru the bars.
The Moon is not looking.

She is fogged out . . .
Of the city I had to go
The pressure on my head
The bust coming
Felt the siege
But my knowing
Wouldn't stop you.

You could not trust the season
Of sage, the feelings.
The thrust of words.
The reality of them
Guards you thru this
Imprisoned night.

The "Bay Poems" have many surprises. There are love poems—"All Things Soft" is memorable; social poems: "Mamaism" extols blacks for having what whitey lacks, Mamaism and Dadaism: "it's a tar-baby world." In the hilarious "For Sale / Coldwell, Banker" Mariah settles a score with the phone company. Perched on top of an abandoned building near the San Francisco-Oakland freeway sits a phone booth dropped there by vandals. Mariah decides not to spend a dime to tell the company where the booth is: "You never listen to outside voices / Unless they plug you with dimes." Moreover, Pacific Telephone does not service poets: "Poetry is not Big Business."

In the "Bay Poems" there are poems on writers who have influenced

Mariah's work: Robert Duncan (he attended Duncan's writing workshop), Spicer, Olson, and Gertrude Stein. His "homage" to Stein is a tour de force, a writing *to* Stein and a writing *like* her. The poem to Olson is preachy and insufficiently outrageous. "Yr Night Mare," to Duncan, apes Duncan's obsessions with weird mythical figures ("Gllave," who "bridled the Golden Three"), esoteric mental gymnastics, the role of the poet as *vates* ("What the Irish call FILI, a seer"), and Duncan's penchant for verbal encrustations ("gold torques and honey-cakes"). In "Stringing the Lights," also from this section, we see our vulnerability as invisible strings wound about our heads. When it's "almost too late / to measure the pulling" we "collect ourselves / to see how whole we are."

"The Gay Heretic" poems have probably kept this book from receiving much critical notice. I do not imply that Mariah is a writer of gay life documentaries. But there is a problem, and as a writer myself who happens to be gay (as distinct from being *a gay writer*), I am puzzled by the reticence of the straight world to receive a world that contains so many of their brothers. There are times, yes, when Mariah fails to see that a good romping sex poem is only that, and that a terrific poem should be more. His outrageous "Figa," is both obscene and more. He generates meanings—and a longer essay would explore his fascination with the art / poetry of French surrealist poets who have touched this poem. His primary theme, underlying all of his craft, is erotic self-discovery. Making vigorous love to a lover, from all angles, in all weathers, is a creative act. Deviance does not count.

Recall Mariah's stay in prison. See the prisoner as outlaw. See the poet as outlaw. See the poet returning again and again to outlawed sexual acts. See the poet returning to the "crime" of writing poems in a hostile culture. In Mariah's world, we begin to discover lost basics: the soles of other men's feet, the heft of their testicles, their firm/soft throats, the stubble of their beards—all produce spurtings of the spirit and of the body—of art and life.

THE POEM AS SPIRIT-MEAT:
MICHAEL MC CLURE'S CORPUS OF POEMS

AIM: McClure's poetry has been better understood by the lions at the San Francisco Zoo at feeding time than by American poetry-lovers.

BLAST: No contemporary poet has

1. Written with more energy than Michael McClure.
2. celebrated a sheer physical existence as a means of spiritual enlightenment so persistently and tellingly.
3. better synthesized the conflicting female-male elements of our natures— Jean Harlow and Billy the Kid being archetypal. McClure is a major love poet.
4. moved as deeply into madness: he destroys in order to recreate sanity.
5. employed sheer sound as *Mantra*: McClure writes a pure *Mantric Poetry* without any trappings OMwise from the far east or from Jeremiah and ranting Old Testament prophets.
6. been so unabashedly *romantic* in these cynical days: McClure is a son of Blake, Swedenborg, Shelley, Whitman, cummings.
7. Etc., etc., etc.

THEREFORE: McClure's writing is like action painting: spontaneous. The reader is to re-experience the excitement McClure felt writing the poems. The energy screaming (streaming at other times) is as important as any traditional poetic statement. McClure fractures the preconditioned poetic response. Communication, obviously, is a tone, an excitement, a fear, a sexual connection, a discharge. The act of the Poem is *Mantric:* chanting, caressing, shouting, shitting, or breathing. The poem is cleansing and spiritual. Non-verbal ideas spread like warm honey on the slab surfaces of the mind, zapping from my mind over to yours, from McClure's over to ours.

As *mammalian communicator*, McClure ennobles Man, since he (man) re-achieves or recognizes linguistic *Mantric Forces*, The Lamb's *baa* responds lovingly to the *graaah* of the lion and meshes with it. Jean Harlow responds with lascivious purrs to Billy the Kid's growling and chest-beatings. Declaiming the delicious sound *graaah* freshens our spirit-nodes; we vibrate with recharged life.

McClure's beast (mammal) language is *love*: we are to form these animal sounds with abandon and pleasure, with love explosives, love-verbal-fun-ejaculations:

> THE PINE CONE IS PERFECT. IT STANDS BY
> THE FOOT OF THE MAIDEN.
> No, it is upon the table. The furniture is
> grahoor. The light is grahoor.
> This is in bliss eternity. Oh calm gahrr groooh nahrr
> la ahhr NOOOHH ! Marr sum vahhr grahrraiee hrahhr
> nok-thorp naharr. No rise up ! No stand out !
> BUT STEADY !
> STEADY ! STEADY
> as she goes
> I am thy-my flagged flesh ship.
> GRUHH. NOOOOH ! HAHHR ! BLOOW !
> Bluhh
> !
>
> —(Ghost Tantras No. 30)

Like "The Pine Cone Is Perfect," the 99th of the Ghost Tantras must be read according to its individual sounds, without our worrying about whether we understand them or not. Poems are not necessarily always meant to be recollected in tranquility, rendered into prose equivalents, read in a vicar's tone, or worshipped: they are to be *lived* as part of one's blood stream. As founts of energy well up within us we luxuriate in pure animal sounds. We are spontaneous and sensuous (sensual). We grow childlike, trusting, innocent, and Blakean. We resonate *spirit, body,* and *mind.* Life may be bleared and seared but it is uncontaminated.

McClure's poems are restorative, and as we read, the actor in all of us emerges. This actor is the *agent extension* of our *meatspirit selves. A primal scream* releases us into life. McClure would free this *agent,* thereby enhancing poetry as a sung-shouted-declaimed-primal experience. Here is a portion of Ghost Tantras No. 99, the final one of the long series:

> IN TRANQUILITY THY GRAHRR AYOHH
> ROOHOOERING

GRAHAYAOR GAHARRR GRAHHR GAHHR
THWOSH NARR GAHROOOOOOOOH GAHRR
GRAH GAHRRR ! GRAYHEEOARR GRAHRGM
THAHRR NEEOWSH DYE YEOR GAHRR
grah grooom gahhr nowrt thowtoom obleeomosh.

The poem is strangely formalist despite a rampant structure and design. In his essay "Reason" (in *Meat Science Essays*) McClure describes his *spontaneous man* as one who lies in sunlight on the forest floor with his eyes closed. He exercises, stretching as yogis do. He gives himself completely to the sheer pleasure of his muscle-life. "He groans, writhes, twists, denies himself nothing that the sinew and tendons and lung and heart request." His consciousness is a "blank field." He ceases to measure time as an animal play of muscles establishes a rhythm, creating a pattern in space.

(McClure's most avant-garde poems have neo-classic rhythm patterns, echoing Milton, Marvell, and Dryden). He repeats patterns, inducing a delicious animal heat: bright colors play inside his skull, and he growls, raising his arms to the sun. He makes animal-pleasure noises at the sun. "He is *mammal!* He has touched "a ball of silence" within himself and knows he is *Man*; but he is also tiger and lion. He knows what his primitive forbears felt. His *deep reason* is unrelated to the "intellect...except as it furnishes the notes for a melody of reason. "Reason is "the liberty of human flesh moving in the universe."

To McClure, poetry "comes straight in through the senses and combines imagination with distortion." McClure's equation is: the greater the joy and pleasure one experiences, the greater the life one feels. He hates moderation. The human stretching his muscles and snarling mammal sounds acknowledges that there have always been "secret hopes and desires." The notion of "levels of existence" McClure rejects as a "kind of modern psychological folklore." The mammal-man portrays his belief "that matter is spirit and the meat is the container." We are so conditioned to think of meat as something sold in supermarkets or fed to animals that we have almost lost the positive overtones— these McClure seeks to restore. His aware, vibrant man requires no logic to comprehend his destiny; "stretching his leg and twisting the muscles of his arm in pleasure creates reason. The pearl gleaming on flesh in the light is an act of reason!"

This statement is central to McClure's work. Until we are spontaneous, and reject conventionalities, we shall miss a unique experience. Poetry is Action. Poetry is Explosion.

Of course, there are earlier models for McClure's elan: Shelley's romantic exclamations and his willingness to risk overstatement for a fervid personal truth. Whitman's unabashed energy: his "urge, urge, urge" is reflected in McClure's "The Surge" (*Star*). McClure's own note below suggests his fascination with the poetic act as engendering protein organisms. The poem, he implies, must fall short of an absolute beauty—it remains a step towards a "fully achieved" or perfect life:

> This is the failure of an attempt to write a beautiful
> poem. I would like to have it looked at as the mind-
> less coiling of a protein that has not fully achieved life
> —but one that is, or might be, a step towards livingbeing.
> "The Surge" begins
> THE SURGE! THE SURGE! THE SURGE!
> IT IS THE SURGE OF LIFE
> I SEEK
> TO VIEW...

In "Under The Black Trees" he dares to declare pain and joy without apology:

> My chest is weeping—and I do not cry longer.
> There is only the kneading of my chest
> and I know it is moaning. The lobes
> of my lungs draw upon one another.
> And "White Bread Gleams upon Heavy Tables" humorously imitates Whitman's fondness for French words to convey an emotion an English word wouldn't quite convey: the puns on "ass" and "massage" are choice:
> The smoothness of thy toes,
> thy chin...
> THY AMBASSAGE!!

McClure's perpetual use of OH OH OH OH reflects a Romantic poet's fondness for self-declamation. This example appears in *Dark Brown*: "OH BRAIN OH LOVE OH GOD SHIT PAIN OH HEAT FIRE OF CONFUSIONS." Such explosions (with their attendant humor) are a "BUILDING," McClure writes, "TO A HUGE GLORIA ROMANTIC CRY, NEW BAROQUE SHAPE / halls of graciousness and beauty unseen before." McClure's cries move towards that "baroque shape." Their frequency, and their sequential juxtapositions with crude words deny a full return to a Romantic sentimentality. Yes. But how are we to respond to such unrestrained writing? Is he putting us on? Should we proceed to a far corner of the cocktail-party room? Pass Go and go home? Gossip about McClure behind his back as a super-romantic slob and lousy poet? McClure insists that we FREAK OUT:

MANTRIC WORDS AND SOUNDS
UNBLOCK THE CHOKED AND
CLOGGED BODY CHANNELS
TO THE SPIRIT!

If these poems were merely one long personal wail we'd avoid them; but the *love* and *humor* attract us. We relish the mammalian joy.

His blocked capitals McClure obviously borrows from pop culture: movies, comics, newspapers, television commercials, and posters. Life is perpetual verbal circus of headlines, mottos, and hyped messages: The *poet as barker.*

We laugh as we enjoy McClure's *giantism* as well as his *mousiness.* Lion and Mouse romp together in Eden; as do Devil and Angel. Jean Harlow and Billy the Kid. Eden is in the here and now in the sense that in the world's nooks and crannies contain Paradise; and that lost echelon of senses Blake insisted we shucked at the time of the Fall may return in full measure.

At the Fall, Adam put away his cock and persuaded Eve to cover her cunt with a fig leaf. From that moment man denied muscle-knowledge, muscle-grandeur, and *mammalian joy.* Superb orgasms simply happen: jert, jert, jert. You needn't pump, bump, jump, grind, and sweat. You don't even require another body. You don't feel the pool of honey on your belly until you return to the human (from the mammal) state. Stir the honey with your fingers. Smell it. Taste it. A Gift from God. Poems are *sperm* and *maiden juice* meant to be savored! Your *vesicles runneth over!* REJOICE!

No poet writing today is a better love poet than McClure. *Foils and poignards?* "Valentine's Day Sonnet" is representative of his feelings about women. As a hymn to Woman it is ostensibly conventional, suggests Blake in its language (and not merely because McClure says *lambliness*), and in its playfulness reminds us of that master love poet e. e. cummings. The poem is tender, intense, and Venusian. Here is how it starts:

GLORIOUS DIVINE CREATURE, I'VE JUST
SEEN YOUR NAKEDNESS,
Your womanly-muscled flesh, and lambliness again
in a new light

I SMELL THE SULFUR AND SPRUCE
in your hair. And the dream-scent of your sleek waist.
but it is the relaxed light upon your brow and cheeks
               that tells me
YOU MUST BE PROTECTED
from Rippers and Devourers.

This erotic moment is from "Fuck Ode" (that concludes *Dark Brown*):

ALL IS QUIET BUT MY SONG TO ME, YOUR
                         SONG
        to you. This is our touching. This
is the vast hall that we inhabit. Coiling,
standing. Cock into rose-black meat. Tongue
into rose meat. Come upon your breasts, Come
     upon your tongue, Come in your burrow
Cavern love snail breath strange arm line

I see McClure as the Jim Dine of poetry. "Oh Fucking Lover Roar with Joy—I, Lion Man!" incorporates a pop mode with a traditional one. In one passage there is an echo of the popular song "I'd walk a million miles for one of your smiles," The image of the "two meat clouds" is humorous and surreal. The third line is a parody of one of Shelley's in "West Wind." Amusing also is McClure's seeing Oversoul as Undersoul:

I GROAN, I AM, UPON THE CONE SHAPED
                        BREASTS
     & tossing thighs !
—AND SEND MY THOUGHTS INTO A
     BLACKER UNIVERSE
OF SUGAR !

Thy face is a strained sheer Heart twisted
     to fine beauty by thy coming.
It is a million miles from toes to thighs !
     (Our bodies beat like the ultimate movie
slowed to blurs of two meat clouds becoming
     one—and the Undersoul is joined
         by kissing mouths.)
                      OH !
                      OH !

McClure's motifs affect me as Claes Oldenberg's works do: the artist's zest for life triumphs over all absurdities. Both men rejoice in transmuting the threatening, the desiccated, the horrible, the funky, and the ugly into joy.

"Grahar Mantra," a celebration poem, reveals McClure's Concrete-Word Power. Letters of the alphabet are Mantras. *Grahhr* is a joyous release concretized by the adjectives surrounding or attached to it. *Grahhr* evokes celestial matters. It is vapor, and it is sexual: a "White Mount." Blood Wisdom particularizes the abstraction, *mammalizing* it, detaching it from bread-and-butter meanings:

> Blue Black Winged Space Rainbow GRAHHR
> Black Winged GRAHHR Toes Kiss
> Pink Leather GRAHHR Blue Rainbow
> Vapor GRAHHR Vapor GRAHHR
> Hahr Rainbow Space Black Yahr
> GRAH ! GRAH !
> White Mount Toes Kiss
> Toes Kiss Star.

While McClure avoids self-pity, he does experience despair, doubt, and anguish. *Dark Brown* displays torment, which McClure's Vesalian man triumphs over:

> THAT I AM A FLOWER DOES NOT MEAN
> THAT I AM RESPONSIBLE
> FOR THE AGONY OF THE ROOTS !
>> ("Poisoned Wheat")

> Sickness and guilt must be cast off!
> Guilt is a luxury.
> Being sickened is meaningless.
>> ("Poisoned Wheat ")

> Each man is a mess and a fuck-up
>   with hideous ideals
> serving his perverted individual
>   HOLY GHOST
>   with a twisted smile!
> BUT HOW BEAUTIFUL ! HOW BEAUTIFUL !
>   —And what grace !
>> ("For Anger")

"Mad Sonnet 3" (there are 13 in the series) reveals a delicate, gentle, and fantasizing McClure. His language moves freely among levels (*tits to dew-drop*). Skilled rhymes (Both as superb camp and as complex rhymes; sometimes he is archaic; at other times he is experimentally fresh: *hollyhock, thought, stalk, not*). Tiny mammals hear "the sugar run in the stalk of the lily." Finally, *meat is beauty*, the very inner source of our spirit-beings:

> TINY MAMMALS WALK ON WHITE BE-
>   TWEEN THE YELLOW
> BOULDER GRAINS OF THE LILY'S
>   POLLEN....

> I am obsessed with the thought
>   THAT I AM SANE
> and men are not

> IF BEAUTY IS NOT MEAT THEN WHAT IS ALIVE
>   is not imagination!
> AND IF MEAT IS NOT BEAUTY
>   then save condemnation
>   and drop your bombs
>   &
>   spray the rays!
> PEEK OUT !   PEEK OUT !

Many clues to McClure's aims as poet lie buried in his prose pieces, most of them gathered in *Meat Science Essays*. These remain one of the crucial documents of the early 'sixties. Here is his conclusion to "Revolt":

> There is no Cynicism that may stand in judgment.
> Revolt pushes to life—it is the degree farthest from
> death. Stones do not revolt. There are no answers.
> Acts and violence with cause are sweet destruction.
> And the sadness that there must be any death.
> There is no plan to follow. All is liberty. There are
> physical voices and the Voice of Meatspirit speaking.
> There are physical voices of the dead and the inert
> speaking. The dead is the non-vital past that lives within us
> and about us. There is liberty of choice, and there is,
> or is not, a greater Liberty beyond this. But there is

constantly revolt and regimen of freshness.

Yes, praise to all things that bring the UNIVERSE near! Praise Michael McClure. Praise Us. GAAHHHHHHHHHHR!

THE MACDONALD-EDDY NATURE POETRY SYNDROME:
JUDITH McCOMB'S
AGAINST NATURE: WILDERNESS POEMS

As a rule, male poets have seen far more sermons in stones, intimations of immortality in aretes, tarns, and teepees, and more arousals of passion induced by Alpine storms and exploding volcanoes than women poets. That men have had an edge on natural affinities puzzles me.

None of the great nineteenth-century nature poets were women. Men alone removed nature's clothing (was not nature "the living garment of God" as Thomas Carlyle said)? And the removals were not necessarily erotic. When Wordsworth in his skiff was frightened by a louring Mt. Skiddaw he was responding to incredible forces beyond himself, forces he read as a Universal Consciousness innately responsible to and caring for him, even in its hostile moods. Following Wordsworth and Carlyle, Emerson and Thoreau set the pattern for generations of Yankee poets to pluck Transcendental buckwheat in the wilds. Transcendentalism has been a man's province. Despite her nosiness, Margaret Fuller was pretty much left out of it, albeit she did own a cantankerous heifer at Brook Farm.

Nature's nymphs and seraphs, in their diaphanous gowns and garter belts, continue to lure male poets to twitch their last garments off; and poets in our time have continued to yank, snap, pull, and tear, revealing hints of warm nature-flesh: viz., Gary Snyder's peregrinations up, into, over, and through the Rockies, feasting (metaphorically) on centipedes, lizards and manzanita berries; Howard McCord's romantic returns to the navel of the universe, that primitive omphalos located somewhere in Iceland; my own poems inspired by northern Wisconsin lakes and forests, by arbutus patches in snow, and by deer drinking amidst the lilies; and William Stafford's and Wendell Berry's domesticated landscapes.

What I'm probing is what strikes me as arrogance in these poets (and others who take cues from nature); they assume that nature cares! A useful term for the phenomenon, perhaps, is the *MacDonald-Eddy Nature Poetry-Syndrome*. It's an old but not very well understood disease. Let me explain. There's a scene in the movie "Rose Marie" in which handsome Canadian Mountie Nelson Eddy seats himself on a mountain peak beneath a scintillating full moon. He begins to sing.

Across a sizeable valley rift sits Jeanette MacDonald comfortably positioned on another peak, wearing one of those marvellous hats and a gauzy frock. Eddy and MacDonald soon begin to sing to one another. Like gypsy moths sending sex signals, they bathe the Rockies with delicious chocolate-covered sound. Nature herself is immersed in human love trills, lilts and vocables. The bears forego rending stumps for ants and honey, deer perk up their ears and interrupt the flow of fecal droppings, and weasels allow freshly caught partridge to flop free. The singers *inspire* Nature; Nature *inspires* the singers.

There's sentimentality here, of course; and the treacle is male-induced. (Wasn't Jeanette an Indian maid?) The question persists—why does the male artist rather than the female call these mountain tunes? Women are generally back at the main camp, brewing the coffee, whipping up biscuits, or taking saunas with one another and their kids. Here are some possible explanations: Since Nature is female (Mother Nature) women feel repelled by getting it on with her. Lesbianism. Also, if Nature is female, a woman should feel she already possesses whatever estrogens it is that attract men to Nature. Also, American males have had a rough time displaying emotions; women have not. Women are supposed to be sensitive, drizzly, and emotive, even if they have to force these feelings as a display for their males. Nature for these repressed men serves as a kind of female safety-valve; emotions they fear to display in their everyday lives are there sanctioned. Exhausted burly linemen and oil-pipe conduit builders and fire fighters, as they guzzle down their Buds and Coors, gaze at the wilderness and are stunned. The mountain side trembles, chilling these hunks. Nature as safety-valve.

Which brings me to Judith McCombs. An American poet has put the thumb-screws to Nature, and a woman has done it. McCombs is no filmy-gowned, floppy-hatted Jeanette MacDonald. She has earned her right to be "against Nature." These poems should be displayed in all Sierra Club shelters and recited in the main lodges of the U. S. Forest Service as parties of back-packers take off for the wilds. McCombs herself is an indefatigable woods-person; she's gone on survival outings in winter. She teaches wilderness classes at the Detroit College of Art and Design. "Against," in her lexicon, has at least two meanings: the one I've already implied, that she *opposes* Romantic notions of Nature; another is that she is a minutely observant peregrinator of the wilds and projects herself "against" those immense backdrops. This second view is the dominant one. Let me illustrate.

Here she nags a male friend who finds glaciers "messy." In the face of glacial shifts, human warmth is slight and fleeting:

> Why can't you take Nature as offered?
> Shut up & be grateful, you can't afford
> your private dynamite, so don't interrupt
>
> Out on the ice it's our one chance to listen
> to whatever the glacier is muttering, to see
> how this great swollen hunk & its Neanderthal drains
> are ploughing the bedrock   Here we can notice
> how accidentally the glacier creates
> soil & water, valley & life
>
> Look we are mammals, tramping the surface
> The warmth we have
> > > is small & not lasting

She is satiric about the equipment male backpackers think they need for survival, a mark of their vulnerability and of their exclusion, finally, from the Nature they idealize:

> What are you proving, importing yourself
> & your gear to the wilds? Your daily calories
> exceed the environment   What you can gather
> is sour, or breaks, & besides you are queasy
> about killing
> > > You stop on a ridge & the safe water gurgles
> out of your plastic container into your mouth
> In your left breast pocket the keys to the car
> are jingling
> > > You can always go back
> You can always go back

Earlier in the same poem, McCombs exposes the common Romantic fallacy that stones babble as much as brooks do. Here she dumps several manure cart loads of these phony poems:

> The hawks don't want you out here, they're too ignorant
> to beg for your garbage   The bears & the clever
> mammals avoid you   The trees are just trees,
> they all look alike   The stones have no numbers
> no shapes you remember (but they seem to multiply)
> Did you come all this way to gibber with stones?

A main trope for nature poetry is the Garden of Eden. If Adam and Eve were versifiers, and if God were giving Pulitzers for poetry, chances are that Adam's efforts would resemble Wordsworth's or Snyder's; Eve's would commemorate the small disasters of fallen rose petals, flies trapped in spider-webs, and the mushy deaths of raspberries. Here is McCombs on Paradise:

> Nature is not like you & me, dear,
> whatever its virtues it doesn't have hands
> & it isn't our garden   If the inhabitants
> squeak to each other, if the stones understand
> what hooks them to earth, that does us no good
> The clever things hide when they hear us, & the rest
> move so godawful slow, we can't notice, or follow
> A strange kind of time is elapsing, outside
> of our watches   We can't make the mountains conform
> to the lines on our maps   They slide in the night
> & when we're not looking   Between boulder & boulder,
> forests & scree, summit & summit,
> There aren't any numbers women
> There is only the earth
> There's a perfect night view of the mountains behind us,
> a real panorama, just like the brochures,
> but it's bigger & colder & harder than us
> Let's talk about something more human: my hands
> in your pockets, you're ticklish, & who left the grease
> in the stewpot again, & why is the bedrock
> on my side of the tent   My watch says it's 8
> & here comes the moon with her merciless light
> so where is the flash
>
> No matter how far in we go, how long
> we are what we are
>   unnatural, human

Her realism is refreshing. On one of her backpacking trips, she retrieves an old table. When she rights it, it collapses into the lake. Conclusion?

> Aristotle was right
> (& my shins are learning): a thing is its usage:
> & a table that is through with being a table
> is not a table at all

How refreshing! McCombs is a female Thoreau!

Lest I misrepresent her though, let me say that she never chucks out transcendental possibilities. Only after she has dispelled arrogantly sentimental readings of Nature can she celebrate the mysterious "natural flowing" of the world "which feeds on life & tends ever towards life." She praises this "flowing," both with "gratitude & bitterness," Humans are minuscule against Nature's scope. McCombs performs basic human acts: feeding a baby, loving a man. Her celebrations, consistently Aristotelean, remind us of a basic problem: mountains don't care whether we love them or not:

> the mountain is there, a mountain. It is not
> inside you. It has all it can do
> being a mountain. It does not want
> to be loved.

McCombs is a small but potent figure on this earth; her loving is intensified by an unblinking realism. Humans require succoring. She lights a match in the dark—a paradoxical act, since her own brief flame of life prevents her from *seeing* what hostile forces wait among the Ponderosas:

> In the blackness a lapping
> of water or muzzle; the air says something,
> gibberish or warning, & quits when I move,
> matches in hand, to strike open the fire
> that stops me from seeing.

McCombs' songs, far more moving than MacDonald's, evoke dignity and beauty. If this book receives the readers it deserves, American poets will write less sentimentally of Nature. Male poets should turn to the best of Frost, D. H. Lawrence, and Gary Snyder. They might memorize McCombs' poems and kick their traditional nature-habits of pruriently poking and probing Nature's parts. I'm nagged (and pleased) that it has taken a woman to get things right.

ON DIVINING ROD:
McKUEN IN THE PANTHEON

The object of this literary quiz is to spot the passages penned by Rod McKuen. A score of 15 will be amazing. I have appended a key and place my readers on the honor system, at least until they have completed whatever identifications they can. In addition to McKuen, the following poets are represented: James Wright, Galway Kinnell, Robert Creeley, W. S. Merwin, Denise Levertov, Adrienne Rich, James Merrill, Howard Nemerov, Robert Lowell, Richard Howard, John Ashbery, Tess Gallagher, Derek Walcott. Here are the passages:

1.   Sometimes I feel sometimes
       the Muse is leaving, the Muse is leaving America.
       Her tired face is tired of iron fields....
       I am falling in love with America.

2.   The hills rise up
       like water walls,
       waves in solid glacier.
       Held in place
       by pasted plankton
       seen as grass.

3.   A starry frost will come
       dropping on pools
       and I'll be astray here
       on upsheltered heights.

4.   We'll all go home when winter comes
       for now the seasons will not change
       they are a shawl of ribbons,
       paper, rags
       a willow dragging branches in the water....

5.   Years from now you'll not remember why,
only that it happened and on time
underneath protective touch and arm.

6.   When you look back there is always the past
Even when it has vanished
But when you look forward
With your dirty knuckles and the wingless
Bird on your shoulder
What can you write

7.   If I take a lover for every tree, I
will not have again such an
opening as
        when you flew from me.

8.   To have been loved once by someone—surely
there is a permanent good in that,
Even if we don't know of the circumstances
Or it happened too long ago to make a difference.

9.   We scattered over the lonely seaways,
Over the lonely deserts did we run,
In dark lanes and alleys we did hide ourselves....

10.   I know the roadway to those towns
the mind imagines or puts off
it lies a little way beyond the cities
hands, not hearts, have formed.

11.   This is mid-autumn,
the moment when insects die
instantly as one would wish for a friend.

12.   Here where all is frozen over,
taken in the January glass
that cracks and falls to pieces,
we see every bird that stops to rest
               on icy branch
as omen.

13.   My Papa's gone to Michigan
my brother's in the slammer

Mamma's serving fish again,
damn her.

14.   When you do dance, I wish you
a wave of the sea, that you might ever do
nothing but that, move still, still so,
and own no other function....

15. My words reach you as through a telephone
where some submarine echo of my voice
blurts knowledge you can't use.

16. Everything changes; nothing does. I am back
The doorbell rings, my heart leaps out of habit....

17. Brown cricket, you are my friend's name.
I will send back my shadow for your sake, to stand guard
On the solitude of the mourning dove's young.
Here, I will stand by you, shadowless,
At the small golden door of your body till you wake
In a book that is shining.

18. He is the painter of the human mind
Finding and faithfully reflecting the mindfulness
that is in things, and not the things themselves.

19. Most San Francisco tragedies stay unadorned.
This lack of advertisement
                    is what makes The City great.

20. A tall black lady, fashion's captive,
Is passing, passes, passes on
the smell of mingled blossoms
                    lingers in her wake.

21. But the Lady is indefinable,
she will be the door in the wall
to the garden in sunlight.
I will go on talking forever.

22. Before I enter the rooms of your solitude
in my living form, trailing my shadow,
I shall have come unseen.

On Divining Rod

Rod McKuen, who has published over twenty books of poems, in 1984 published *Suspension Bridge.* The first printing ran to 40,000 copies, and enjoyed a $40,000 promotional budget and an author's tour. All this would green the most generous-minded of poets with envy. Poets who grace the pages of *APR,* or the lesser lit mags, or who teach in writing programs, or who are officers in the Poetry Society of America and the Associated Writing Programs sneer at the book.

Publishers Weekly (Sept. 7, 1984) has a devastating unsigned review followed by a glowing take on Denise Levertov's *Oblique Prayers.* This passage by Levertov earns praise:

> They make mistakes:
> they busy themselves,
> anxious to see more, straining their necks to look
> beyond blue trees at dusk,
>   forgetting it is
>   the dust at their feet reveals
> the strangest, most needful truth....

Now, a quick scrutiny of these lines (penned by a Euterpe of contemporary verse) reveals sins generally seen as McKuen's: the cliches ("straining their necks," "busy themselves," "most needful truth"); the romantic times of day—here it's dusk with its "blue trees"; the sleazy/easy rhymes—"dust," "dusk"; the hollow abstraction "truth." When poets of Levertov's stature write this badly, it's often written up, as it is here, as evidence of genius.

I am not defending McKuen against his flaws; many poems suffer from poor editing. Others sound like jottings tossed off while eating pastrami on rye. And his ego can be cloying.

Yet, the hypocrisy of poets and critics who praise poets writing worse than McKuen irritates me. This passage, by much-touted Charles Wright, is from his *The Other Side of the River.*

> I want to sit by the river,
> in the shade of the evergreen tree,
> And look into the face of whatever,
> the whatever that's waiting for me.

David St. John, in *Bookworld* (May 20, 1984), extols Wright as "a poet of great and subtle humor"—as the "little song" quoted above, "excerpted from the dazzling title poem," shows. That's irresponsible—both poem and sycophantic critique should be wrapped and tossed in the garbage.

The hostility towards McKuen is in part sour grapes and in part ignorance. He has to be the only poet in America who is dismissed out of hand by peers who won't read him. The assumption (and I confess to having shared it) is that someone so popular must be bad! If poetry sings out in the cafes, night clubs, and the streets it sullies itself.

Yet, I do recall the rush of academics and poets to the pop culture of the 50's and 60's, academics who donned Guatemalan beads, fringe buckskin jackets, and who attended perpetual performances of *Hair*, dropped psychedelics, and smoked dope. Bob Dylan, Mick Jagger, and John Lennon were master poets. English Departments anxious to attract students sponsored courses in "the poetry of Rock." It seems obvious now that those Dylan and Lennon lyrics were simple-minded.

McKuen is as much of a musician as he is a poet. Not only has he written and recorded fine symphonic and classical compositions, but many of his songs are pop classics, Academy Award and Emmy winners. His tradition is that of cafe singers and jazz artists (Piaf, Brel, Coward, Dietrich, Garland, Kitt, and Bassey), and of poets (Whitman, Lorca, and Neruda).

A fair critic will discern the positives in the cafe-songs and ballads and will dismiss poems that are jottings rather than finished pieces.

In *Suspension Bridge*, "Heartland" is disarmingly simple in both image and form. While innocence and experience juxtaposed are as old as Blake, McKuen's re-fashioning is fresh:

> The ditch between experience
> and innocence
> is not so wide.
> Each has its outer edges
> and its other side.
> The sound that works to resonance
> and later echo
> must have that first initial strike.
> And what of oceans,
> tide and tidal,
> that first vital sign a trickle
> or a stream
> must start the motion.

> Experience is only an exaggeration
> of that first dent in innocence.

In "River House" McKuen scrutinizes nature: gooseberries, Indian artifacts, ants, and an

> Albino butterfly on branch,
> a speckled roach inside woodpecker drilling.

The country, McKuen writes, "keeps erasing its own heritage."

"Backpacking" is a reworking of the notion that all journies, whether by foot or by train, are new beginnings and new endings. McKuen descends a train near the region he's about to explore. "Rainbow droppings" to the north signal the spiritual / physical adventure awaiting him on his climb:

> Many-colored and odd-angled,
> slices of some larger framework broken up
> still shining, though, and perfect
> in their imperfection.

His quest was after a "stranger," a lover, rather than "secrets in a landscape." He fails, and the train waits to return him to civilization. "Wait, and You Will See the Night Sky" resolves the dilemma of a private quest. True, the quatrains are faded, and the abstractions nebulous—but there is sufficient appeal. McKuen inverts the image of night-fear (this line is reminiscent of Robert Frost: "Night never meant its walkers any harm…"):

> Each body is but harbor for a time,
> each harbor's depth is measured by its sound.
>
> Do not believe the old dividing line
> You will find your own line soon enough.
> Out of darkness, further darkness
> unlike the dark behind.

Implicit is a tough-minded view of one's life and aging.

Not everything is pretty in McKuen's work. In "Christchurch to Duneden," as he drives along a New Zealand road, an eagle, feasting on a possum, is struck by a speeding auto:

The eagle leaps and dances
for a moment on the hook,
an ornament awry

McKuen subtly interweaves the plight of the bird with his own pain:

What I wanted and I want
is your head on,
> belly, belly up
in anteroom or acreage afar.
I would that I could say it better
Hand about, let go of it.
There is no new way
to tell timeworn stories.

Oh heart, you are much quicker
than the eyelid flickering
but never, never fast enough.

His love poetry has matured. "Lillian at Fifty" shows transformations: Lillian's hair is graying, her voice is "thickthroated," her eyes are lined, and her breasts "bend and curve / and fit into her body curve, / the way a lover's arm was meant / to cradle that so perfect head...." While he can still be turned on by youth, viz., in this vignette from "Down Montgomery Street," the earlier silliness over nymphettes à la Leonard Cohen (who has many parallels with McKuen, as composer, poet, and performer) are gone. In another poem, he displays a moving empathy for a "Joe" who scribbled an advertisement for love on a "shithouse wall" at Morro Bay. The message is a cry of lonely pain, and through a winsome humor ("You can be faulted only / in your penmanship, / not for your pencilled and outreaching cry."), McKuen reveals empathy:

I hope a dozen ring you up
and bring Utopia to your first meetings.
Myself, I send the season's greetings.
Would it were myself.

I do not claim for McKuen a more exalted place in the poetry pantheon than he deserves, but I urge that he be read. Perhaps in these decades, when poetry is trapped in tedious confessional modes it is time to reanimate ourselves through what we have hitherto dismissed as poetry "outside poetry"—populist, or cafe, or street poetry. McKuen is a good place to start.

Key to Quiz

1. Derek Walcott, "Upstate"; 2. McKuen, "The City as Ocean"; 3. Seamus Heany, "Unsheltered Heights"; 4. McKuen, "The Voice of Independent Means"; 5. McKuen, "Wait, and You Will See the Night Sky"; 6. W. S. Merwin, "It is March"; 7, Tess Gallagher, "Willingly"; 8. John Ashbery, "A Wave"; 9. Galway Kinnell, "The Avenue Bearing the Initial of Christ.... "; 10. McKuen, "Open Invitation"; 11. Robert Lowell, "Circe"; 12. McKuen, "Last Refuge"; 13. McKuen, Over at Our House"; 14. Richard Howard, "Move Still, Still So"; 15. Adrienne Rich, "The Lag"; 16. James Merrill, "After the Fire"; 17. James Wright, "Poems to a Brown Cricket"; 18. Howard Nemerov, "Beginner's Guide"; 19. McKuen, "Going Home"; 20. McKuen, "Lower Montgomery Street"; 21. Robert Creeley, "The Door"; 22. Denise Levertov, "The Presence."

THE GREAT AMERICAN POETRY BAKE-OFF,
OR, WHY W. S. MERWIN WINS ALL THOSE PRIZES

It's always easy to deal with persons who aren't offensive in any way; and if these persons are poets who write unerringly and weave a superb style around cliches, you have a poet easy to honor. In fact, judges nearly tumble over themselves to decorate these poets. A boy-scout ethic prevails: poets clean in heart, clean in mind, clean in the hearts of their countrymen....

I have been an avid follower of W. S. Merwin's writing for years. His translations are consistently first-rate; and his several volumes of original work contain a number of masterpieces. Only now, however, after intensive readings of *Writings to an Unfinished Accompaniment* do I understand his formulae for success. He seems to be settling for less than his best; I mean to be constructive.

I have—quite rightly—loved the intense purity of Merwin's diction; there are no obscenities, no jargon from science or technology, no words smeared or bleared with trade or toil. His language is basically conceptual. A Puvis de Chavannes world we might say, as distinct from Van Gogh's. Also, his music lulls me into believing that such exquisitely-manipulated sounds are deep. In a real sense, Merwin is a modern free-verse Swinburne—his technique is so fluent you forget what he is saying, marvelling at the technical brilliance. And the tone is always somewhat formal, *grave* (in a French sense), seldom humorous, never offensive. But when you scrutinize the flawless surface, and divorce the ideas from the craft, you find a series of postures. I shall describe these, for they reveal Merwin's recipe for whipping up prize-winning delectables for the great American bake-off competitions.

The Merwin landscape: comparisons with paintings don't help, since there is almost no color in these poems; and there are hardly any details, except for vague bandages, clouds, asters, worn-brick surfaces, a paw print, smoke, gold, a doorstep, and a crack in a wall. Perhaps parallels with drawings or etchings are more apt than ones with paintings. But here too the scenes they enshroud (Merwin's dominant tone is empty, stoned, elegiac) are so uncluttered they hardly hold our attention long. Here is how one such drawing might look: a flat foreground landscape with a hint of a mountain in the background. Near the mountain shines a light, possibly from a lantern, shedding beams of a sufficient thrust to suggest divinity, or the light up the road. In the foreground a stele with the initials W. S. M., or your initials, on it, and possibly a quick scribble of a wolf chasing some pale sheep, or a flea carrying a Riding-Hood basket of miniature diseases. To paraphrase Richard Howard's illuminating back-cover blurb, Merwin's landscapes are *not,* therefore they *are;* and since they are *not* we may justifiably call them *visionary.*They have, says Howard, "a quality of life...which must be characterized by its negatives, by," he helpfully explains, "what it is not, for what it is not cannot be spoken."

Merwin's landscapes reflect his versions of what the French poets he translates and reads are like. I find it helpful to call them *Beckettian,* a Samuel Beckett landscape reduced to even fewer essentials than Beckett's possess, a space with vague bits here and there amid which the doomed of the earth, or the gently betrayed, wander searching for light, or for the voice with news of chance / fate loose against them. There is little dramatic in Merwin's land of the lost.

Merwin's images: At least fifteen poems have mountains; almost as many have clouds, lights, doors and windows (both shut and open). There are many clouds, almost no rain, dogs (they seem to be his favorite animal), stones disappearing in flames, all meant to speak in some mysterious, mystical way. I'm not averse to a poet liberally sprinkling objects through his poems; none of Merwin's, however, is well-defined. He presents *cloud,* say, and we must determine its properties—cumulus, sagging-with-rain, cirrus, sunset-stained? An important element in poetry is the image, something concrete, a thing seen. Most readers translate an image into a object which may carry several concepts. An egg in a basket represents more than breakfast.

Merwin's counting: He loves to count, as a means, I guess, of suggesting concreteness. Counting requires little involvement. Also, counting evokes the Orphic, the cabbalistic. There's magic in numbers; you needn't ever find a person behind the numbers. For whatever reasons, Merwin loves numbers: 1 window, 17 men with shovels, 70 tongues, 1 star, 10 changes. 1 cloud, thousands of languages, and 1 or 2 eyes. At one point, at least, Merwin sensed the pointlessness of counting. "Exercise" is an admonition for us to drop the abacus. A "list" passage suggests a talismanic medieval riddle, telling you how to lose warts, acquire a healthy mind, or minimize the pains of childbirth.

Merwin's metaphysical paranoia: Through pain we purify ourselves, poor suffering bastards forgotten and despised by the gods. The universal whine is born of an injured sense of betrayal by forces larger than ourselves. The whine is as old as Noah. I had assumed that hydrogen bombs had blown it forever out of existence. Its pallid cry sounds anachronistic.

"Habits" is the most explicitly haunted of these poems. *They* (are *they* gods? other people? demons?) keep handling him: they cling to his memory, they use his eyes for their own sockets, they borrow his tongue, and they loan him ears so that he can hear them.

I admire these suggestions of the mythic and the antique: Oedipus losing his eyes, the slaughters in *Titus Andronicus.* It's comforting to observe a self pursued by the Eumenides. A sow loves her mud; and the gods have always had it in for us. And, since Merwin's theme dates from Orestes and Job, he has to be profound: his hamstrings have unarguable ancient latching points. He's a poet, a lemonade mystic (a little sweet, a little sour, on the gray side). Such ideas are eminently teachable and reviewable.

Wallace Stevens was equally religious, mystical, and conceptual. But when Stevens borrowed a Platonic or a Shakespearean concept he invested it with verve and twisted it around in his splendid head so that the thought came out strange and rare. Merwin seldom brings his conceptions off as well. My comparison with Stevens is speculative. If, however, Merwin is a religious poet, I expect him to be a superior one. When he turns oracular I want him to be as good as Moses, and I don't mean Moses wearing bluejeans, chic western boots, and a frilly-lace shirt open at the throat. I mean a Moses-Vates (as Carlyle saw poets), one wearing a nightgown, a truth-serum mystic who changes human lives forever. And I do not have R. Crumb's "Mr. Natural" in mind.

One more example: "Words" is a poem built around easy cliches. Technically, the poem is flawless. To flex one's stylistic muscles is fine, but the result should be seen as an exercise and should either be kept for selling to the archives at Buffalo or Texas, or consigned to the flames. When the world's pain speaks to Merwin, the words express joy. Often, taken in, we learn his words by heart. Just as often we turn from these deceiving vocables "with hands of water."

Merwin's never-fail ingredient image: If the poets of this country were to assemble in New York or Washington D. C. for a bake-off, and a prize were given to the author with the most dependable, never-fail images and metaphors, Merwin would receive the sequined apron. Here is what I mean. "Bread" is a concoction of safe ingredients. His loaf looks perfect. Readers who think poems should be worked before they're properly digested, but not worked too hard will love the product. The crust looks hard, but once bitten into collapses. Each face in the street, Merwin writes, is a slice of bread wandering, searching for nutriment. This sounds clever. Do these slices of bread crave a toaster? a butter-knife? some jam? an ocean to jump into? Do they hope to become Communion wafers?

Light is another never-fail image, a nice leavening for mystical purport. True, *light* is vague, because it may appear anywhere from the bowels of the earth (as radium) to the molten core of the sun. This light, says Merwin, is "the true hunger" passing these bread-folk by. "They clutch"—what, we don't know—possibly their own soft middles, or each other's soft middles. *Caves* is another of these images. Thanks to Plato a poet won't go wrong, ever, with this archetype, and particularly when we have a choice of caves: first, the ones bread-people find to hide in, and second, the "pale" kind bread-people long for in their dreams. Reality v. reality, folks. Where is the scrim? The home-cave contains the foot prints left behind when bread-folk are off wandering the streets; the foot prints wait their return. Also, these caves are hung with "the hollow marks of their groping...their sleep...and their hiding," assorted fish-nets and Spanish moss.

At the end of Bread-People Street a tunnel symbolizes "the heart of the bread"—it's either pumpernickel or whole wheat, since, Merwin suggests, it's "dark." The people "step after step" hear the stuff just ahead of them, as they move through "ragged tunnels" coming "alone" to a wheat field "raising its radiance to the moon." The poem is up-beat. Ladies from Woods Hole to Pasadena can be assured that verse is not dead. W. S. Merwin here offers a half-loaf short on nutriment.

Merwin's light at the end of the trail: We've just seen one instance of this light, the illuminated wheat-field. The termination of struggle as insight? Again, the easy idea.

"The Way Ahead," a messianic-light poem, begins with a paradox—in winter small creatures by hibernating inside the bones of larger creatures "will be the largest of all / and the smallest." One Monday, people will be shaken into spiritual awareness, some broken, some stroked and blessed. An eye will reveal "what was never seen...beholding the end." A voice will charm nature. Toward this place (wherever it is), feet—I assume they are ours—"are already marching." Corn throw up their hands (why not their ears?) weeds leap up from their ditches, eggs press on towards "those ends" (omelettes?). Nightmarish flowers—and Merwin is forceful here—will usher in an apocalyptic light.

Technically, once again, "The Way Ahead" is fine; its rhythms, their hesitancies, advances, and withdrawals, well-wrought, lull one into feeling that this is a terrific poem, when, in fact, it flaunts stale ideas. The Merwin recipe of parts (ingredients) for a celestial dessert is tried and true. The Biblical tone, prophetic, is masterfully handled. And the conclusion, spoiled by the funny image of eggs pressing on, is vivid.

Merwin's sound at the end of the trail: Sound, like light, works mystically as someone or something calls to us, emitting a dim voice through our wretched universe. If we could catch the message we'd be saved. Unheard melodies are sweeter than heard melodies—Shelley's *chanson!* On these terms, the best of all poets would be totally deaf. Disregarding blind Homer and Milton, silence is golden, as the popular song goes. Let's not deny Merwin his idea.

"When the Horizon is Gone" treats with originality the frayed motif of Existentialist man dropped into total absurdity. When the horizon disappears (a truly freaky idea) man will receive comfort from the horizontal earth. There'll be no mirages out there. Man's blood, since his veins, too, are horizontal, will sink. The problem is, alas, that the blood finds "no center to sink toward." I can't quite see a connection between the absence of an horizon and the absence of a center. How does one measure it? In truth, there's something attractive about lost horizons.

But man's traumas aren't over; whatever his hands hold must be viewed vertically, and since hands can't feel "it" they free "it." The eyes, too, since they project upwards from a supine skull, also see vertically, but don't recognize "it." "It" appears to be the sound of the universe (also vertical), and since two parallel vertical lines never meet... "The Silence Before Harvest" and "Beyond You" share the theme. "A Door" (the last of the four poems in a sequence) is the most explicit of these voice-hearing poems, and the most uplifting. We may come to feel at home in the universe. I'm almost reassured.

Merwin's Ezy-Myth Mix Method: At times Merwin's facility for concocting poems appears as an overly literal translation from the ancient Ainu or Greek or Cherokee, a self-conscious act. When such poems succeed they carry authority; the poet is a shaman for the ages wearing a poem-mantle adorned with cowrie shells.

He tells us the origins of the gods, fire, and religions. The writer as Carlyle's *vates,* a difficult role for a mid-twentieth century American poet to assume.

"Division" is a frustrating example of the Ezy-Myth Mix method. A story-teller tone puts me off:

> People are divided
> because the finger god

named One
so he made for himself a brother like him ...

This is rhythmic prose of little distinction set out to look like poetry; and saying "familiar ground" does not suffice. God must begin somewhere, so God creates out of Himself. No news here. Think of God's surprise had an Otherself leaped from his belly, or his testes, without any need for His will at all. Load on surprise, W. S.! God's early responses to his partner-twin are jealousy, fear, and threat.

But why is he a "finger god?" Why not a toe god? an ear god? a pancreas god? What was One doing with that finger? The appeal is facile. Poets are supposed to sound mystical! We love being myth people; and if we can sound like rewriters of *Genesis*, embellishing here and there, readers in the great cupcake audience are regaled, comforted in their acedia. We aren't so far after all from primitive roots.

Merwin's god drops big god-tears on the sand. A twin of himself fails to suffice. His selves are lonely. He creates two more look-alikes—twins. Fearing they'll lose each other, their hands secure them to one another, and arms, understandably, connect the hands. Their hearts, though, fail to merge against loneliness. This is poignant. Too bad the Chingachgook opening isn't more original. As the Shakers knew, being simple is a gift. I carp because Merwin's achievement is so impressive. A note: his device of starting numerous lines with *and* is an easy device suggesting a primitive style. See the *ands* as raisins in the plum pudding. Yet, even when prose masquerades as poetry, he's usually apt.

Merwin's totemism: Totemism smacks of the primitive, and I don't put it down—when it works. Why not set up poems as totems portaging glyphs of the spiritual? To load a mundane object with religious freight could be a positive act, for it is the antithesis of whimpering.

In "The Unwritten" Merwin renders the common pencil as a totem. Poet as *schreiber/* scribe. Words not yet written "crouch" inside the pencil, *weissnichtwo*. These words, though alert, won't appear because the pencil-wielder wants them to. None of his magic will bring them forth: "not for love not for time not for fire." To decipher their speech we'd need a gift of tongues. Frustrating, locked inside perhaps is that ONE! the word poets and philosophers have sought for centuries! Merwin implies that any writer may release The Word. Like Goethe's Faust, however, the poet may be scribbling so hard the Word may flash past his ken and all will be lost. Yet, we poets continue to worship the pencil, ascribing wonders, and by extension, extolling our miraculous selves.

Merwin's Big Theme [cf. "The Door"] poems are forced and clever, especially when a paranoid self takes over:

> they need your ears
> you can't hear them
>
> they need your eyes
> but you can't look up
> now
>
> they need your feet oh
> they need your feet
> to go on
> they send out their dark birds for you

The vagueness fails, despite the interjections. There is beauty, but the poem evasporates. Merwin's voice wastes itself in shallow feelings. We are lost and wandering in a colorless, vapid, landscape. Persecutors we can't identify pursue us. Yet, there's a blessing: when you open your mouth manna drops into it. There's a beautiful stew of mysterious ingredients, well-seasoned but short of sustaining nutriments.

Merwin's figures are brothers to Samuel Beckett's. Merwin's lines seem depersonalized in the way that Beckett's are depersonalized, in chrome. There is also a spaced—in the sense of dope-spaced or stunned—quality (I'm not accusing Merwin of being a head—you can be of the devil's party without knowing it). Lost folk wandering after some remote voice or light, some with bandaged physiognomies, sound like partially lobotomized, dispirited Dicks and Janes seeking for a lost Spot (an anagram for GOD?). "Dogs" with its "Happiness is a warm puppy" echoes is relevant. Notice the numbing effect of the repetitions of "dog" and "at last," and the facile rhymes "alone" and "your own." "Loneliness," Merwin writes,

> . . . is someone else 's dog
> that you're keeping
> then when the dog disappears
> and the dog's absence
> you are alone at last ...
> but at last it may be
> that you are your own dog
> hungry on the way
> the one sound climbing a mountain
> higher than time

If we are "the one sound" climbing the mountain (are we also the one hand clapping?), our lives are minuscule Existentialist acts. Although climbing a mountain, packless, and bookless, can be wearing, it doesn't quite symbolize Sysyphus' efforts. The need for struggle is generic to Man. Shelley's idea of Beauty, in its origins and combinations, created an image of a forest lake: bubbles begin at the bottom and where they escape to combine with other bubbles emanating from other lakes to form finally a Symphony of Universal Sounds. In their highest ascension these reach the One, the All. While this may not be good chemistry, it's pretty good art.

I think of no better way to conclude this essay than to quote from the final stanza of the last poem in Merwin's collection. "Gift" moves to a prayer uttered by the speaker (Merwin?). Shelley's symbols (and even Shelley's language) reveal Merwin's sources. "Shadowless mountain" is the Romantic mountain seen as the Ideal in full light; Night—silence is the alembic for Romantic mystical awareness; the Eternal—the mountain is "no child of time"; Morning—Romantic symbol of refreshment. These, Merwin says, are "gifts." From whom do they come? There is no apparent answer. Merwin closes with a pure Shelleyean prayer:

> I call to it Nameless One O Invisible
> Untouchable Free
> I am nameless I am divided
> I am invisible I am untouchable
> and empty
> nomad live with me
> be my eyes
> my tongue and my hands
> my sleep and my rising
> out of chaos
> come and be given

This is "neverfail writing." Like so much else in *Writings to An Unfinished Accompaniment*, it's a Can't-Fail Concoction.

THE POET AS MATISSE:
BERT MYERS' *WINDOWSILLS*

Bert Meyers died of cancer on April 22, 1979, at age 51. He was a gifted poet, one of the best, and was unacknowledged in most poetry circles. He cared less about fame than any poet I have ever met. His earlier books were with Alan Swallow (*Early Rain*, 1960), Doubleday (*The Dark Birds*, 1968), and Kayak (*Sunlight on the Wall*, 1976). Bert looked with extreme disfavor on the hustling so much a feature of the American poetry world. He never had himself listed in the Directory of American Poets, for example.

Windowsills reflects Meyers' characteristic themes: life as a series of lovings tinged with threat, the positive beauty behind common objects—leaves, hands, tools, boats, flowers, and children. His voice was closer to some European, South American, and Oriental poets he admired—Jammes, Laotzu, Akhmatova, Basho, Tu Fu, Neruda, and James Kavanagh. Among American poets, he favored Robert Bly, John Haines, and Thomas McGrath. He responded especially to poets with a philosophic import. The flower in the glass, the boat shimmering on the waves, the blue teapot in the old oak cupboard symbolized for Meyers the permanent beyond all that is transient.

Windowsills is about *looking*, and about framing views through and beyond sills. The poet, the book assumes, is a passive viewer, a Matisse of poetry. A world of meaning transpires beyond his windows. Before we can *know*, Meyers implies, we must *see*. Nor is he sententious. His book is full of visual delights. His motto, from Goethe, is apt: "Best of all, merely to look."

The first section of *Windowsills* contains a dozen short "Images." Bales of hay are "cartons / of sunlight fading into a field." Leaves suggest "shreds of a giant eraser"; shadows are fences; a passing snowfall transforms windowsills all over the city. Frequently, Meyers' vision turns on some slight disturbance, as his poem moves from metaphor and scene to metaphor and scene. Here is VII:

> A flock of crows
> dissolves in the mist—
> a cigarette's ash

in a glass of water;
and sunlight
twitching in a puddle.

The tenth "Image" turns on two metaphors. Hands are "twin sisters"

to whom everyone's
a wrinkle
that needs to be smoothed,
a stranger who should be fed.

Hands, those humble wings
that make each day
fly toward its goal;
at rest, still holding
the shape of a tool.

The second half of *Windowsills* is a series of "Postcards" from France. Here Meyers' painter's eye regards the sea:

When calm, the sea's so blue
you could paint the sky with it.
Sometimes, it's a green tablecloth
laid on the wind.

"Island" evokes an exotic, bustling landscape. Each stanza is a variation on the theme of wavering vanishing points. Dwarfs and hunchbacks load wagons in the heat:

Gardens drip...
Flowers burst from the walls.
An ox appears
like a hillside in an alley.

This tourist's point of view continues as we move inside a grocery store:

So poor, box
of baking soda's
smaller than a cigarette pack.
Next, a scrawny young priest follows a double file of boys down a street:
Pale girls lean on their windowsills,

framed like the earliest photographs.

The tourists leave at twilight. We stay behind observing the retreating tourist-ship. People on the pier wave lighted matches as the boat, "a huge altar," loses itself in the fog.

A series of nine village vignettes follow. Through strokes as simple as those in a Hokousai print, Meyers evokes a village cemetery:

> The cemetery's such a pretty town—
> old, quiet, full of mansions.
> People, flowers, crows, everyone comes.

Meyers' inventiveness is a whimsical celebration of life. He writes of fruits and vegetables with great affection—after all, they are the basics of life, the "walls of France":

> A market in the street.
> Bananas rest their Midas hands.
> Herbs, those quiet housewives,
> wearing their modest prints,
> were found in the fields at dawn
> Clods of garlic, the kitchen's diamond,
> hang from every stall.
> Cheese, like the walls of France;
> red peppers with a plastic glow....

This is a rare one-liner. Any poet who has tried to write one of these knows they are difficult:

> Frogs croak "twenty-one" in French all night.

Meyers' image-making works best in the final long sequence, "Paris." Each of these eighteen vignettes sparkles with vibrant seeing, each fixes absorbed impressions. Here is a sample:

> An old dog, a four-legged
> bundle of straw,
> leaves the cafe and goes
> to the gutter for a drink.

> When he returns, his footprints
> are a crossed row
> of tiny vases, each one
> with four flowers, on the sidewalk.

Meyers economically captures a seamy Paris in "Postcard":

> And here are also filthy streets,
> leprous walls that sunlight
> never touched, smeared with crud,
> battered like garbage cans...
> the cracks in a stone
> are a landscape of nerves;
> the air's a perpetual fart
> and even the shadows wear rags.

I am tempted to quote all of these poems, for they have been lingered over and honed. Once Meyers found the right phrase, metaphor, detail, he applied his personal fixatives of tone and style.

Because of his early death from lung cancer, Meyers' poems assume even more meaning than if he were still alive. While our mortality tricks and dooms us, we rejoice in the sheer seeing of what is immediate, simple, and direct. Our windowsills hold incredible vistas within their frames. Bert knew how mortal he was. He had battled emphysema for years, and I recall one walk with him and his young son, when the latter pleaded with his dad not to go into a convenience story for yet another pack of Marlboros. Bert wrote rare, wise, and beautiful poems; their beauty is intensified by the fact of his death.

I visited Bert for the last time three months before he died. He had been reading a book written by an Israeli on how to face dying. As always, remarkably frank, he told me that he feared what he had to face. He realized that his life's awful irony was ready to drop the sword. As this book shows, there were glorious flowers, sunlight, water, in abundance beyond his windowsills, pointing to some far less ghastly place than planet Earth, a home for Bert's spirit.

LEONARD NIMOY WRITES
VERSES WITH POINTED EARS

What kinds of poems would you write if you were Leonard Nimoy and had little pointed ears? Would the mastications of your soul be drenched in planetary cosmic schlock? Or would you have managed by radar tapped into the celestial rhythms of the universe in a superhuman way? Well, dear reader, you won't have to go far to find the answer; Leonard Nimoy of *Star Trek* fame presents himself to the world as a poet. *Will I Think of You?* is an absolutely darling ana of soul belches and eructations, accompanied by photographs snapped by Nimoy.

Before moving into *Will I Think of You*, let me speculate on the fantasy some celebrities perpetrate, that they are *poets*. Has the hitherto lowly office now exalted itself? Nimoy is one of several non-poet folk who have published their orifice-verse-pickings to the world. John Boy of "The Waltons" is one; his slender *Poems* actually isn't too bad. I gather that most of these verses he wrote before he was famous. Then, I hear that Robert Mitchum once published verses; these I've not found, but, since he is one of our greatest actors, if they do exist, they'd be good. And novelists, too, write poetry. John Steinbeck reputedly did, under the pseudonym Amnesia Glasscock—a baker's half-dozen extolling the virtues of the "beauty of breeches on sailors." And Ernest Hemingway. And James Joyce. And Ray Bradbury. The latter billows along on his numerous laurels, scribbling verses for his adulators. He even hired an orchestra to orchestrate them. I heard him read his concoctions at a Comic Book Fair in San Diego; he was embarrassingly derivative of dime-store Swinburne. His ideas were slick undergraduate ideas. *I* can't remember what orchestra leader, probably Previn, Bradbury "commanded" to "arrange" his verse. Then, consider the rock and pop singers who call themselves "poets." Donavan called himself "Your Bard." Jim Morrison wrote middling verse. And teachers and academics hoping to be in with their students once included Bob Dylan and Beatles songs in the curriculum. Poetry, in these realms, is akin to masturbating; the fact that you whip off your own batch makes it worth someone else's scrutiny. If your ego is sizeable, you expect fans to shell out cash for same.

Why do celebrities want to be poets? Does this mean that poets have supplanted architects, doctors, politicians, and singers as the ultimate turn-on profession? In a dismal world crashing to the ground, does the pursuit of verse, implying as it does the ethereal and the free, rank as the highest of human pursuits? As a practicing poet I like the idea. Soon, women's magazines will glamorize poets, forgetting that Dylan Thomas was a slob with women, that James Dickey was said to devour women the way other men devour tootsie rolls, that Robert Frost was a disaster in bed. And we all know what Ted did to Sylvia.

Poets, my dear, are not all Chopins. Nor are they all Byrons. Byron, you recall, spurning his wife's marriage bed proposals, tormented her on their wedding night by screaming that he was in hell. He kept a candle burning by their bedside all night, and declared that he didn't mind actually sleeping with women as long as they weren't too plain. He preferred men and boys.

Poets are in, it seems, and that includes the grubby ones.

So, welcome Leonard Nimoy! Through the greedy paws of Dell, the mass media publisher, Nimoy's volume is available in several forms, depending on what you feel like paying. The cover-blurb informs us that Nimoy addresses his beloved, "hoping that somehow she will hear. These are the eyes of a man seeking his beloved in every place where life and beauty dwell. This is the magic of love itself, transforming our world into a place of miracles."

Why the lover doesn't show up seems obvious: these poems are shameless and tedious. The worst of them scrape and shiver the old fiddle of romantic sentiments. The absent lover has better taste than Nimoy the versifier.

If you imagine a verse (don't call it poetry) cuts below Benton or McKuen—cold cuts below! you have Nimoy. Pomposity comes through in the el slicko titles of Nimoy's sections: "Daybreak and Darkness," "Seasons," "Joys and Sorrows," "In Places," "At Times." Here is an example of jug-gurgling verse, where the beloved is a jog of fire juice and the poet is another: firejugjuice female stokes firejugjuice male:

> Will I think of you?
> Only when it's cold
>
> and I'm shivering
>
> against the wind
>
> And suddenly from inside
> The core of me
> From my deepest depth:
> Comes
> A small warning flame

Which wants to grow
And I fight it

                              Until I realize I need it

Want it

          To flow through me

To fill me

               because

                   It is you.

A glance at Nimoy's language reveals that he doesn't know that cliches are despicable: "You shiver in the wind," "deep inside the core of me," "a small warming flame," "deepest depths." Worst is a coy image of rain on a window as God's tears drenching Nimoy's misery. The result is a forget-me-not poem: "If this you see, remember me." Yes, these verses contain lines so maudlin they resemble those that raunchy country school boys scribbled on pencil tablets, wadded up, and flung across the aisle to Becky Thatcher. What these poems need is some of the juice those same boys carved into the walls of school outhouses!

Nor does Nimoy, despite his trekking, know the value of precise, telling images. Here's the Good Samaritan theme once again:

           If we can help One Who finds the way

                        Too hard or too long

       Then it is Worth all of being

               And I will try to help

               Because someone helped me

      Someone who cared more

          About the brothers on the road

                       Than about

     the Gifts at the end

               And that someone was you

               So I will think of you

Who is the *you?* What *brothers* on the road? What *Gift* at the end? What *way* is lost? At least the parables in the Bible had an original cadence and a vital language (in the King James Version). Nimoy's poems are dime store paste rings. Love is a sexless mutual weeping. Only a cretin would respond. Or, if it is still true that love is blind, then I suppose you can fantasize on that handsome dude with the funny ears; the Star Trekker is nibbling on yours. That's your trip, reader, not mine. To repeat, I resent the glutting of what little poetry market exists with dreck like *Will I Think of You?* I speak for a host of poets who can't find publishers, poets whom the biggies like Dell, Random House, Simon and Schuster, and Time-Warner persistently ignore. They'll publish celebrity poetasters like Nimoy and Bradbury and Susanne Schutz and John Boy; for they make bucks. It's that simple.

CHARLES PLYMELL:
BEAT NEON POEMS

Charles Plymell's origins are in the American heartland of Kansas, providing a locale and a voice that reverberate in the poetry he has written over the past thirty years, including over a dozen new poems, printed here (in *Forever Wider*, his Selected and New Poems, Scarecrow Press) for the first time. There's a prairie literalism of form and idiom, often accompanying some of the most sophisticated writing of his, the Beat, generation. A poem by Plymell is "news," an intimate journal of lives touching a spectrum of readers.

There's a refreshing plebeian quality to Plymell's writing, which often echoes folk-art. He is steeped in country music, jazz, juke box ballads, rock 'n roll, and grand opera. He delights in exact rhymes, dropping them in unexpectedly. Their appearances seem spontaneous, as a riff in a jazz piece does. He thumbs his nose at pretentious poets and critics who prefer hermetic verse congealed in complex forms requiring explicators. Plymell's affection for Rod McKuen is but another instance of his giving the raspberry to pretentious poetry piranhas who dismiss accessibility as evidence of bad writing. He has feistily encouraged writers who stand outside the academic confluences of American writing. In a poem on an exhibition of Modigliani's paintings, he spies an old bag man near the museum door. He asks the guard if the man is dead:

> No, he says, not really...he
> Sleeps on the grates, you see,
> Otherwise his flesh may freeze.
>
> His belongings were rotten feathers.
> His bed old pillows and rags
> Army blankets tethered with bags.
>
> I asked if he was all right.
> He looked at me in fright.

What do you feel in your heart
About these patrons of the arts?

Plymell writes as if the bag man himself had composed these lines—they are antithetical to the sophisticated, chic art-lovers in the gallery. Paradoxically, Modigliani himself would have preferred the company of the bum to the sophisticates.

From the 'fifties, when Plymell moved to California and became a central figure in the Beat Movement, he has played the role of poet as gadfly with a delicious verve. He is both a proletarian poet (as Ferlinghetti and Ginsberg often are) and a poet of aesthetic purity. "Kindergarten Lessons" concludes with this stunning interplay of Magritte-like images: eagle, mountain landscape, sun, and all-encompassing sky:

Snow in the head of an eagle
in the beak and on the eye
and the mountains and the
clouds are glass broken with
the eagle still on it.
* * *
Curtains and wood, glass broken
and the sun still on the glass
what's out in the sky
because it got painted on.

In all of his peregrinations, West, East, North, and South, Plymell's universe has been that of protestors, dopers, jazz musicians, hookers, and other underground souls. He has a scathing contempt for politicians, tycoons (these are "hoggers of the harvest"), despoilers of the environment, and academics. The latter he delights in tweaking whenever he attends their readings.

See his delicious "The Dream of the Academe."

At times, Plymell seems to have stepped from the pages of Burroughs or Kerouac. We can imagine him waiting, distressed in mind and health, in Dr. Benway's Waiting Room of the Doomed Universe, hoping for relief. Once in the Doctor's presence, however, patient-doctor roles reverse—Plymell is something of a shaman trickster. He will have zapped Benway, the fake, and will depart the loathsome office restored to health, and return to fresh streets and crash pads new. His world is not pretty. And he is paranoid about the future. Among his fears is a fear of science. If the biologists can create a one-sided guinea pig, what are the implications for humans?

I'm afraid of science
afraid to point my head north
that the one-sided guinea pig will die.

I'm afraid of the streets at night
that a landslide of barking grease will
chase me past the carbon copy of the blue light.

In the midst of his paranoia, his intimacies with others—friends, lovers, passing acquaintances who zap him with some unforgettable nuance—keep him sane. His defiance of forces in a world gone mad provide an insulating cocoon around himself and those he loves. Some of the finest of these poems are elegies to family and friends. One of the most moving commemorates a painter friend, Bill MacNeil, who died recently in San Francisco, of AIDS. Another vigorous poem, in long free verse lines, "Not a Regular Kansas Sermon," is to his ailing mother.

Plymell's place in the Beat Movement is secure. His first prose book, hailed as a classic and given cult status, was published by City Lights. Ferlinghetti wrote of Plymell's *Neon Poems* that Plymell continues that early Beat vision fashioned and rendered visible by Kerouac, Ginsberg, Corso, Whalen, McClure, Burroughs, and Ferlinghetti himself:

These are the poems of his vision of the apocalypse rose of
America—Brooklyn Yellow Pages, Hollywood blacklight sun,
Second-hand Rose on the juke, Gough Street Blues, wild rose
of Utah, New York iron city, Kansas madman's dream, eternity
in the groin...and the vision goes on.

To paraphrase Plymell himself, his poems are "flashlights," searching the street maps / in dark seats of Volkswagens." The Beat Vision continues, as thousands of sensitive young men and women seeking alternatives to a stifling middle-class culture leave the sedate, safe towns of America for the metropolises. Plymell's poems illuminate their travels, inspiring them on their difficult quests, and showing them the majesty of taking great risks in pursuit of personal values. To be among the enormous band of the unwashed seekers after the naked lunch is, Plymell implies, to be among the blessed.

BONE DENTS:

HOW TO READ GARY SNYDER

Since the 60's, platoons of young poets have imitated Gary Snyder, adoring him with the fervor they bestow on Rock Stars. Some even change their names to Moon Dance, Sun Bush, Basting Spoon, Axe Handle, and Little Elk. Many visit his northern California acres to imbibe creativity, drink manzanita tea, and eat granola al fresco amidst the raccoons, skunks, and possums. At a wave from Snyder, they would gladly lick the sweat from the planks in his sauna, or stand guard all night against the wee ring-tailed beasts demolishing his outdoor kitchen. Perhaps he might, in return, zap them, like a hearty Mr. Natural, with all manner of talents, real and imagined.

Obviously, a poet isn't responsible for his imitators. But the traps exist in Snyder's work, as they do for few other contemporary poets: a surface simplicity which the imitators misread; his reportage; the spare, no belly-flab style. The difference between Snyder and followers is that when Snyder takes a sauna, it's an experience; when the acolytes do it's merely a bath.

So much by way of preamble. The occasion for this piece is the appearance of Snyder's first book in almost ten years, *Axe Handles*. How have the years treated Snyder? Pretty well, I'd say. Despite a few limp efforts (included are throw-away poems about Jerry Brown's visits to Snyder's yurt, nature trivia, and Snyder's role on the California Arts Council), some of these poems are among Snyder's best. There is a quieter, mellower tone than we find in of the earlier work; and he now writes of what he scrutinizes before him, without much reminiscing. It's as if the passing years have made the immediate experience more valuable than ever—a deeper delving in the earth itself as a means to awareness.

"Getting in the Wood" is vintage Snyder. His trade marks are all here:

l) The effortless, non-sentimental beginning. The phrases, shorn of their definite articles, are subtle ink-strokes on the page. They possess a marvelous tactile quality. Snyder gathers wood-rounds which have aged on the forest-floor, and splits them with an iron wedge driven by a sledgehammer. The poem opens as easily as a greeting, evoking a quick mix of smell, color, and the kinetics of spurting water:

The sour smell,
>
> blue stain,
>
> > water squirts out round the wedge....

2) Argot from the trades, from the survival arts. These ("peened," "wedge," "axe," "peavey," "maul," etc.) he employs with a zest like that of Gerard Manley Hopkins in his sonnets to Welsh laborers. Here Hopkins glories in the physique and skills of a ploughman:

> Hard as hurdle arms, with a broth of goldish flue
> Breathed round; the rack of ribs; the scooped flank; lank
> Rope-over thigh; knee-nave; and barelled shank—
> Head and foot, shoulder and shank—
> ...He leans to it, Harry bends, look. Back, elbow, and
> liquid waist
> In him, all quail to the wallowing o' the plough...

What Hopkins and Snyder say (also see Hopkins on variegated loam in "The Windhover") is this: if you aren't meticulously observant of physical details, you miss important spiritual signs. Details become symbols. In such naming Snyder fuses both his Zen Buddhism and his American pragmatism. Tu Fu and Thoreau.

3) Complex evocations of the senses: how the skin feels as sweat drips, the smell of "crushed ants," the sounds of wood tumbling, the cantering sledge emitting the ring of "high-pitched bells." Snyder is a poet of the synaesthetic effect; he can be as esoteric as Baudelaire or Swinburne charging poems with a highly orchestrated synesthesia. On his level, Snyder is a pure art-for-art's sake poet. And I love him for that.

4) The incredibly compact music created as Snyder joyously names tools, flora, and fauna. These moments create exciting verse music. This passage is highly cadenced, accentual, rampant with raw energy. Snyder is in full control:

> Wedge and sledge, peavey and maul,
> > little axe, canteen, piggyback can
> of saw-mix gas and oil for the chain,
> > knapsack of files and goggles and rags....
> And a bit earlier, this:
> ...the complex duff of twigs
> poison oak, bark, sawdust,
> shards of logs,

And the sweat drips down….

5) The celebration of human effort as intense energy spent towards both
survival and spiritual growth (What I call the John Muir Syndrome: see Snyder's
poem to Muir in *Rip-Rap*). Here, with a relish again reminiscent of Hopkins (one
of the latter's favorite words was "delve"), Snyder's "young men" make wood,
four cords of it:

> the young men throw splits on the piles
> bodies hardening, learning the pace
> and the smell of tools from this delve
> in the winter
> death-topple of elderly oak.
> Four cords.

Their pride is their *arete*, that old Greek word for a skill superbly employed.
Here the unerring skill of the woodsman is enhanced by his excellent tools. There
are echoes of sprung-rhythm in the alliterative design, a lovely stress on liquid
sounds, and an avoidance of regular iambs. The enjambments are subtle, and the
long-vowel music contributes much. The second line, in its trochees, dactyls, and
caesura, is akin to Hopkins' more original devices, ones that reach back to Anglo-
Saxon accentual verse. "Four cords" is a neat tying off, a closure for the
sophisticated passage.

In lesser hands, Snyder's triumphs over the physical worlds of forest and
machine, rendered almost with eyelids peeled, might seem silly, a phony
primitivism engendering a Grease-Can School of Poetry, or, as I have called it
elsewhere, Ugh-Poetry. This verse Snyder himself avoids through a zestful music
which at times almost makes the meanings of his words superfluous. We must
resist enjoying these effects if we are not to miss the didactic beneath much that
Snyder writes. Aren't pure effects, though, what good poets aim for? an avoidance
of sermonizing? a transcendence of raw materials?

Another poem, "Working on the '58 Willys Pickup," includes matter
appropriate for a Whole Earth Catalogue (how to mulch your sterile ground with
sawdust, gravel, and chuff so as to make it fertile):

> Now to bring sawdust
> Rotten and rich
> From a sawmill abandoned when I was just born
> Lost in the young fir and cedar

> At Bloody Run Creek
> So that clay in the garden
> Can be broken and tempered
> And growing plants mulched to save water—
> And to also haul gravel
> From the old placer diggings,
> To screen it and mix in the sand with the clay
> Putting pebbles aside to strew on the paths
> So muddy in winter—

Finally, the old truck is repaired:

> The rear end rebuilt and put back
> With new spider gears,
> Brake cylinders cleaned, the brake drums
> New-turned and new brake shoes...

After a "tough-handed" job well-done, Snyder looks forward to reading Chinese philosophy.

In "The Cool Around the Fire," Snyder prunes underbrush in a season of drought and imminent fires and meditates on his labors, equating them with "heart" and an emergent spirit-elevating "cool." The result, arising from surface simplicities of diction and cadence, again suggest brush-strokes, signs for the transcendental:

> Burn brush to take heat
>   from next summer's wildfires
>   and to bring rain on time,
>   and fires clear the tangle.
>
>   The tangle of the heart.
> Black coffee, bitter, hot,
>   smoke rises straight and calm
>   air
> Still and cool

Brilliant techniques in themselves do not, of course, constitute a whole poetry. Tone matters, as does theme. The pragmatic, self-reliant voice so characteristic of Snyder never pushes or bullies the reader—in his best poems he never overtly urges us to march, axes in hand, out to enroll in woods-survival courses, or to build our personal lean-tos, saunas, yurts, and field kitchens. Like

John Muir and Thoreau, his mentors, his experiments are his own (Thoreau never intended that anyone else live his experiment, stake a claim at Walden Pond, plant beans, or eat wood-chuck raw). Snyder's experiments are uniquely his. Yet, while he does not propagandize, the life he creates, evokes, and extols is so appealing we feel welcomed to join in, creating the ecosystem he envisions. He plants his own apple-seeds. And his self-reliance is a most endearing strength. His awe / respect for nature, for spirituality, for each human life, drops into these poems almost casually, at times with humor and gentle ironies, often at his own expense. Those who choose to harvest his apples may. Feel free. But you'll have to use your own ladders and pails, and your own hands, not his.

Another dimension is thematic. A lesser poet would be content merely to record his quests after the mythic omphalos of the universe. Snyder's framework is far more ambitious; he is always a mere breath away from universals. He finds a poignant continuity in all experience, from the most primitive ancestor to the squalling, puking infant recently emerged from the uterus. His efforts to create a self-sustaining ground-earth-house for his family echo an ancient Oriental existence, physical and metaphysical. In an unforgettable image, Snyder describes a prehistoric woman seen in a Stockholm Museum:

> Knees up in an easy squat
> > your body shows how
> You gave birth nine times:
> The dent in the bones
> > in the back of the pelvis
> mother of us all,
> > four thousand years dead.

This bone-dent connects us to our ancestors. Our life is "quick," Snyder observes, and followed by a "long slow / feeding" of time, symbolized by a "woodpecker's cry." Life-death is a simulacrum. The "corruption, decay, the sticky turnover" we witness everywhere, passes into eternity, as a form of "glacial rubble, / crumbling rocky cliffs and scree." Snyder's tenacity, his faith in his immediate time—locked experience flowing and smoking towards the transcendental and his love for the earth (one ecosystem for all) inspire those of us lacking his gifts and trenchant wit. All of this, of course, is quite apart from the beauty of his writing; his themes and techniques are a rare fusion for these times. By imagining Nature as a "sweet old woman" who gathers her firewood (for the Heraclitean fire?) in the moonlight, he celebrates his life and reassures us about our own.

JACK SPICER HAS AN ATWATER KENT
IN HIS LIVING ROOM

Billy the Kid is to Jack Spicer what Adonis, Childe Harold, Alastor, and Werther were to the nineteenth century Romantics. Prettify him; forget the fact that Billy was an idiot, a moron, sadist, and incredibly naive; pretend that as a symbol for the POET he threatens the bad guys who think that poets are faggots or worse, and who are out to git 'em; and assume that Billy's body is so pure that he never bathes—no jockey shorts cramp his balls beneath his tight, patched jeans. Yes, Spicer's out there confronting vast panoramas: the Western U. S. landscape is Spicer's equivalent for Byron's Alps or Shelley's Euganean Hills. Billy is also the Poet as Christ: Billy has *stigmata*, bullet holes, three in the groin and one in the head, "dancing right below the left eyebrow." Billy as Romantic Poet-Figure carries a touch of the comicbook person; but Spicer's writing is too deft, and his shifts of voice between speaker and Billy too subtle to fashion Billy of cardboard. Spicer writes kaleidoscopic poems, or, rather, to use a word he liked to characterize his own work, *collages*. In *Billy the Kid:* Part II, Spicer characterizes his poem:

> A sprinkling of gold leaf looking like hell flowers
> A flat piece of wrapping paper, already wrinkled, but
>   wrinkled again by hand, smoothed into
>   shape by an electric iron
> A painting
> Which told me about the death of Billy the Kid.
> Collage   a binding together
> Of the real
> Which flat colors
> Tell us what heroes
>   really come by.

Once he has set up a collage, with Zen-like fondness Spicer contrasts the opposite of what he's just said, paradoxically:

No, it is not a collage. Hell flowers
Fall from the hands of heroes
        fall from all of our hands
                        flat
As if we were not ever able quite to include them.
His gun
        does not shoot real bullets
                        his death
Being done is unimportant.
Being done
In those flat colors
Not a collage
A binding together, a
Memory.

Yes, Billy is Spicer's invention. Yes, the bullets he shoots aren't real. But since a collage is made up of actual swatches of paper, cloth, plaster, if a poem *is* its inventions and, hence, imagined, you can't have a collage. Yet, at the same time, one has a collage. Clear?

What of Billy as *enamoratus?* Spicer underplays the homosexual motif. His speaker is rather mindless in his love for Billy. Love feelings are as direct as those in a valentine:

Billy the Kid
I love you
Billy the Kid
I back anything you say
And there was the desert
And the mouth of the river
Billy the Kid
(In spite of your death notices)
There is honey in the groin
Billy.

In homosexual parlance, of course, "honey in the groin" is sperm.

Spicer was sufficiently influenced by Robert Duncan and Charles Olson to appreciate Romantic myth-motifs. Among them are the eternal river, the holy grail, and the poet as a shaman and sensitive plant. Let's examine Spicer's river image: near the river Billy the Kid is to be shot. Dry grass and *cotton candy* appear at the water's edge—death motifs, possibly, of the real world (grass) and of a fantasy world (cotton candy), the latter, essential fluff imagination material derived from natural fact. Moreover, cottonwood trees in the distance resemble cotton candy.

As he approaches the river, Billy, aware of his doom, meets his Romantic doppelgänger and secret sharer *Alias*. Bill tells Alias that "somebody" wants him "to drink the river / Somebody wants to thirst us." Alias says it's not the river that desires their deaths:

> No river
> Wants to trap men. There ain't no malice in it. Try
> To understand.

Billy and Alias doff their shirts, a sort of courtly or knightly exchange frosted with homosexual overtones. Billy says:

> I was never real. Alias was never real.
> Or that big cotton tree or the ground.
> Or the little river.

Flashing on sophisticated neo-Platonic notions of the Real and the non-Real, Billy opts for a way of driving deep into the perplexed cortices of despised Philistines the inference that art and poetry possess true Reality and that all else is woeful illusion. Again, Spicer wants it both ways: illusion and fantasy (dancing) are fun:

> Our lady
> Stands as a kind of dancing partner for the memory.
> Will you dance, Our Lady,
> Dead and unexpected?
> Billy wants you to dance
> Billy
> Will shoot the heels off your shoes if you don't dance
> Billy
> Being dead also   wants
> Fun.

I find Spicer's tripping with Shelley's Platonism valuable since two giants war in his imagination: one giant (both are lucky and green) represents Reality as Absolute shot off and beyond and towards and eventually into some Hyperion over-world of Intimation and Intuition. Giant two is earthly, concrete, evoking Williams (and Olson). This giant speaks through Spicer in a letter to Garcia Lorca (*After Lorca*):

I would like to make poems out of real objects.
The lemon to be a lemon that the reader could
cut or squeeze or taste—a real lemon like a
newspaper in a collage is a real newspaper.
I would like the moon in my poems to be a real
moon, one which could be suddenly covered
with a cloud that has nothing to do with the poem
—a moon utterly independent of images.
The imagination pictures the real. I would like
to point to the real, disclose it, to make a poem
that has no sound in it but the pointing of a finger.

Here is his poem (#4 of "For Poetry Chicago," *Book of Magazine Verse*) about
the problems he confronts with that lemon:

The rind (also called the skin)
      the lemon is difficult to understand
It goes around itself in an oval
      quite unlike the orange which,
      as anyone can tell, is a fruit
      easily to be eaten.
It can be crushed in canneries into
      all sorts of extracts which are
      still not lemons. Oranges
      have no such fate. They 're pretty
      much the same as they were. Culls
      become frozen orange juice. The best
      oranges are eaten.
It's the shape of the lemon, I
      guess that causes trouble.
      It's ovalness, it's rind. This
      is where my love, somehow, stops.

Fascinating! Particularly the notion of the poem "that has no sound in it but
the pointing of a finger." Spicer's ideal poem is as near as your nearest camera
loaded with film. Wind film forward to hand with finger pointing towards up-
coming # 1 photograph. The finger-hand predicts the dozen or twenty photographs to follow, even before they are recorded. This ultimate poem (the hand-
finger on the film) allows, nay, demands the most complete Romantic act: the
reader is to create his own poem. To use one of Spicer's words, the reader creates
a *serial:* there are as many frames as one would care to follow after the hand on

the film appears. And these would contain sensitively rendered lemons, oranges, cottonwood trees, moons, etc., evoking the vegetable and mineral existences they enjoy in nature.

Let's try moving our mind around *lemon*. See the lemon as a third eye of the citrus world, anent Spicer's fondness for layers of meanings. First, though, circulate your mind over, around, under, and through (vertically and horizontally) the *lemon*. Taste, touch, lick, bite, pinch, hit, smell, squash, and suck *lemon*. Make rhymes for *lemon: one, done, swimmin', wimmin, agamemnon*. Have *lemon* fall from branch of lemon tree onto grass. Carry lemon into house. Lemonade, hand lotion, fuck lotion, etc.

I'm saying that I don't understand—to my satisfaction, at least—how Spicer's lemon becomes the "object" in the poem he means it to be. I am also perplexed by the Romantic vagueness when I try to see Billy the Kid as OBJE CT, or Merlin, or Garcia Lorca, or Henry Rago, or Huntz, or God as Coleridgean *ommjects*. I conclude that Spicer absorbed some of Lorca's talent for allowing objects to determine fresh routes within a poem, an earth-talent route. Perhaps, then, Ph.D. linguists (Spicer was one of them) disappear in quicksand, those blatant morpheme-addicts. No wonder that Spicer's best poems are transliterations of Lorca.

Spicer characterized his failure to achieve that clarity of image passing all understanding in part 10 of his "15 False Propositions about God":

> I do not remember the poem well but I know that beauty
> Will always become fuzzy
> And love fuzzy
> And the fact of death itself fuzzy
> Like a big tree.

The "blurred forest" frustrates him. He wants to tear it down with his bare hands. And in the concluding portion of the letter to Lorca mentioned above, he explored the connection between the natural object both in maturity and in decay:

> But things decay, reason argues. Real things
> become garbage. The piece of lemon you shellac
> to the canvas begins to develop a mold, the
> newspaper tells of incredibly ancient events in
> forgotten slang, the boy becomes a grandfather.
> Yes, but the garbage of the real still reaches out
> into the current world making its objects, in turn,
> visible—lemon calls to lemon, newspaper

to newspaper, boy to boy. As things decay
they bring their equivalents into being.

He finds his resolution in a principle of correspondences, much like the *correspondances* that excited Baudelaire:

Things do not connect; they correspond. That is what
makes it possible for a poet to translate real objects,
to bring them across language as easily as he can bring them
across time. That tree you saw in Spain is a tree I could
never have seen in California, that lemon has a different smell
and a different taste, BUT the answer is this—every place and
every time has a real object to correspond with your real object
—that lemon may become this lemon, or it may even become this
piece of seaweed, or this particular color of gray in this ocean.
One does not need to imagine that lemon; one needs to discover it.
Even these letters. They correspond with something (I don't
know what) that you have written (perhaps as unapparently as
that lemon corresponds to this piece of seaweed) and, in turn,
some future poet will write something which corresponds to them.
That is how we dead men write to each other.

Love,

Jack

In his conflict between illusion and reality, Spicer found an escape: a burrow with two exits and two entrances. Actually there are two adits; both are located at the base of a tree Spicer called "God." By exiting from one hole, the poet is responsible for the success or failure of his poems…as verbal constructs (phoneme morpheme delights) conveying images, thoughts, and Jungian materials. From the next exit he emerges as—and this is Spicer's metaphor—"a counterpunching radio" ("Sporting Life"). The poet

is a radio, the poet is a liar. The poet is a
counterpunching radio.
And those messages (God would not damn them) do
not even know they are champions.

In a portion of "Vancouver Lecture #1" Spicer amplified the metaphor. Essentially the idea resembles ideas we find in Shelley and Wordsworth, albeit

Spicer's are couched in a modern lingo. Spicer dissociates the radio program from the radio set:

I don't think the messages are for the poet ... any more than a radio program is for the radio set. And I think that the radio set doesn't really worry about whether anyone is listening to it or not and neither does the poet. And I don't know what the poem does.

The radio program, obviously, has a sponsor who does his thing(s) to get his program heard. The quality of a program doesn't affect the actual radio set playing it. So, if the poet is a radio, the poet transmits what he receives from somewhere outside him, from some New York, Chicago, or San Francisco Studio of the Soul directed, paid for, and arranged by numerous ghostly sponsors.

Later in the lecture Spicer deals with these ghosts. First, metaphors aren't meant for humans; they are meant for "ghosts." Metaphors make specific the individual transistor wires (as in radios) reaching as silver from "the end of the beautiful as if elsewhere." This remark has the lucidity of a sentence tossed off by Gertrude Stein as she observes Toklas whipping up another batch of cookies. There *is* an absolute *beautiful*. Says Spicer, "The wires in the rose are beautiful." Wires connect the *beautiful* with physical objects. Silver filaments quiver in the radio-poet who makes them audibile through his language. His readers tune-in. But who are the sponsors?

> Poems were written for ghosts. The ghosts the
> poems were written for are the ghosts of the poems.
> We have it second-hand. They cannot hear
> the noise they have been making...
>
> Finally the messages penetrate
> There is a corpse of an image—they penetrate
> The corpse of a radio. Cocteau used a
> > car radio on account of NO SPEED
> > LIMIT. In any case the messages
> > penetrate the radio and render it
> > (and the radio) ultimately useless.
> Prayer
> Is exactly that
> The kneeling radio down to the tomb
> > of some saint
> Uselessness sung and danced (the
> > radio dead but alive it can
> > connect things

> Into sound. Their prayer
> Its only connection.

Is this clear? Spicer seems to say that Beauty, Sound, Grave, Past, or Death quivering in poems constitute the individual "ghosts" of those poems. Yet, a super-ghost lurks behind each poem. Spicer devotes his "15 False Propositions about God" to the theme. The question? How responsible is the poet for his writing, good and bad? Is he simply a radio through which intimations from the universe broadcast themselves?

A motif of the "God" sequence (or *serial*) derives from Ezra Pound:

> Beauty is so rare a thing,
> So few drink at my fountain.

The lines become a refrain. God, King of the Forest (Oh! shades of Regenerative Myths, Vegetable and Fisher Kings) has one leg longer than the other. His forest contains poets and their lovers: young trees are young lovers, old trees are old lovers. The poet struggles to find "a new Song / Real / Music." He has "A pain in the eyebrows. A visiting card." The departure of one of Spicer's lovers occasions a complaint to God. At the moment when the *serial* turns metaphysical, or meat-aphysical, Spicer asks:

> Why
> Does
> Your absence seem so real or your presences
> So uninviting?

The question's not subtle, Sandy. "Arf. Arf." Send the young hustler packing, Jack, and find yourself a mature poet to love. Spicer, instead, argues with that Daddy Warbucks in the Sky who declares Spicer's poems to be "real bad." Spicer's response?

> "Dear Sir: I should like to.... "

God declaims that hate and love, since they suffice as clarifications, don't belong in poetry and merely embarrass both reader and poet since they "lack Dignity." Spicer replies:

> Dear Sir: I should like to make sure that everything
>   that I said about you in my poetry was true, that

> you really existed....
> That you were not an occasion
> In a real bad scene
> That what the poems said had meaning
> Apart from what the poems said.

Does this sound like a Romantic poet's cop-out? An easy way to dissuade your opponent from cornering you by declaring that you hadn't meant to argue: my poems have meanings quite apart from what they say, and, you, incredible dummy (D, if the Dummy is the Deity) you should understand them?

Should we condemn poets who use sleazy thought and sleazy image-making to weasel out; who masquerade shallowness by saying that their profundity is too precious to be verbalized? Isn't this a mere step away from the slap-the-forehead-gad-I'm-sensitive school of authorship? The impact of art is so esoteric that attempts to describe it sully it? Obviously, to lack an intellectual substrata is a delusion. And, Spicer, stance does not equal substance. As a Doctor of Philosophy in Linguistics, Spicer understands the dilemma without really resolving it, except in vague Romantic terms. God, he says, is the nearest tree. Okay, I wander outside (I happen to be at Yaddo in Saratoga Springs, New York, right now). I approach a large white pine. It has its concrete properties, and if the tree is God, God for me is a living organism, one quite vegetable.

So far, so good. What next? Do I climb my tree? Pray to it? Rub against it until I come? Chop it down?

In concluding the fifteen poem series on God, in a rather sloppy line, Spicer reports on his psychic state: "No thought coheres or sensation." Perhaps he wrote the poem—or, since he believed in *dictated* poetry, perhaps he received the poem at one sitting, and, since it is long, was too exhausted to revise it properly. His inability to see God beyond "treeness" he blames on the "abysmal toyshop" of the world, full, as it is, of the gawds and geegaws, distractions and entertainments. Spicer again denigrates "Dear Sir," confessing that he once believed in a "three-headed God...sometimes both when talking with you and living with you." Spicer puts things evanescently, with a flicker of self-pity. While he doesn't exactly fall upon the thorns of life and bleed, by stepping among them he scratches his calves.

There is something old-fashioned in another of his ideas. In the Vancouver Lecture, he explored the notion of the dictated poem. A poem, he reports, nudges him on the back and starts coming through, scaring him, particularly when it delivers the opposite of what he thinks he believes. "Even a practicing bad poet," he declares, knows that "something from outside" produces these results, sneaking in details we never intended.

I won't analyze the ramifications of Spicer's theory (see the treatment of it in *Caterpillar* 12), but will simply suggest that his thought, which, he admits, is as old as the proverbial hills. Does he display any fresh insight? No. But his statement is valuable since it transpired before a live audience—no ghosts this time. He is baldly Romantic, and connects with Olson, Creeley, and Projective Verse. Also, he attaches the idea of an external creative push to Wordsworth's wisdom of the primitive and the wise child. Such folk are better "poets" than educated, well-read scribblers. Says Spicer: when you're "hooked up" with universal sources it's best if you are uneducated and a little dumb:

> "because an uneducated person often can write a better poem than an educated person, simply because there are only so many building blocks, so many ways of arranging them...in the long run, for really just good poetry and sometimes really great poetry—an infinitely small vocabulary is what you want..."

Of course, there is always the possibility Jack may be putting us on. But I don't think so. The judgment we must make, finally, is on the quality of the house Jack built.

Since he knew so much about language, in this sense, his primitivism works: for he never quite allowed himself to appear in public convincingly as the primitive dummy he extolled. The Vancouver Lecture shows both his awareness of and his distrust for his vast learning. One of his best linguistical poems is #3 of the series "Graphemics" from *Language* where those silver threads conveying a false or plastic reality: the object is a red light warning the poet that he observe limits; the connections between crossing a street against a traffic light, tying a shoe with a granny knot, and the need to snarl—symbolize the poetic act:

> Let us tie the strings on this bit of reality.
> Graphemes. Once wax now plastic, showing
>   the ends. Like a red light.
> One feels or sees limits.
> They are warning graphemes but also meaning
>   graphemes because without the marked
>   ends of the shoelace or the traffic signal
>   one would not know how to tie a
>   shoe or cross a street—which is like
>   making a sentence.
> Crossing a street against the light or tying

a shoe with a granny knot is all right
Freedom, in fact, providing one sees
or feels the warning graphemes. Let
them snarl at you then and you snarl
back at them. You'll be dead sooner
But so will they. They
Disappear when you die.

When Spicer tries to be simple, as he does in his poem to Ginsberg ("For Down Beat," *Book of Magazine Verse*), simple-minded statements suffice for simplicity. Look at this opening line: "At least we both know how shitty the world is." The concluding sentiment is a glitzy reflection of Whitman's cranky twists of language: "Fight the combine of your heart and my heart or anybody's heart. People are starving." On the other hand, this insight works:

"The poet has an arid parch of his reality and the others.
Things desert him."

Spicer then, alas, proceeds to bathos, the occasion his obsession with a lover: "I thought of you / as a butterfly tonight with clipped wings." Not only is the sentiment silly, but "with clipped wings" hangs out there sloppily, too detached from its subject *you*.

The start of one of his God-poems ("For the St. Louis Sporting News," *Book of Magazine Verse*) is a refreshing contrast:

God is a big white baseball that has nothing to do
    but go in a curve or a straight line. I studied
    geometry in highschool and know that this is true.
Given these facts the pitcher, the batter, and the
    catcher all look pretty silly.

There are many moments of such quality in Spicer. One discerns the aesthetic silence he loved, a silence, in fact, he celebrated in *A Book of Music:*

Ridiculous
How the space between three violins
Can threaten all of our poetry.
                                        ("Cantata")

And we

> Can learn our names from our mouths
> Name our names
> In the middle of the same music
> ("Duet for a Chair and a Table")

Throughout Spicer the poet, finding himself in a collapsing world, hopes to maintain sanity through his art, knowing, at the same time, that you have almost no audience. (Spicer apparently never copyrighted his few published books). Spicer treats this theme most movingly, and by my focusing on his Romanticism, I ignore much else that moves and delights. He is a master-writer, and it is no small wonder that young poets, particularly on the West Coast, revere and imitate him. He is the West Coast Frank O'Hara. Spicer's sense of a collapsing world was real: shredded wheat and paper maché (sic), and fuzzy trees and fuzzy people, and fuzzy wars and revolutions. His Arthurian poem, "The Book of Merlin" is his most revolutionary piece. He uses passages from a German marching song popular with the Army of the Second Internationale during the 1930's: "Heimat, du bist wieder mein," references to Sacco and Vanzetti, and to Hitler's *Koncentrationslage*...these surround the central motif of the Holy Grail. In the modern world we must choose between the Grail (Love) and the Bomb. Though Spicer is pessimistic, confronted by collapse and immanent disaster, he nevertheless, prompted by "someone" out there, builds his house. His most apt statement on the theme occurs in the 5th section of "15 False Propositions." The passage is clear, at least on the surface. There are two houses: the house you live in (or the world), and the house you construct with your poems, a palace of art. When house #1 falls down you find yourself shivering in the timbers with "the vacant lumber of your poetry." The rarity of Beauty—the ubiquitous Romantic idea—is a sad consolation:

> When the house falls you wonder
> If there will ever be poetry
> And you shiver in the timbers wondering
> If there will ever be poetry
> When the house falls you shiver
> In the vacant lumber of your poetry.
> Beauty is so rare a thing, Pound sang.
> So few drink at my fountain.

More durable than this passage suggests is the house that Jack built, a house with a decor determined by Romanticism. These inherited concepts of creativity, god, and passion are varied by furniture and decorative bits from the twentieth century. His house, therefore, is sufficiently contemporary. The rooms are spacious, filled with air and light; and the jointures are true:

> This is the melancholy Dane
> That built all the houses that lived in the lane
> Across from the house that Jack built.
> This is the maiden all forlorn, a
>   crumpled cow with a crumpled horn
> Who lived in the house that Jack built.
> This is the crab-god shiny and bright
>   who sunned by day and wrote by night
>   and lived in the house that Jack built.
> This is the end of it, very dear friend, this
> is the end of us.

TIME-STOPS OF THE SPIRIT:
CAROLYN STOLOFF'S *SWIFTLY NOW*

In this, her fifth book of poems, Carolyn Stoloff's primary motifs are sun, wind, seeds, and small creatures—ants, moths, and birds. The landscape is New Mexican. As resident of Taos, she considers and absorbs scenes and events with unusual clarity. She scales herself down to the minute in nature. Her emotions exfoliate from seeds of feeling, desert weeds and poppies germinating from hard seeds in the baked earth, caressed by wind and thunder-storms, coming to fruition as a wealth of petals.

Stoloff, a New Yorker, is entirely at home in her Western locale; and she might have lavished her time rendering the vast, monumental sweeps of deserts and mountain ranges—scenes so vast one can gaze for miles of an afternoon and observe half-a-dozen vivid thunderstorms transpiring at once. She might have echoed the painter Georgia O'Keeffe, who spent a long life evoking Western grandeur; her close-ups of bleached skulls and flamboyant flowers are monumental. We respond to O'Keefe as we do to vistas of great landscape reaches. Stoloff's approach is different. While O'Keeffe works for the grand transcendental form, Stoloff prefers the more Aristotelian look—her vision focuses on a patch of earth rather than the expansive sky. Small birds and insects peregrinate over, under, and through her scenes. Seeds burgeon. She scrutinizes moments of exfoliation. After a vigorous afternoon rain, pupae unfold into butterflies, and a weed-stalk bursts forth with a shimmering ephemeral blossom. She is a poet of the intimate close-up. Her *takes* define her immediate space; and, at their best, her definitions evoke psychic landscapes of force and beauty.

A short poem, "Vespers," displays her mode. Present are both vastness and restriction; the former makes sense only in terms of the latter. A bird flashes past and, for a moment, "mars" the "lustrous rose" of the sunset. A meadowlark sings. These swift impressions lead to this potently expressed wish for a deep union with the earth:

> I'd like to thrust my spine
> like a spear in earth
> let it leaf!

The wish itself, via a natural germination and flow, eventually glides "like sound" into the horizon, into its "running gold" wound. The result is *spiritual botany:* the transcendental occurs via the germinative, from the loam upwards. And since the flow in "Vespers" occurs within four short stanzas (eleven lines), the result suggests time-stop photography: the tension of the poem moves from *spine* to *plant* to *flower* to the sunset.

In "Evening Meal," the sky is a "banquet of color." Stoloff's small house has become "all window." She smells the spiced aroma of sage, as she steps (a concrete act) into the "still balm" of evening, a balm that soothes the ants on their hills and the birds roosting in trees. With her feet "firm on the land" she regards the sky, discerning "radiant pheasant-clouds" and lambs "from the fatted flock." She devours this rich feast, washing it down "with a cool quart of sky," and is restored in spirit. The clouds turn to "peach fluff" as the twilight falls.

A longer poem, "A Piece of Light," interweaves her motifs in complex ways. An ant attempts to carry a fly, "big as a truck," up a wall. The ant never succeeds. He climbs part-way, drops the fly, and has to start all over again. As she observes, Stoloff recalls an acquaintance, a counter-culture pilgrim, who reports on her two-year trek towards wisdom. The woman's tough bare feet reveal her life. She's lived under pine branches and tarps in the mountains. Axes, she says, are "more honest" than chain-saws. People, particularly Indians, have been good to her. She's thrived on nuts, beans, grains, and boiled lily-buds.

As Stoloff recalls the woman, the present intrudes as a car passes, throwing dust all over the phlox outside her window. She returns to the ant struggling with the fly. Why does the creature make its home up in the beams of her house? She casts some of the light hitherto illuminating the ant and the hippie over herself now. Her seed-plantings are equivalents for the repetitions of ant and woman. Whether the seeds will produce light, i. e., germinate, is always unclear. Stoloff plants in good faith, and is nervous as she searches for sprouts. She sees none. She must learn patience, as ant and woman have had to. Her urgings of the seeds produce this wry observation: she also shells her "articular nut / for a piece of light." Experience, then, is a matter of repetitions performed on the hard, resistant plane of this mineral-vegetable earth. Our destiny is to foster growth, believing that we shall flower.

In "Passage," vividly rendered particulars lead Stoloff to transcendence. The sunlight she walks through on a desert road is "solid butter." Pebbles, "barley size," impede her walk. She observes a rosebush and imagines its feet drinking deep down in the desert soil. She walks all day. At noon the hills "slip" into a "yellow skin." When afternoon arrives, Stoloff feels a sense of someone (a lover?) absent. The glaring yellow light reflects the actuality of her days. And the days, like pebbles, resemble barley-grains in the sweep of time. Dusk arrives with its "shadow-spills," followed by "night's ocean." Interesting here are the hints of a private longing, one that might easily have turned confessional. But Stoloff is too much the artist to allow this. Resolutions of personal doubt, longing, and pain appear to shave off into a natural event (lightfall, shower, storm, sunset). In a sense, she steps outside her private cravings for clarity. The result is a universal experience, one that satisfies us greatly.

A most effective concretizings of vastness appears at the close of "Behind the Hour." Once again, Stoloff focuses on a patch of brightness. In the "fine flour" of this light, numerous "ragged locusts crawl," symbols of old private "quirks." At the same time, desert gusts shake a tree. "Green-gold clusters" of ripening plums fall. Stoloff takes up a bleached animal skull:

> four firm teeth
> no strings attached
> no sour grass scent
> or mobile lip
> sawdust from broken rock
> spills
> from its holes

If there are "poor Yorick" tones here, they are greatly underplayed. The memento mori is Stoloff's own:

> dry bells rustle
> I exchange breaths
> with the dark nostrils
>
> behind every hour

"After Labor Day" envisions human mortality through a grasshopper about to deposit her eggs and die. Stoloff's excitement arises from a lyric energy, evidence again of her feeling herself into an object. She is not, however, a mere word-painter or an embroiderer of purple passages. Her techniques resemble those found in the paintings and drawings of Paul Klee and Joan Miro, where a precisely but quicky-rendered detail evokes an entire bird, flower, or landscape.

Stoloff observes grasshoppers proceeding "this way or that," all "up...around...and under" pigweed stems. A hopper in flight excites her. There's a "gasp of vermilion skirts" when the creature leaps. Another hovers nearby, "clacking her castanets" before plopping to earth. One hopper will shortly "sink" her "ovipositor" into clay, and, once her eggs are laid, will become a "tatterdermalion" crawling beneath a "dirty rosette" and die.

The concluding stanza is affectionate; and in its simple tone produces a chill—for Stoloff is writing about us:

> I used to wonder where you go
> I guess I know
> a spring   a summer   and one fall
> that's it

"Swiftly Now" reflects this same theme, of the grace of dying into nature, as a natural process. Distant horses seem like small "piano hammers" silhouetted against "chill gusts." There's another brilliant sunset. Nearer, "a bird drops / to a brown fist / asway on its hairy stem / to tug a seed from its cell." Heads of flowers, "darker" than night, fall to the asphalt as a "litter" of notes. The poem closes with this composed moment:

> what won't give gracefully
> breaks I guess

Stoloff's perceptions make her a botanist-biologist of the spirit. Her special curiosity emerges from her fascination with life's concreteness. She never gushes, and knows when to rein in a visual effect for enhanced symbolic properties. While she is primarily a celebratory poet, her wonder leads her to a tough-minded view of the cyclic sweep of events. Her time-stops on nature occur with the shutter of her camera wide open. Because she is never pre-programmed, her surprise (and awe) often unsettles her. When this occurs, Stoloff is merely doing what painters and poets have always done who have guided us to *see* their visions as induced by minutiae. Holbein observed a pink in a man's hand, Dürer a hare, Burns a mouse, Dickinson a robin eating a worm, Rossetti a three-cupped woodspurge. Each of these *seeings* generates its own conundrum: Is the man holding the pink greater than the flower he holds? Does the flower exceed the man? Is the poet observing the mouse or the robin larger than those creatures? Stoloff confronts conundrums with artistry. She is larger than events because she contains them. She has seen, heard, tasted, and felt them, and loves their profound overtones.

COFFINS OF WIND:
MARK STRAND'S *THE LATE HOUR*

My pleasure in poets transcends conflict: poets are not my natural enemies. But, a critic must play wolf-roles, especially when poems generate tedious conjugalities. I wish I could help Strand feel less lost, elegiac, submissive, and sad. How many times an hour, reader, can you face mirrors of snow and fading light, little stabs of sorrow, wind-coffin miseries and not feel dulled? *A body of bliss?* We find on our tongues instead: "Ah, poor me!" We are "such small beings" travelling "in the dark/with no visible way/or end in sight." I want Strand to explode graves, to shiver his flesh, to scream negations in tornados, to rev up his moon-pallor with rainbows, to cease graying his tepid visions into ashes before they are born. I miss *seams* in most of *The Late Hour*. And, seamless poems lack savor. A bored God from His Celestial Armchair spins forth such verse. Though laced with ambrosia and frosted with ichor, God's saliva might better impress us if there were an oyster or two. In *The Late Hour* no thrill zooms from foot-sole, up past navel and nipple to one's topmost follicles.

It follows, as surely as Atheneum Inc. followed Strand, that literary criticism is a form of speleology. Our entry into the subterranean world of the book is its cover, cave-cover as adit.

Among the twenty-five poems here, two are adaptations from Charles Dickens and one from de Andrade. Inside Strand Cavern, stalactites and stalagmites, like geriatric lion's teeth, are worn down. In this "kingdom of rot," there's much room for roaming. Numerous poems sit like shrouded ashen tombstones. In contrast, "About a Man," "Exiles," "Where are the Waters of Childhood" have a tenuous grace. Clearly, Strand has meditative lyrical gifts. In the good poems your face shines back at you as glimmering pools, not tombstones. As in most caverns, the mystical is very misty: glimmers disappear at the moment you think you snag them. Can you be sure of their depths? Can you wade through without drowning? Do they contain eyeless fish? Where is the guano?

When poems lacerate language, energy booms. American poets, like Merwin, Kinnell, and Strand, confuse philosopher poets with poet-wizards. Alexander

Pope gave the lie to the act: poets aren't philosophers: when they try they merely warm over last week's soup. When Strand complains that in "these days...there is little / to love or to praise, " or refers to that "place / beyond / beyond love, / where nothing, / everything, / wants to be born," I feel conceptually underprivileged. Nor does his cutting up these pallid thoughts into macaroni lines achieve for me the momentousness he desires. Camus and Sisyphus have tainted too many creative minds. And there is no booming when Strand "mirrors" well-known moments from other poets. Consider the trivialized Rilke of "Pot Roast" where Strand almost changes his life and no longer regrets "the passage of time;" or, the nod towards Roethke's far field in "the field's edge" ("Poem of Air"); or, the trivializing of de Andrade by the lather of first-name allusions to friends; or, the Eliot tones of "White"; or, the echo of Shakespeare's "bare ruin'd choirs." Finally, there are Dylan Thomas strokes "in the drift and pitch of love." Strand's "adaptation" of a passage from Chapter XLVIII of Dickens' *Bleak House*, since it raises issues about such adaptations, is worth scrutiny. Always, there is the problem of quality: is the adaptation an improvement over the original, be it poetry or prose? Strand's adaptation of Dickens is inferior to his model. Here are a pair of instances: Strand substitutes the flat "on deserted roads and hilltops" for Dickens' "dusty high roads and on hill-summits"; Strand substitutes "thousands of stars" for "a multitude of stars," and dissipates energy by adding a vapid passage not found in Dickens:

> It is a still night, a very still night
> and the stillness is everywhere.

This echoes the sleaze of Matthew Arnold's failure, "A Summer Night." What Strand contributes in adapting Dickens is the ecology theme, one merely hinted at in the original—mildew, oil slick, urine, empty bottles, tires, and rusty cans. The rich-poor contrast concluding Strand's piece is energetic. My guess is, though, that C. D. would never approve of this:

> And the poor in their tenements speak to their gods
> and the rich do not hear them...."

Strand lacks the imagination either to match or surpass Dickens, so drops between trying to evoke Dickens and being himself. Here's the problem: if you write "adaptations" and the result is mere "writing" needed to pad a slim book, why not write an original poem? Don't whittle away at Dickens with your dull penknife.

The casual critic or reader, being fashionable, will uncritically accept new books by well-known poets like Strand, no matter how derivative, enervated, pompous, slight, or expensive. These poems are fetishes, and fetishes demand little except admiration, particularly if they are popular with females on college reading circuits. Fetishist Fun keeps many American poet hacks in motion. Fame rests on a prostatory glow—you rub mine, I'll rub yours. If poems were girl-scout cookies, these poets would spend hours brushing crumbs from their faces.

Strand has whitened images almost to the point of invisibility, engendering the opposite of excitement. In "Poor North," Strand's wind "beats around in its cage of trees." I perk up. In another poem, a woman in bed beside her lover "stares at scars of light / trapped in the panes of glass." In "Snowfall" snow is "the negative of night." In "Seven Days," the person addressed appears inside "a glass pillar filled with bright dust." A fine image ensues of gulls wheeling "in loud broken rings." But isn't that a near-steal from Yeats' "Wild Swans at Coole"?

A poet traps himself inside an *insidious heroism* when he sees himself as an *Ur-Mensch*, as Adam, *exteriorizing* the universe *ur-ly*. He thinks everything he writes is pregnant with meaning. He spews forth narcissistic little phrase / word droplets, personal pronouns—as in this random assembling from "Pot Roast":

> I gaze upon the pot roast...I spoon the juices...
> I sit by a window...I do not regret...
> I see no living thing...I bend I think...
> I tasted a roast... when I finished...
> I remember the grave...I taste it again ...
> I raise my fork...I eat.

Or, here, in a briefer poem, "Lines for Winter," Strand *narcissitates* for Ros Krauss:

> tell yourself...you find yourself...
> what you know...your bones play...
> you will be able...you cannot go on
> or turn back...you find yourself /
> where you will be at the end...
> tell yourself...you love what you are...

Certainly, to be fair, there's an implicit courage in locating selves precisely in *les deux glace* of existence—physical ice, spiritual ice. The insidiousness transpires when the proportion slips, when the personal pronouns dull by their omnipresence and the poem becomes a Chinese water torture experience. No poet is an Adam. An Eve, perhaps? Feeling spreads like cream over a Proustian *madeleine.* In fact, one can read "Pot Roast" as a verbal play on "Proust"; a chunk of meat rather than Proust's cookie inspires Strand. Birds have a way of appearing far less ungainly in flight than when they waddle on the ground. As a critic, I've tried in this experiment to ground the elusive goose of poetry without clipping its wings. Towards worrying my bird, I have chosen Strand's book—but without explaining it. Poems are not isotropic. Another critic would approach the goose differently, either pressing numerous eggs from its anus or wringing its goose neck for the sake of pressing its liver. Perhaps I have merely been dream-reading, and Strand did not write the book I've critiqued. I leave the last word to Strand himself, who sees the problem most perspicaciously in "No Particular Day"; he writes of "moves of the mind/that never quite/make it as poems.... "

PAUL TRACHENBERG'S
MAKING WAVES

In this, his second book, Paul Trachtenberg continues the highly personal mode of *Short Changes for Loretta*, published by Cherry Valley Editions, 1982. In *Loretta*, Trachtenberg assumed the persona of a trashy southern California femme fatale who winsomely, and sometimes hilariously, spread her confessions over pop poems resembling carved bits of ivory. Loretta moved from a Catholic girlhood to careers as actress and poet. Even in desperation, she is iconoclastic, coloring her recollections with a tone and a diction reminiscent of Mickey Mouse cartoons and fey animals cavorting in a world structured around fantastical illogicalities. Loretta fails at love, as an actress, and finally contracts cancer, which she is cured of by the Beatles' "Magical Mystery Cure." She finally wings off into space, losing her socks—which are floating up there now as intergalactic junk. We assume that Loretta herself, dressed in a beaded gown and ocelot furs, is wreaking her funky charm in an unnamed galaxy where kinky sex-goddesses fly after their death. The reader suspects that more of Trachtenberg resides in Loretta than he'll admit.

By using a female persona for his first book, Trachtenberg could be more inventive, more surreal, than he could by limiting himself to an autobiographical work. In *Making Waves*, on his Southern California life, his tone and inventiveness remain remarkably like that of *Loretta*. Trachtenberg's poems are not interchangeable with those of any other poet, no small achievement. When I asked him what he sought most to convey in *Making Waves*, he replied that he wished to capture the "feel" of growing up in the Southern California of the Beach Boys, Annette Funicello, Dick Dale, and Anaheim's Disneyland. (He has worked as a candy man and a pickle-seller in the Magic Kingdom). Amidst the surfing, fast cars, semi-nudity, and cheeky Disney animals, there are dark themes—isolation, loneliness, dope, and a drifting past conventional social norms. Like Edward Fitzgerald, Trachtenberg sees his Paradise as a wilderness, as well as a place ("enow") of joy, love, and fulfillment. He sees much of the trash amidst the glamour.

He grew up in Lawndale, a suburb of Los Angeles, now given over to freeways and ugly industrial plants. Whenever he drives north he passes over the exact spot where his family home once stood. Isolated as a youth from the beach (developers forced his family to move inland), the lure of sand, sun, and surf was eventually consuming. He was shy and dreamy, "besmirched" by "an insane modesty." Growing up was difficult:

> The wind finally wafted the leaf.
> I began to see naked bullies
> and wimps of all sizes.
> I warmed to this stark reality.

He discovered pop music: Funicello's "room was furnished / with sand to sand carpeting, / palm-to-palm walls, / Dick Dale in stereo." Sexually alert, he began hitchhiking to the beach. Jan and Dean and the Beach Boys obsessed him. Jan's decimating car-crash made him feel he had lost a family member:

> Sadly, Jan lost his balance,
> not on a board, on wheels—
> supine in twilight.

Finally, he bought an old "wooded Chevy." The resulting freedom intensified his lust for surfer bodies. By writing in the mode of a surfing song, he minimized his pain:

> Skimpily dressed beach boys
> balancin' blithefully in the blue.

Uncle Sam had other plans, however; and, warned by his high school coach, he was called before the draft board and was rejected as "a strange one." Shortly, the reality of the draft hit, and he appeared for inspection, one of a number of youths in jockey shorts

> conveyed like coke bottles
> to be filled with
> whatever Sam desired.

His homosexuality saved him, the Army doctor deciding that he "was a bottle / they didn't need to fill"—hardly a situation for treating lightly or humorously. Feeling euphoric, he left the induction center in a queer bliss:

My clipped wings grew
once again. My feet,
my hair like Mercury's helmet,
endowed me with six wings.
I flew Sam's factory forever.

He escaped deeper into Southern California life, immersing himself in
hibiscus blooms, sexual, the showiest of area flowers. A job at a supermarket left
him little time for the surf, so he quit, spending most of his waking hours in
Huntington Beach, the surfing capital of Orange County. When his funds ran
out, he found a distasteful job in a hospital laundry counting soiled linen.
Eventually, almost as a gift from God, he was hired by Disneyland! This desirable
world he entered at full throttle:

Jamborees, dances, characters & bands
adrenalized the land—a passion
for protoplasm and synapses
of eclectic visions.

Soon, his quizzical sense took charge and he satirized the Disney fetish for
cleanliness: the "hunt for spilled popcorn" is "a must performance in Everyland.
/ Not a kernel unpreyed upon..." Sanitized fantasy animals, fantasy "topiaries,"
shamed the natural world of privets. The latter felt "mistreated and misshapen."
Workers, bored gathering trash and debris, turned for sexual excitement to the
"monorail girls." Kinky sex things transpired in the Magic Kingdom:

Pinocchio made hay with the dwarves.
He nosed the bosoms of tour guides.
Dopey varnished his wood into flesh.

Much partying occurred. The three little pigs doffed their hot costumes,
Mary Poppins wore street clothes, and Mickey Mouse and Alice in Wonderland
carried on, the latter shocking the Candy Man when he realized that both Alice
and Snow White were not virgins. He had an affair with a lavatory cleaner (a black
female), resisted the advances of gay Rudy who played ragtime piano, and fell in
love with a superbly tanned lollipop girl:

She was bronze with rosy cheeks,
delicious in her candy pink dress.

He drank too much, lost Toni, and through his dad's intervention worked in an Alpha Beta warehouse, "a new Alcatraz." He still spent weekends at Laguna Beach "where the gay boys lay," stoned on sunshine, salty sea air, and creme de menthe.

His gay world was a "wild toad ride" of booze, dope, and sex. In Laguna, he met an older poet who encouraged him to write, calming him. He flirted with Christian Science, with hippie transcendentalism, and with the Timothy Leary crowd. He became an avid reader of the *Urantia,* and practiced the Parahansa Yogananda brand of meditation. Self-quests continued:

> Did I swallow too much salt water?
> "Who are you?" asked a big tomato worm.

He emerged as a poet in "a purple jungle," watching beach creatures hulahooping and dancing passacaglias:

> I was on the crest, ready
> to kick out, taking a left side.
> Grabbin' the rail, I avoided
> the curling wave.

He was relieved he had not gone under. He moved in with the older poet, wrote "odd" poems on "fiber-glass boards," and built word castles by reading dictionaries, encyclopedias, and books of facts. He studied vocabulary cards. His growth as a poet was an autodidact's development, one always outside convention.

THIRTEEN WAYS OF LOOKING AT
DAVID WAGONER'S *LANDFALL*

"The blackbird whirled in the autumn winds. It was
a small part of the pantomime. " —Wallace Stevens

I

"David Wagoner seems to me one of our best poets,
perhaps one of the best we have ever had in this country."
—Robert Boyers, jacket blurb for Wagoner's
Collected Poems: 1956-1976

II

David Wagoner is a prolific poet. *Landfall* is his eleventh book of poems. He
has also written ten novels, has edited Theodore Roethke's *Notebooks*, was
chancellor for the Academy of American Poets, and has edited *Poetry Northwest*
and the Princeton Poetry Series. He was twice nominated for the National Book
Award and once for the American Book Award —so the jacket blurb informs us.
He has yet, however, to receive an ermine tippet. We'll be patient.

III

What is Wagoner's poetry like? Little Brown, Inc. touts it as "timeless and
arresting." Let's scrutinize this blackbird of verse. Like all blackbirds, he dips and
soars with such grace he scarcely ever misses the nest or the twig he opts to perch
on. A blackbird's behavior is never as stunning, or as inventive, as an egret's, or
a macaw's, or a hummingbird's, or a shrike's. I must resist, therefore, expecting
more of this fairly commonplace bird than I would of a more flamboyant one.
The *Britannica* characterizes a blackbird's song as "mellow."

IV

Wagoner reflects a middle-class sensibility fast approaching middle-age. His reposes fall within the framework of the entirely possible, noncontroversial, and secure. He sleeps in gardens, stands around in swamps and in woods and on lake shores, and evokes a calm, productive, and pleasant existence. Life, one feels, has been good to him; and his meditations on man and nature evolve from a fixed center. While he writes, a faithful wife is often nearby, asleep in her bed. Spiders, moths, and genteel birds await his attention. His nights and darkness, minimally threatening, are occasions for reverie and a gentle metaphysics. His imagination is domestic. He's never far from home. The paths he takes are all well-beaten. Survival trips are not for him—he likes the stroll or the day's excursion, all within a whistle distance of the boat-landing, the cabin, or the look-out tower. His creatures are most noiseless and patient. Recall that Jonathan Edwards was not far from home either when he observed those spiders drifting out to sea and started a fad among American writers for botanical and biological minutiae.

V

A Poet of Middle Age feels superior to younger poets. (Poetry of Middle Age, from prestigious houses, is often written by the Young). In "Elegy Written in a Suburban Churchyard" Wagoner observes the young "living it up" to Beatles music: "Ringo instead of bingo." The young, he says, litter squashed beer cans. Thomas Gray, enamored as he was of church yards, might have reflected negatively on the young of his day for trashing gravestones. The Poet of Middle Age seems obsessed with a pallid aging. In "Elegy," Wagoner, on that downward side of life, as a tomb-chill sets in, writes his own commemoration. Though his energies may not diminish, he moves slower, is more urbane, and avoids excess either in feeling or language; in short, he takes few risks. His expanding middle requires new protective antics—he sits, observes, and meditates a lot. I'm writing metaphorically; judging from photographs, he's in fine physical shape.

VI

Looking back at Wagoner's poems, one detects a Middle Aged sensibility present all along. He's never been inventive and has generally worked within the confines of restricted themes and motifs. He's an onlooker, not an activist or experimenter. Perhaps that's why he's a good editor. He's an easy poet to admire, as praise of his work shows.

VII

Wagoner belongs to a group of American poets who write of agrarian and working-class lives. The middle-aged poet from Tennessee, the lyricist of the mid-western trapper-farmer ancestor, the family historian of the Detroit assembly plants... These poets bestow self-compliments by showing how sensitive their progenitors were, despite their having been brutalized by industry, the farm, and lousy or non-existent educations.

I challenge readers to find one such poet who confesses that his progenitors were stupid, callous, mean, and despicable, persons quite other than Gray's "mute, inglorious Miltons." Wagoner's father, a smelter in a steel mill, sought to prevent his brains from melting in "those tyger-mouthed mills." Yes, that "tyger" is the ghost of William Blake's feline. Wagoner's dad was a sensitive bloke (feminine?) who brought "flowers" home from the mill: gears, cogwheels, ballbearings. Wagoner's "fire" catches spark and generates from his father's.

Such fascinations with roots may reflect a poet's uneasiness about his being insufficiently macho in a culture that expects men to act like men. If Daddy was a hunter, miner, smelter, or welder you've inherited his macho genes. Wagoner doesn't linger over his sexual identity, which implies he has no doubts of his manhood. Reading him is like reading William Stafford—you feel secure with the Geritol content of the verse.

VIII

Wagoner's new poems stitch together into an afghan of verse. Afghans, though beautiful, fall short of being works of art. These are cheery, well-crafted pieces hooked together by easy formulas (patterns). Most "afghan" poems are naturals for anthologies assembled for people of unsophisticated tastes—books used in school literature classes where the visuals are as crucial as the verbal, and in sentimental gift books meant for the mass consumption on holidays. In such poems (and they do acquire their hermetic lives and shapes) there's often a wry, easy humor; and there's nary an off-color word. Nature, particularly in its small manifestations, flourishes; Wagoner's menagerie includes squirrels, spiders, moths, and cuckoos. There is wholesome fun when Wagoner focuses on some uncanny attribute of the creature or plant he describes, usually in human terms.

IX

Everybody loves cuckoo clocks. In "Cuckoo," Wagoner's is frozen, *"kaput,"* and belongs to "the Black Forest of *our* nightmares." Its parts are stuck. This well-crafted poem is likable, frosted with good feeling: there's a "slaphappy" doorway, the house itself is "a flop-house for gnomes," and the cuckoo is "bird-brained"— effects uncomfortably close to the worlds of Dumbo and Thumper. Wagoner emerges as a man crammed with *Gemütlichkeit*. His sentiments are always "poetic" and benign. He spares the cut worm by tossing it over the fence; the spider goes on about its business unharmed; and the moth occasions empathy rather than distress. As Wagoner meanders through his landscapes, reciting the names of plants and birds, he's more like Eve than he is like Adam; he tends, one imagines, "the droop'ng flowers all."

Our most successful (widely accepted) poets have always been inoffensive and ingratiating. Charles Bukowski is a glorious exception, as Ginsberg is. Though Wagoner's poetry is cuts above light verse, he is too eager to induce comfort and belly-glows. He should be better than he is.

"Note with the Gift of a Bird's Nest" is generic Wagoner. A gray-haired poet and his wife (her hair is still golden) cut off tresses and put them where bucktits can retrieve them for a nest. The poem devolves into a corny love compliment, a literary lapse. God! How far we've spun from Donne's bright hank of hair about the bone. I fault Wagoner's adulators more than I do him. On one level, he's fun to read; on another, he's avuncular, self-indulgent, and coy.

X

Coy moments in *Landfall* (and there are many) usually reflect the pathetic fallacy—that device so loathed by Samuel Johnson when he determined that John Milton's use of the device in "Lycidas" was "easy, vulgar, and therefore disgusting." Here's what I mean: In "Return to the Swamp" Wagoner describes a striped bass as "a splashing-master / Ringmaster of refracted light." A bullfrog, in the closing lines, awards Wagoner a "green princely attention." Thumper and friends! In another poem, swamps have "an underlying answer"; reeds have "good lost lives"; wrens "decide" what the poet is and "slowly excuse" him. (Dylan Thomas was also coy). In a good poem, "Sleeping on Stones," Wagoner demonstrates that he needn't always be ingratiating: a dog salmon shreds her tail-fin as she fashions a spawning place.

XI

One of Wagoner's features, one we've already seen, is the naming of plants and creatures: scarlet sporophyte, clubmoss, bittercress, rush, sweet-after-death, quillwort, spikerush, lobelia, milfoil, and caddisfly. Here he's a Ewell Gibbons of poetry who does our nature-living for us, and his naming of plants and creatures absolves us of guilt over being so urbanized. We need to start all over like tiny first Adams, giving names, or matching up what we see in the marshes with our field-guides. As reassuring as it is to know that we are still not totally exiled from nature, we detect a residual superficiality in Wagoner's naturism. Merely to name an object is not to invest it with either magic or profundity.

In his closing poem, "Landfall," Wagoner attempts to raise enigmas: once we've named and renamed the trees, birds, plants, and animals, they turn hopelessly nameless again, leaving us alone with our hearts.

XII

Carole Landis, in the forties, was noted as the Ping Girl; Wagoner can be called the *Ing Poet.* I am not being Confucian, reader; rather, I stress a recurring device marring these poems. Most poets eschew the easiest mellifluous present participle. Whitman remains the model for this practice. Two poets, Theodore Roethke and Thomas McGrath use the device superbly—but, then, they are cuts above Wagoner. Wagoner's poems would improve if he'd throw out gerunds. Within six brief lines, "Dipper" contains these: skimming, standing, dipping, staring, drowning, wing-swimming. Three appear in crucial end-of-line positions. The opening stanzas of "Algae" and "Cutworm" are similarly marred. In a poem I admire, "Song from the Second Floor," the facile device is a jewel of great price displayed an inch or so below the navel.

XIII

Wagoner looks and sounds the way a good American poet should—gentle, a bit melancholy and introspective, wide-eyed, enamored of first-person report-age, eager to name the objects in his Eden (there's rarely a whiff of Hell), and positive in his nostalgia for seasons and generations. The commonplace and the minute carry trite meanings: *we* are these moths, cutworms, spiders. If our roots are smothered we may still survive. I see no evidence that Wagoner seeks to be innovative, or pioneering, or to chill us as his mentors Frost and Roethke (and McGrath?) did so capably. Nightingales, after all, do have necessary places in the sky. Don't ever expect, though, that you'll surprise Wagoner seated with Henry Thoreau on a log eating a woodchuck.

Note: I have purposely not quoted much from Wagoner's book. In my experience, Little, Brown, (and sometimes Doubleday) has proved intractable in refusing to allow critics to quote at all from their books without paying substantial fees—this despite the guidelines suggested in the recent copyright code. This policy does hinder the reviewer, particularly if the poet under scrutiny is not as well-known as Wagoner. Little, Brown dislikes sending out review copies. I received a curt note from them saying that they don't send such copies to "free-lance reviewers." A letter of protest I sent to the President of the company produced the book. I don't feel inclined to take such trouble in the future.

FEMINISMO:
DIANE WAKOWSKI'S *SMUDGING*

Diane Wakoski's province is utterly female, frequently self-parading, and full of little bushes quivering with cunts craving cocks. Wakoski is the Boadicea of modern poetry. Her country behaves according to her rules. By comparing her to that legendary British queen I am not hinting that she should experience Boadicea's fate: weren't the queen's limbs tied separately to different horses dashing madly off in all directions?

Wakoski is a marvelously imperious poet! To use another analogy, she presides over the distaff side of contemporary verse like the Queen of Swords, smiling, yes, and with charm and (I hope she'll forgive the crudity) balls. Wakoski's energy is terrific, and her personality, as it emerges from the poems, is unique, despite the sometimes vast and frequently annoying self-indulgence. Wakoski understands the correlation between being a character and luring readers to her work.

An irritation I felt in earlier books I feel here. I call it *feminismo.* In "Ladies, Listen to Me," a poem with a Carrie Nation title, Wakoski tells "ladies" how to behave, to cultivate and employ their *feminismo* with a vengeance. She begins by splitting herself apart in a sort of Ovidian (Ovarian?) way. She "snaked up" (an atrocious pun; such tend to *sneak up* on Wakoski) and saw herself as a cottonmouth snake (ho, shades of D. H. Lawrence, that feminine sensibility obsessed with his own maleness and the maleness of the world) looking at a woman—herself. Folks, we must be in the Garden of Eden and Diane-Eve invents her own snake for achieving self-awareness as a woman bent on finding the knowledge to lord it over man, that loathed but essential creature.

Then appears another myth: her ugly-duckling appearance. In a poem memorable for these two lines: "I have the spirit of Gertrude Stein / but the personality of Alice B. Toklas," Wakoski confesses that in society she has little to say. Poets are supposed to scintillate. She's "usually taken for / somebody's / secretary." Far out, Diane! In "Ladies, Listen to Me," she moves into self-deprecation: Just see me, people: "a plain ordinary woman" who wears glasses, lets her hair grow "to change the shape of her face," is neither fat nor thin, is equally shy and aggressive, "self-righteous and self-effacing." If a poet continually stares into the orchid (or pitcher plant) of the self, he (or she) risks alienating readers. And, what poet doesn't feel like an ugly duckling? Isn't that why poetry in the first place? "Nobody Loves Me, not even the Voles, Hyraxes, or Elephants" is particularly apt.

In "Ladies, Listen to Me," Wakoski boasts of a secret "only a few men have / and all women, if they were not soft and spoiled and foolish / could have." Eve's wisdom relates to prisons and "iron gates against the body" which turn body, "or its counterpart / the mind" into "a coiling spring." I'm not sure the image works: it assembles too much around it. One is reminded first of a coiled-spring bed, automobile, teeter-babe, and next, because of the cottonmouth image, of a snake readied to *spring* on its victim. Finally, one thinks of Robert Frost's *pasture springs* cleared up or returning to their sources. Wakoski reports that this spring is "no source of water then, / but the crystal container, / the cup which holds / everything." I am confused, unless this is a new image meant for gluing objects to it, as a piece of assemblage art. The passage needs clarifying.

Wakoski delights in her "tough" image: Diane, not of the moon, but of motorcycles, symbolic Leather Jacket Queen. She is the eternal woman deluding the man near her who feels he is "the firm enclosing the soft," when, in actuality, the woman is "the soft encasing iron." Who is duped? Is this news? Even the Marlboro Man before he died of lung cancer probably sensed that in the midst of a good lay the vagina is rough and that the mons veneris rises over hard bone. Men know that the lashings, and the will, of even the weakest-seeming woman are Boadicean.

Wakoski's *feminismo* takes the form of Gossip-Poetry. The poems that suffer much as Gossip-Poetry are "Greed: Parts 3 & 4." Moments are embarrassingly private: "Robert Kelly is overweight." Diane "the wife of the Hawks' Well Head...told me she'd never pay $30 for a dress..." Carol Bergé: "that beautiful black orchid of the Chelsea" who sent a poison pen letter so vexes Diane she finds it "necessary to say nice things about her / even when no one else wants to." These across-the-back-fence moments have little to do with poetry and would be better inscribed in journals or letters published during the senile years of the principals. Wakoski knows that she is sufficiently visible in the literary world to know that any eructations she wishes to see in print will *see* print. A sort of verbal *Dianarrhea* results.

Another side of Wakoski' *feminismo* is regressive in these feminist days. The woman intent upon *feminismo* feels enormously threatened by homosexuality (each homosexual is one male less for her to dominate) and protects herself (and womankind) by name-calling and by boasting of her boudoir skills. Wakoski's love poems, particularly "Anger at the Weather," "The Moon Explodes in Autumn as a Milkweed Pod," and "To bed," are powerfully erotic. Wakoski feels compelled to translate her female sexual energy into violence, tenderness, and hate, producing equivalents for the threatening physical energy of the male. "To Bed," a superior love poem, flashes images of violence: a cut-off finger, blood— and, later, bleeding on the sheets, a nose nipped off, a sharp beak kissing a human mouth, and a bleeding face.

Wakoski is always aware of tight, deep moments of touch, taste, and hurt passing between the sexes. In "Water under the Bridge" her lover, watching the light on the river, passively receives Diane's love-making:

> you watch it
> with the sun sparkling on it
> as only your eyes are when you first wake up
> and I am kissing the soft parts of your body....
Tender, intricate, simple, and beautiful.

Her response to homosexuals appears in "Poem for Judy Garland Which is A Field Guide to Butterflies." The butterflies are cliched gays who lament Garland's death—weak-handed amorites of "Over the Rainbow." Because of the stereotype, Wakoski's effort to expand the image to include "we—craftsmen and admirers of accomplishment" (by which I assume she means poets) fails. The concluding pathos is false: the young men, again, "with weak hands" (gratuitous information), clutching their sheet music hope for a "dispersal of energy" from Judy's spirit.

Beneath many of these poems there's a tremendous female persona obsessed with keeping a (the) penis close and, preferably, erect. If through her sheer strength she drives men away, her potent feminism will give her life meaning. Sisters don't suffice. A penis present, with attendant bitterness and rage, induces more life than a cockless placid life spent entirely in the company of other females. This, I would say—this struggle with men (Wakoski's *feminismo*)—is what makes for much of Wakoski's originality. When men are absent from her life she feels useless: see "Handbook of Marriage & Wealth"—excellent Wakoski. The moving "The Joyful Black Demon of Sister Clara Flies through the Midnight Woods on her Snowmobile," one of my favorites, concludes with a potent prophecy-curse against the man who betrayed the nun:

> The man who betrayed you
> opened his book to the wrong place.

When he turns the page
he will find your name spoken,
his hands will turn black and his beads crumble
                    like dust in them.

Feminismo provides, I think, a useful yardstick for current views of many of today's liberated women; the contradictions fascinate me. The antagonist male must be dominated (short, of course, of actual emasculation), he must be enticed and coerced by the woman's softness (which is actually iron), and he must be utterly virile. Without him woman is sterile and miserable. A cynic might recommend female masturbation as a way out. But, carrots and dildos don't fight back, nor do have they hearts. In a total male-female engagement, life finds much crazy meaning:

All the earth
rushes
with water
            but
I am the moon,
Diane, dry
waiting to be taken care of.

Price: quoted on inquiry.

WILLIAM WANTLING: THE DOGGED POET,
OR, THE POET AS DOG

William Wantling was forty-one when he died on May 2, 1974 of a heart attack brought on by codeine and wine. He was introduced to heavy dope, he said, through the military; when he was hospitalized in Korea he was given morphine. "It was beautiful," he said. "Five years later I was in San Quentin on narcotics."

I first heard of Wantling via Marvin Malone's *Wormwood.* I heard little else of him until I received a copy of his last book *7 On Style* from his publisher, A. D. Winans of Second Coming. Wantling published ten books in his brief life—all of them from small and almost inaccessible presses. In fact, Peter Finch, of *second aeon,* Cardiff, Wales, emerges as the publisher who has published more of Wantling than anyone else. Finch's press, in collaboration with Caveman Press, Dunedin, New Zealand, published *San Quentin's Stranger,* the first generous sampling of Wantling's work, edited by Trevor Reeves. At a Small Press book fair in San Francisco, I once talked with Winans, Len Fulton, and Doug Blazek about Wantling. The tragedy of Wantling's death struck me, as did the irony of his being ignored in poetry circles. To assist in making him better-known, I shall assess his poetry, the bits and pieces of it I've been able to assemble. Three of his books were loaned to me by Paul Mariah, no stranger himself to Wantling's life.

I

There are photos of Wantling in his books: a burly fellow of sensitive mein with an aura of rambunctiousness. His passions were obviously huge: dope, alcohol, sex, and poetry—he would have been right at home on the Merry Prankster Kool-Aid Acid bus. But what did he know of verse? A good deal, much of it learned from anthologies in the San Quentin prison library. Throughout his work he's fascinated by traditional forms and diction. And this polarity between the literary and the realistic (his word) is useful for understanding him. Rarely, though, did he let formality dominate; his best poems have unique urgencies. He was seldom the tatty scribbler who writes for the sake of writing, jacking off as the Muse sniggers into his ear over an obscene telephone.

It is easy to dismiss Wantling as a minority poet. Often, kind folk outside the walls—the mother-hen editors and anthologists—are sentimental over these men; and much published prison writing is bad. Wantling is the exception.

II

The earliest of Wantling's books, *The Source,* was published by Len Fulton in 1966. Fulton's introduction compares Wantling with Dostoyevsky, another incarcerated writer from "the utter crush of the cave." Wantling is "a tiger, raucous." He "springs with a certain prodigious elusiveness from the page; he needs discipline and yet,[once] achieved will certainly mark Bill Wantling's decline." Fulton needn't have worried, since Wantling himself resolved the issue by dying young.

The title poem of *The Source* addresses a Venus or an Atlanta in Calydon figure, and extols a mythic woman, a muse of poetry, love, and life. His capitalization of pronouns is entirely old-fashioned; and behind his cadences one hears Swinburne's "When the hounds of spring are on winter's traces." Phrases like "wild imagining," "rose to light," "mare-white thighs," "hounds of destiny," are connections. "Her love about Her like a field of frozen fire" is an echo of Swinburne's "Laus Veneris." From this point Wantling moved to create his incredible work. Here is "The Source":

> and She we know yet have but seldom seen
> rose from the sea where all paths lead
> rose in Her robes of lucid silver light
> Her cornflower eyes of wild imagining
> rose to light all the cities of this earth
>   with Her mare-white thighs
> Her love about Her like a field of frozen fire
> Her whimpering hounds of destiny straining at the leash

The second poem, "Heroin," is in a new mode of reportage, and is projective and colloquial:

> High, once I ate 3 scoops of ice cream
> high it was the greatest

greater than the Eiffel tower
greater than warm sex, sleepy
early on a morning....

A Shakespearean sonnet follows. Despite the quaint language, the drift is
Existentialist:

How is it, though the mind extend
few plans that Time may not erase
when we have wandered to our barren end
and left no trail upon the sands of space,
How is that we, cut to life's bare bone
and protesting our unjust fate as Man
fearing emptiness and O alone, alone
outlines against the emptiness we scan,
How is that we hold our heads so high
and explain the emptiness away
and fill with myths the empty sky
that endless cipher which we wander day to day?

Yet we are only puzzled by the myths we spin.
Why not deny The Myth and face the Emptiness again?

"How to Make a Molotov Cocktail" is a taut political poem, artful in
cross-echoing sounds and cadences:

the Bitch-ridden cliche that tightly
turns the hidden twitch of truth remains the same—only Quick of Death
is prone to know the new—& seldom
bidden change seldom does it change
—the same today as when the Bolsheviki
bullets flew & all the gutters flooded
crimson With the Czarist blood....

Moments here read like parodies of Swinburne's assonance, the consonants
twisting back on themselves humorously. Also, the "as when the..." is faded Pre-
Raphaelite writing. I have the feeling—one I have throughout Wantling's
work—that he loves pastiche.

Towards the close of "it's cold for August," a rampant energy emerges
as Wantling rages against society:

& what if the dam should
            suddenly burst
if suddenly I should run
            headlong, frothing, haphazardly
hurling shrapnel grenades
into high-noon crowds?
if suddenly tossing aside the
            dead ugly ache of it
all, I equalled the senseless
with my brute senseless act?

O My, wouldn't I
shine?   wouldn't
I shine then?
wouldn't it be I then who
had created God
at last.

This is not successful. The literary stuff is pretentious: "brute senseless act,"
"the periodicity of," and the locutions "dead ugly ache of it / all" and "if suddenly
I should run." The last stanza drifts deeper into the sophomoric.

"The Dog as Poet," however, is superb. There's a raunchy energy. The poet's
birth was easy:

as a pup
I was popped forth
like a clean new cork
from a poisonous suppurating bottle
no hard & angry birth here
an easy lay
begot an easy liar
dreamer, scoundrel...

Fucking bitches became Dog's "raison d'etre." His first bitch was

blue & easy
she thought me hers, said
I could cure the melancholy
            of her timid soul
spur on to glory the timorous genes
                        that were her lot in life

When the blue bitch kills him creatively, he lopes off, hunched, "wild and free." In a tour de force Dog becomes Don Juan:

> Is there one the insolent pup
> won't lay ? !
> the whispers went:
> his mother was a bitch's bitch...
> his father was unknown...

> Yet which of us would itch of this
> when bitches free & easy, hot-tail
> cool-tail, slim or overblown
> lay before us every night
> begging us to cork their bottles
> & cork them stiff & tight
> & so many bitches, be it known
> that spending night upon spent night
> would never know them all, their pretty ways
> their tortured groans
> the way they spread without a fight?

> & after many an exciting night
> I filled my belly in their kitchens
> & slipped away
> before the dawn advanced to burn the dark
> & turn it into day
> before the sun exposed my bitchings
> & gave the target for a shotgun blast
> before my days of happy rut & ditching
> were put to end at last....

Yet, clever dogs too grow old:

> before I start my singing I ensure
> my spot is where the sun is warm
> yes, in the sun is where I lay
> only in the sun, day on endless day

III

Sick Fly (second aeon, 1970) takes its title from a passage by H. L. Mencken: "The Cosmos is a gigantic Flywheel making 10,000 revolutions a minute. Man is a sick fly taking a dizzy ride on it." Wantling now writes *disquisitional poetry;* ie., poetry in journal form—autobiographical snatches in non-poetic language. He has abandoned the earlier literary posturing:

> It was Tuesday morning
> I was flunking out of school
> The February sun was hazy
> I went to bed with 2 jugs of white port
> to drink myself asleep
> but I kept flashing back to the day before
> ... I kept letting my dog off her chain
> & she kept running out in the road to
> chase the gasoline tanker
> & she kept clipping under the rear wheels
> & she kept yelping with surprise as she
> sat in the road with her guts hanging out
> between her back legs & her eyes
> never stopped looking at me with shamed surprise
> as if she'd got caught shitting on the rug
> & then the sun was bouncing off her eye
> like a handball off the blank concrete wall
> flicker / flicker
> death
> flicker....

Because of the animal's violent death he pops pills, "half a handful" of them, "all colors." Sweat streams down his legs. He fights puking. His trip is a bummer: "things" emerge from corners. There's a black hole in his wrist. His artery gushes blood two feet in the air. The blood pustulates. The din of 10,000 steel-heeled boots stomping. Two days later his wife finds him under his bed, curled up, in feces and vomit:

> But here I am now fairly calm
> full of tranquilizers & group therapy
> It evidently wasn't my turn after all
> What I wonder is, why all the hassle?
> Why all the bullshit?

> I never wanted to be a poet anyway
> I'd carry a lunch box like everybody else
> if only the muttering would stop

Dope conditions these poems, evident in the disjunctive forms. And perhaps that's what poems written under the influence of dope do, produce a jumping, flashing chaos. There are few successful such poems—some are by Ginsberg, Corso, Wieners, and Snyder. Wantling gives us the exteriors of these experiences; in other words, he doesn't invent hallucinations. We see what he *does* before, during, and after a trip; he's even funny—read him on riding a bicycle while he's stoned. In an elegy for James Dean, a fractured line, probably dope inspired, is appropriate:

> parts of your torn jacket
> are still offered for sale
> and
> a boy just pimping into
> pictures
> keeps your twisted
> body steering wheel
> on his
> L.A. wall
> and still we hear
> your muted icy hipster snarl
> ... see the soft smile breaking / and guess your rage and
> wonder at it all

The concluding poem, brief, almost a colophon, is startling:

> actually
> to sum up 35 years
> Billie Holiday
> is the only sane person
> I ever met
> & shooting heroin
> the only sane thing
> I ever did

IV

San Quentin's Stranger reflects fine bookmaking, and is superior to the other
perfect-bound Wantlings I have seen. Len Fulton has assembled what remains
the essential Wantling, incorporating poems from *The Awakening* (Rapp and
Whiting), *Obscene & Other Poems* (Caveman Press), *Sick Fly* (second aeon), and
10,000 r.p.m. & Digging it, Yeah! (second aeon and Nola Express).

"Poetry" presents Wantling's conflict between his allegiance both to "good
word music and rhyme" and to his gut-wrenching prison life. In non-rhyming
couplets, the piece shows Wantling under the strictures of a form; even so, a slack,
midwestern voice prevails:

POETRY

I've got to be honest, I can
make good word music and rhyme

at the right times and fit words
together to give people pleasure

and even sometimes take their
breath away—but it always

somehow turns out kind of phoney.
Consonance and assonance and inner

rhyme won't make up for the fact
that I can't figure out how to get

down on paper the real or the true
which we call life. Like the other

day. The other day I was walking
in the lower exercise yard here

at San Quentin and this cat called
Turk came up to a friend of mine

and said Ernie, I hear You're
shooting on my kid. And Ernie

told him So what, Punk ? And Turk
pulled out his stuff and shanked

Ernie in the gut only Ernie had a
metal tray in his shirt. Turk's

shank bounced off Ernie and
Ernie pulled his stuff out and of

course Turk didn't have a tray and
he caught it dead in the chest, a bad

one, and the blood that came to his
lips was a bright pink, lung blood,

and he just laid down in the grass
and said Shit. Fuck it. Sheeit.

Fuck it. And he laughed a soft long
laugh, 5 minutes, then died. Now

what could consonance or assonance or
even rhyme do with something like that?

"The Cold War" employs a bizarre image to suggest America and Russia at odds:

> The Cold War
> today i saw a strange sight
> i saw a set of mutant ugly siamese twins
> joined from hip to shoulder—
> they were hissing, snarling, sneering
> each mouth spoke hate for the other
> and the one with a right hand
> waved a dagger at the one with a left hand, who
> also waved a dagger...
>
> they were duelling

In prison, Wantling's braggadocio kept him functioning. He early sensed that his best chance for survival, facing shock therapy and other prison brutalities, was through ironic detachment. "Who's Bitter?" expresses this:

when Judge Lynch
denied probation
& crammed that 1-14
up my ass
for a First offense
I giggled

when Dr God
stuck 7 shock treatments
to me for giving my chick
in Camarillo
2 joints
I laughed aloud

now when the State of Illness [the prison was in Illinois]
caught me bending over
2 jugs of Codeine
cough medicine
& charged me w/   Possession
and Conspiracy
I shrieked
in idiot joy
 a bit worried
they all inquired
—What are you Wantling?
—A goddam Masochist?
I, between hilarious gasps
O howled—No,
—I'm a Poet!
—Fuck me again!

Joy is paradoxically real in "Dionysus in Summer," where he shouts out his
elan—this despite Dionysus' mangling of a hare. In "Obscene" Wantling writes
a poem that will get him busted, a grenade.

Obscene
her sweat mingling with mine
I slowly slide along & down
find her navel with my tongue
& her only eye of love
        form a tiny pool

her mindless legs fly open
I tongue her cunt, her
      musk a pungent funk
          part flower
        part rutting beast, & I
a wolf involved with winter moon
      howl soundlessly
a serpent

                  climbs my spinal tree
rooted in my balls
flowered in my skull
I know the Unicorn
some itching prick of its
ivory spiralled horn & mount
that mythic beast, am one with it
surge deep   into her cave
pouring through her center
      her abandon
             approaching adoration
the look of love about her
like a field of frozen fire
the ecstasy of Spring
damping down her thighs
&
a documentary
on deep-sea fishermen
who, angry at their luck
come upon a herd of Sea-lions
& their highpowered rifles
firing into the herd
& the carcasses
      float
          useless
          undisturbed
their heads bobbing the waves
          like footballs
their dead eyes staring
      the horizon
          their sea
          their skies
their
      "spindrift gaze toward paradise"
          their dead eyes

as the camera pans
to the Captain
at the rail
& his rifle
& his shining teeth
& the mirth of his tight-lipped
grin
      the obscene abandon
in his eyes
          & the local
public prosecutor
who reads this poem & wishes
"it had been published so I
could take you to court, Boy
on charges of Obscenity!"

V

7 On Style was Wantling's last book. According to Al Winans he was writing it just before he died, after a long creative drought. How appropriate that his final book should treat style. How rare that a poet of such immense disasters should consider style at all. Here Wantling evokes Samuel Beckett:

                  That sentence has
a wonderful
      SHAPE   It is
the   SHAPE
          that matters.

"Style 2," an ambitious contribution, is many things: straight-forward, outrageous, obscene, funny, and intense. Wantling's voice is like a professor's lecturing on Style. To stress that Style "can be found anywhere," he includes a letter a woman scribbled to a newspaper:

I want to tell you
what happened to your cat
after you dropped her off—the
first few days
she stayed just about where you
dropped her
waiting for you to come back

then hunger
drove her on along the road
searching for food & shelter
by now
she eats anything she can find, rotten
wormy, disease-laden ...
dogs & other animals
chase her, &
she is almost hit by passing cars
exposure to freezing nights
almost kills her
but your cat is tough ...
I found her today
she was beside my mailbox
right where you wanted her to go
that nice farmhouse in the country
only trouble was
your cat couldn't see me
her eyes were pasted shut
with infection
                              every bone
showing through her dirty hide
her stomach distended
with worms & starvation
too weak to stand
she made a little noise at me
but it was for you
to hear ... she is dead now

this, indeed, is poetry, not because it speaks
of random, terror, abandon, of
Quick too quickly cut, but
because it speaks of it with Style
because of concrete, sensory detail, stark
outline of emotionally charged events
extreme economy and, woven through it all
a strand of universal raging wonder at
the savage god called Death....

The episode, Wantling concludes, is "Reality imbued with Style." The poem, successful, made Wantling cry. He is, finally, a traditionalist: Poetry as Style (Art) is reminiscent of ancient Greek and Roman Writers: there is a savage god called Death, there are the quick and wiry shadows of our lives, and there is the random terror. Style becomes the Style of the State—the State gasses creatures with Cyklon B:

                                        & I have
                    dulled in 40 years
                                    previously
                    I raged & snarled &   pissed & moaned
                    fuck you, Universe! Shithead!
                                            fuck you I howled
                    you Punk !   I'll rip you off
                                                instead!
                                                    yes
                    once I tried to outrage
                    the random quirks of quick
                    the way they outraged me
                    but now I write of perverse curious things
                    without a curiosity; I inscribe
                    these ugly Random lines
                    with only random anger; I've achieved
                    a certain academic detachment & aplomb
                    my colleagues, now, are
                    more impressed
                                    the Universe
                                            much less ...
                    Oh
                    before you leave
                    you may wish to prepare
                    for next week's lesson:
                    Style 3! please
                    read the entire works
                    of Chas Bukowski.   never
                    mind the
                            Man. . .

In conclusion, Wantling is not a poet on a Parnassian pinnacle, holding an academic prize poetry scroll in one hand and, in the other, his newest book screaming for recognition. Wantling early on accepted neglect. Death is a savage god.

JOHN WEINERS:

THE MIND IN DRAG, THE MIND IN SHAMBLES

Few poets are as legendary as John Wieners. His reputation as a writer who cares little for his fame—one story has him disposing of freshly written poems under the windshield wipers of cars on Boston streets—serves as a corrective to the general run of American poet who keeps all scraps of paper he scribbles on, with an eye on posterity. In the gay world, *The Hotel Wentley Poems* has earned Wieners a place as an almost sainted writer. Literary historians locate him securely in the Beat and Black Mountain traditions.

Behind the State Capitol is an eccentrically conceived, arcane, and self-revelatory book. These poems make a medley of forms: "Cinema decoupage; verses, abbreviated prose insights." Let the reader be warned: You won't easily decipher these poems.

Let's consider Wieners' themes and his style. At the outset, it helps if you have read William Burroughs. The Wieners of *Behind the State Capitol* would be easy in the drug-ridden, psychedelic, sexually bizarre suburbs of Interzone.

The Persona

Wieners writes searingly of his working-class origins, and empathetically of the suffering of woe-begone folks. In no poem does he present his theme more starkly than in "Children of the Working Class," written "from incarceration, Taunton State Hospital, 1972." The deformed, brutalized inmates are like him:

> pinched men emaciated, piling up railroad ties and highway ditches
> blanched women, swollen and crudely numb-
> ered before the dark of dawn

These folk resemble his parents. Other unfortunates, unseen, are condemned to the zoo infernos of mental hospitals and "peon work farms":

> dwarfs, who cannot stand up straight with crushed skulls,

diseases on their legs and feet unshaven faces and women
worn humped backs, deformed necks, hare lips, obese arms
distended rumps, there is not a flame shoots out could ext-
inguish the torch of any liberty's state infection.

From the miserable, the maimed and the insane, children are born crammed
with phobias and manias. A wretched God deserves arraignment for creating
such deformities, and Wieners includes himself as one of them. He confesses that
he will "be punished for writing this": the "rich god," "omniscient," exploits the
poor by keeping them poor. Wieners rejects Whitman's vision of the poet aloof
from life's turbulence. He remains a "witness" to the

poorhouses, the mad city asylums and relief worklines. Yes, I am witness not to
God's goodness, but his better or less scorn.

Other poem iterate this theme: most moving is an elegy to his working class
mother, "By the Bars." Wieners is the poet of the open wound; his authenticity
is never in doubt, nor does he hide from searing pain. He excoriates himself,
endures whips and stings in the burning desert places of his soul and in the world
just outside his apartment, behind the Massachusetts State Capitol where teem
the dregs of Boston life.

The Poet as Drag "Quean"

Over half these writings are obsessed with legendary females, most of them
film and cabaret stars. The grand dame presiding over all is Jackie Kennedy
Onassis featured on the title page. Numerous collages / decoupage of stars both
lend and receive energies from the poems around them; and we never forget that
Wieners is himself, like his alter egos, an outcast and victim. His primary
obsession is for Lana Turner (he relishes the tragedy over her lover Johnny
Stomponato). He is also passionate for Alida Valli, forgotten star of the 30's and
40's, who deteriorated from excessive child-bearing, hepatitis, and the scars of a
horrible Hispanic childhood. Marlene Dietrich, melancholiac of those "Blue
Angel" songs, excites him, as do Marilyn Monroe, Claire Trevor (among the
most gifted actresses of her day), Greta Garbo, Judy Garland, and Bette Davis—
in short, legendary women beloved of female impersonators and drag queens.
Among cafe singers Billie Holiday was a goddess. Another is Peggy Lee. Wieners
is a Charles Pierce of poetry! When he assumes female voices, as he does Lana

Turner's, he can be moving. Through disguises he balances a fragile psyche. Not only is he homosexual (these poems are steeped in homosexual angst), but unlike most gays (contrary to the cliches) he feels more female than he does male. "Yours to Take" contains a vision of himself:

> There's a certain type of men
> > born to suffer as women
> the worst kind
> who never marry and play around
>
> with their own kind....
> > It's the women
> who have struck out in their suffering.

"While Miss Marlene Dietrich Was Singing" contains a gallery of sad, waiting women. Dietrich is herself one, the singer of "seven oceans of sorrow." She waits in a Berlin bar bathed in neon, her hair covered with sequins. Rich and lonely, she paints her nails waiting for a lover who won't turn up. She is "the desperate woman, the / woman left alone."

The archetypal abandoned female (men drove up to "slice off" her "thighs") appeared most unforgettably in Billie Holiday's songs, where Wieners finds paradigms for himself—the descent into drugs and booze, the brutalized life. "Billie Holiday," Wieners writes, "was the story / of my whole life & still is." "Broken Hearted Memorys" recounts, in gentle lyric form, his having met Holiday in New York. He "went crazy afterwards," overwhelmed by her

> sorrow her legacy holding hands under the table.
> Billie's grey-hair was Parisian style and her
> singing Big Apple. She's still rotting nectarines.

In "Does His Voice Sound Some Echo in Your Heart" he sits drinking champagne, taking pills, and considering a paper sent by the state certifying him "mentally ill." To imagine the horror of being utterly alone in such a spot boggles the mind. Rather than wallow in self-pity, Wieners diverts his "feeble central system" to writing poems in women's voices.

In "Gardenias" he gender fucks by assuming Holiday's persona. His failure to "hold" any man or woman occasions the blues; and after twenty years of "drunken futility," he is nowhere, "sick of sickness in the heart":

Despite fur coats, and banquet tables, single ear-rings,
poetry readings across the country, ideal communities
and overseas, the spacious mists pall boulevards to
lone candles in little moon-lit rooms above the city.

He is tired of literary coteries:

it's a womanish heart
growing old alone above the city, parallel horizontal
to the snow
wrapping herself up in the dreams of other men
Have no mercy, they cry on the Fenway,
their mesmerized eyes burn in the darkness,
pushing herself on to the exhaustion of love
for a short eternity.

Most drag performers avoid the illusion that the female they impersonate materializes before your eyes. The image is an outrage—the man wearing the eyelashes, wig, furs, boa, and sequins, remains a man. Wieners maintains this illusion by talking high camp. He "queens" it up with the best of the tea-dance screamers from Manhattan and Fire Island—before the Marlboro man and the San Francisco Levis clone took over the gay worlds. See his riffs on Babs Hutton and the glittering chatter he invents between Simone de Beauvoir and Greta Garbo. What makes so many of Wieners' poems uncanny is that he reveals no five o'clock shadow. To conservatives, bigots, state psychiatrists, and entrapment police, these gender switches are disturbing perversions.

Language and Style

I've never read a book of poems more stylistically eccentric than this one. The "sd," "wd," "cd" affectations of Olson, Snyder, and Duncan are tame by comparison. So far, the passages I've quoted from Wieners have been lucid. Much of *State Capitol,* however, is inexact. At times words are so wrenched and tumbled (as in a laundromat dryer) that they lack overt meanings. First names of obscure friends and acquaintances also rebuff the reader.

Despite my complaints, I find *State Capitol* a book that should be read by anyone interested in Projective Verse and Beat poetry. I shall suggest ways of reading Wieners. "To Allen Hammerschlag" sets up Wiener's aesthetics. This passage begins with two images, examples precisely seen:

> The clenched fist around a crumpled cigarette pack
> Beneath the burgeoning sun's descent
> Absence is failure
>
> A steam shovel with a man in his tiny cock-pit up front
> we rattle by, managing useless controls
>
> beneath grand sun-set.

A meditation on poetry concludes that "lost parts" are images for death. Perhaps the idea is not dissimilar from one prevalent in modern art, from Henry Moore's sculptures where concave spaces speak with as much urgency and beauty as convex spaces. Obviously, this makes more sense as we experience it in marble or on a canvas than in poems where we expect linear flow. Here is what Wieners says:

> And thus poems open an exegesis
> of philosophy, not contradicting emotions
> to be contemplated by graduate students
> living in bachelor flats-by-town.
>
> I miss these lost parts.
> I miss them lost poets.
> They are right, the missing gaps
> as   their deaths.

The gap in the final line illustrates what it is he means, as is the bad grammar of "them last poets."

In "A Living Legend's Intimate Memoirs," much of it spoken by Lana Turner, Wieners seems to turn drunk or stoned:

> E S p e cia 1 lapse in vocabulary bill Bitters
> home brew remedy's sanctify satur-
> day Metro's net gate gross great in
>
> elementary school grade. Ill-non-legal
> 1 = declaims use.
> 5 makes minus
>
> suffering miners, Samos
> 17th sovreign countrite, contrive-
> d, commercial....

I am lost! His lingering over "especial" works as a sign that the poem may shortly zoom off. Once we catch "illegal" and "nonlegal" fashioned into a single word, and that "Saturday" (when she gets drunk) contains "turd," we sense that dear Lana may be in her cups as she rants about Metro Goldwyn Mayer and their "gross" receipts, trying to figure her income with her elementary school math.

Towards the end of the collection (he's been rhapsodizing about Hemingway, about putting Jacqueline Kennedy's brassiere between his legs, Demeter, Mother, and Allen Ginsberg) Wieners provides a fascinating glimpse into his thorny diction. The writing seems calculated to cause "sore throats," which suggests overdone fellatio and traditional lyric poems so sweet they irritate the throat:

> Writing until dark, eather [sic] at the afternoon garden terrace
> seat, or in his room, until the light grew too dim, by the ships
>   dismal funnels, the month of May began quite tranquilly and
> eventually over the stream of the wake, the ship left, reflecting
> verdant brakes of clouds in the reflection and railing lights.
> Composition proves: FALLOw verbs, projective grammatical
> syntax and an opposition both of cosmic generosity to timidity
> of an original sort, leave a course, difficult to pilot.
>   This book in
> its writing is the record of one, stylized and self-conscious, it
> behooves to haphazard twinkling bushes on the phos-
>   phorence, and sore throats.

He cultivates the "ill-iterate" touch, perhaps as a slash at academic poets and critics, the School-Marm Screamers who demand good spelling, complete sentences, accurate grammar. He's for "paganism, lies and heresy," and for a "queer honesty," a "literary dichotomy," "Morphe erroneous untedious mystery," "non-said mistakes," "Revolutionary caval," and "a viscosity submandered." This is plebian writing with a vengeance, as if the caterpillar tractor man scribbled off a few lines whilst eating his bologna sandwiches and Twinkies. These lines also are appropriate for a man sent to jail for being homosexual, thus, incurably insane. "Oh, this is in an / exercise," he exclaims in another passage which reads like a madly-typed writing exercise:

> sentience, surrender, sweet sundered sleep.
> Keep the tryst, trust further
> to his mind's vision where against
> travel, time, ruesome new companions it may
> be contained for the terrain we must encounter
>   and surmount.

The "Disconnected Text," one of his phrases, is probably adapted from Burroughs, from *Naked Lunch* which was formed as decoupage and collage, and written in a junk or booze haze. Weiners blames the Secret Service for his drugged writing: they locked him up for two years, sending him into "drug-induced / collaboration with Apollo and the Nine muses / experimentally on me involuntarily // out of statehood apprehension...."

He owes much to jazz, a motif which runs throughout the book. And the jazz world (he wrote often in jazz bars) is, of course, the world of the outcast black, of an exiled have-not culture that includes homosexuals. Reading Wieners by imagining you are listening to jazz helps. The prolonged musical riff wafts through a dimly-lit, smoke-filled club and requires only sparsely focused listening. Accented moments carry the theme. Perhaps I can illustrate with this passage from "a bloody incident":

> Our BaSement room b-
> ehind the one playing DIRE
> of host Night and Day to His
> murderers, A CROW 'SHAN Milt
>
> KEy, BANDAGing no Latin chrome
> minus one tenthless C E N T U R Y
> for Beverly Bill P A N T A G E S in
> route after our COmm — Algonquin
>
> and Beacon S T reet O' Connor....

Let's assume that the syllables in caps, or the words that are expanded by spacing, resemble stressed musical moments: a seamy world of jazz, nightclubs, Boston and New York Village streets emerges. "Direct" becomes both DIRE (a shouting forth) and "direct".... Wieners directs the tempo by splaying the letters of some words, and by bleeding others. Hearing the poem as jazz facilitates the reading, and makes one less impatient over the absence of mainline sense. Wieners writes as one of Burroughs' Latahs might, seated in a seamy Interzone bar, schlupping drugs, booze, and the marrow/sperm of other Latahs. Eventually, potent political overtones emerge. Wieners is very political, outraged by various national and international injustices, a topic requiring attention. Notice the puns Wieners spins below on Fidel and "infidel," the misspelling of "praise," the disjointed grammar of "while expose," and the play on Bay of Pigs as "camel-bay":

jewel isle Havana, jubilant
in priase [sic] I sing your martyrdom
while expose their infidel reawakening
Cuba, from its majesty aether-borne

merciful American camel-bay.

Another possibility for reading the more experimental poems is to imagine
passages as neon signs—the poems become collages of signs, like those popular-
ized by the painter Stuart Davis (who was also influenced by Jazz and Cubist art)
in the 40's and 50's. The bizarre spacings, again, set tempos and accents. Since
Wieners is first and foremost a poet of the city, much of what he writes occurs
outside a window before which he sits catatonic, enraptured by the feast of light
and sound before him. Here, though, he travels around North Beach, San
Francisco:

22nd S t r e e tgot on The MIS s i o n B O u n d
T H I R D and K e a r n y S T R E E T overland
as I from down T O W N B a y C I T y A R E A
transferred at Market, to re-enter my borrowed S E C O N D
F L O O R Washington   CableCA r train stop. The P U S H
E R H U B had earlier got in, near C I T Y
L I G H T   C   O L U M B U s.... 81

Wieners loves tabloid headlines. He lifts from newspapers and fan mags and
creates collages for his book: "COMEBACK HOPES HIGH / / FOR YVONNE
DE CARLO" is not dissimilar from this upper-case line from one of his prose
poems: "RUMAKER WAS ARRESTED FOR VAGRANCY." It seems obvious
that any of these devices—the stressed moment in a line of jazz, the economy of
the neon sign (particularly on old sign missing letters) and the tabloid headline,
all relate to peaking on drugs or liquor. From the shimmer of one's haze / pain
certain latching points emerge. And, if one trusts the wondrous fragility of the
psyche, one writes it down, and some of it, as with Wieners, gets published.
Behind the State Capitol is a disturbing book, full of personal angst, humorous and
serious posturing, voices, bizarre experimental techniques, and fascinating
connections with popular music, films, jazz, and art. No matter how resistant
Wieners is to ingratiating his reader, the performance remains a unique testament
to a rare out-culture sensibility, one that makes the society that persecutes,
entraps, and exploits that sensibility the truly sick party.

BIOPSIES:

REFLECTIONS ON LANGUAGE POETRY

"I say these things smugly, as if I understand them."
— Lori Baker

1.

I've puzzled much over Language Poetry. I subscribed to *Temblor*, have read *HOW(ever)*, *Cathay*, and *Sulfur*, and receive many books and chapbooks from Burning Deck and Sun & Moon Presses. I've consulted numerous collections and manifestos, including Ron Silliman's *In the American Tree* and Douglas Messerli's *"Language" Poetries*. Practitioners of the mode mumble and evade when challenged to define what they are up to. Some poets and critics fear that such exothermic stuff threatens to smother all other poetries. Their apologist Marjorie Perloff, in scouring them ultra-brite, in *The American Poetry Review*, *Sulfur* and in her books, drawing on her lavish informed intelligence, still obfuscates them more often than she clarifies them.

I've already, I know, tipped my hand—I'm not enthusiastic about Language Poetry. Yet, from the vantage of my sixty-eight years, how can I avoid the old-fogeyism that condemns self-indulgent, mindlessly irrational, pyrotechnical, and smug verse? *Elitism* and *coterie* suit the gaggle of fowl clustered around poets Lyn Hejinian, Charles Bernstein, Brian Watten, Keith and Rosmarie Waldrop, Michael Palmer, Ron Silliman, Barbara Guest, and Stephen Rodefer, among others. Their minimalist burbling, loquacious *texicons* (my coinage for the minds of writers enamored of "text," "lexicon," "semeiotic," etc), and unctuous blathering of life-truths send traditionalists racing up the nearest upas tree.

The anthology *21+1 American Poets Today*, edited by Emmanual Hocquard and Claude Royet-Journoud (Montpellier Cédex, France) features a smorgasbord of "Language" poets. That the volume originates in France also underscores the influence of currently fashionable semanticists, literary theorists, minimalists, structuralists, and post-structuralists: Derrida, Iser, De Guy, and Lacan. I'm told that these influences are already passé in France.

2.

In Hocquard's and Royet-Journoud's collection, Frank Samperi's messy syntax results in Tarzan talk:

> rain not last day
> recalled today
> this blue sky day
> striking pool lake
> generates in
> definite spheres....

Well, let's puzzle through this: why the primitive or immigrant-newly-come-to-America talk in "rain not last day"? Is the rain still pouring? It doesn't seem so, since Samperi refers to "this blue sky day." The day is apparently both rainy and sunny, the latter so super that a pool and a lake generate "definite spheres." Yes, Samperi evokes John Milton's "music of the spheres." But why are the spheres "definite?" Would "indefinite spheres" violate the abstractness Samperi desires. Since his thinking is fuzzy, by giving other ill-disciplined brains the sense that something is "definite," he snares them, much as wet iguana tongues zap centipedes. "Sphere melodies" belong to medieval and renaissance notions of how the universe jells and moves, and Language Poetry is gemmed all o'er with the paste jewelry of lit crit allusions. The poet is too often derivative of college survey classes. Samperi's poem is a mess, intellectually and semantically. He violates one of the first tenets for a successful poem: interest your reader and make him care.

3.

Charles Bernstein has energy, intelligence, and humor; but he can also write poorly. "Type" seems to have been typed out on a narrow strip of paper, like those once used in adding machines. His effort, minuscule, skinny, flashes pretentious words, sops for the reader who feels brainy: "egregious," "machinations," "mesmerized," and "crisscrosses" flop on the page like bulging-bellied toads waiting to be prodded by a love-lorn princess stoned on crack. And there's little music.

Next comes Michael Gizzi. Here's an anoretic moment from "Avis":

Seldom
But like
This
I list
In a cage
Glazed
In a
Pearliness
Persona oscura.

I love the triple squint of "Avis," for it evokes a) "Avis Rent-A-Poem," b) a bird, a rare thing, and c) the caged poem glazed and pearly, concealing the "persona" of the poet. The two whimpering rhymes, "This/list" and "cage/glazed" hardly suffice as memorable, the rara avis bird-throat notwithstanding. And then, the deadening splatter of short, capitalized lines, typical of dozens, yea, even hundreds, of anoretic poems spun ad nauseam from the sallow pens of these writers: not only does one regret the waste of Pacific Northwest pines pulped for printing these, but the effect aesthetically—I don't know about you, reader, but my red blood cell count is swiftly diminishing.

4.

In her contribution to *21 + 1*, Susan Howe peps up nonsense writing with facile alliterations:

Right or ruth
rent
to the winds shall be thrown

words being wind or web...

What I read here may have nothing to do with real estate: you rent "right" [positive] or "ruth" [negative], providing a shelter for your "words." Self-important poets fling words as *wind* or *web* at us. "Thrown" to the winds is a lousy cliche, nor does the future conditional "shall be" excite me. The latter seems promulgated by a seer (or seeress), a pompous, viral touch in lines with no visible anchors of imagery. In struggling to pin this squirming versicle, I think of Shelley's "Wild West Wind" and of Cotton Mather's spider drifting, dragging its web after it, out to sea. Shelley's wind informs the world with visions; Mather's spider, having snared victims (poetry readers?) drifts off to extinction. Such speculations do little to make Howe's verse better than it is. Yet, if you read Howe's *The Europe of Trusts*, you'll see more lyricism and over-all quality than you'll find here.

To show the viral drift-over from writing like Howe's to criticisms of Howe, here is Rachel Blau du Plessis *illuminating* Howe: "whole shadow words, as if visual afterimages, come in her intricate split spell-ings: iris sh' (SHDL) or 'life la/nd friend/no lighthouse   marin/ere (CG)..." This is unreadable. Great intellects have always eschewed darkness visible, darkness inane. Blau du Plessis glories in the umbrageous, suiting the spirit of Kathleen Fraser's dank circular, *HOW(ever)*, in which she appears.

5.

No poet better reveals the enormous debt Language Poets owe to the Mother of them All, Gertrude Stein, than Robert Grenier. Sure, as you might expect, if you've read much of Stein, as I have, becoming an aficionado during my Wisconsin farm boy high school days, you've never forgotten Stein. You know how maddening she can be, and yet, how splendidly original. My guess is that few of her current idolaters and imitators have the training or intelligence to give her more than superficial attention. Grenier, for example, clearly has Stein's famous "A rose is a rose is a rose" in mind here:

grass

there is grass

grass

here is grass

grass

grasses...

Yes, Grenier loses Stein's lean circumspection while ripping off her motif. To say "rose" thrice is to emphasize its beauty thrice and to emphasize the truth that the rose is nothing but itself, shorn of tacky emotional, Romantic associations. If Stein were a mathematician she'd have set the rose to the third power.

Like most Language poems, "grass" glances different ways—there's a snicker (grass as marijuana) and a serious blatt (grass reflects nature's plethora, as seen, possibly, through Walt Whitman's cracked lenses). Be careful; I may infect you in the act of seeming to love you. Stein erects many cautionary signs for her adulators and imitators, signs most of our language poets ignore. They'd appear less silly if they were more alert.

6.

A note on my critical method, through which I hope to deflect objections readers may have: I am inspired by Matthew Arnold's theory of the "touchstone," by which you judge the quality of new poetry by holding it to the touchstone of passages approved as universally excellent. He ransacked Shakespeare and Milton for his purposes. Algernon Swinburne is also an influence; I've always rejoiced in his critical approach (he was a major critic) as he appears in his essay "Under the Microscope." My approach is scientific, as his was, for I borrow from medicine and biopsy procedures. A tiny specimen cut from liver, breast, pancreas, lung, throat, or prostate will discern the presence of cancer or some life-threatening virus at work—you needn't take the whole body, or, in this case, the text. If you do find viral matter you can be quite sure that the entire corpus will soon be infected, if it is not already so. A few lines from a poem, like stabs of tissue from an ovary or prostate, will suffice.

7.

Beverly Dahlen, appearing in Fraser's *HOW(ever)*, writes "A Reading," a poem of 120 parts. Dahlen might just be our latter-day female Louis Zukovsky, for she hints of even more parts to come. When she achieves the googol, Earth's Final Trumpet shall sound. Literary orts of all sorts scatter about her fuliginous writings like so many bone and tissue scraps at a multi-cultural literary dig: Lewis Carroll, Neruda, Freud, Robert Herrick, the old Greeks, Sacajewea, Foucault, Jakobson, Hilda Dolittle, G. Stein, Robert Duncan, and Wittgenstein. When Dahlen speculates on her self as poet (self-consciousness is a sine qua non for Language Poets) note her breathy starts, hesitations, and restarts. Note the solipsistic self-wonderment. Note the facile symbolism: *key*. Note the trendy furniture of "orgone" and the concealed goddess:

> I would not have been a poet.I wonder
> why that recurs,I wonder why I
> don't think about it.the key.a resistance.key,
> Freud knew that even with—
> out the censor there would be symbolism.we
> cannot speak directly as in
> nature,we speak,nature never does,the animal
> that makes symbols,tool-
> master,weaver,orgone.the man who discovers
> her hidden in a tree is...

In another passage, Dahlen dances in eurythmics fashion to the stock images of a new moon and a voodoo doll. When she observes that "All this language is a floating," she helps my argument against her. "It [her writing] depends," she writes. "It is subject to constant modification. It depends." And, then, there's Dahlen's revelatory tone, suggesting a sibylline wisdom, as though some consumptive priestess of Isis or Wittgenstein clad in H. D. garb, or Robert Duncan's gay drag, is holding forth, swinging the palindromes and cut up lines as if they were jammed into smoking censers. Here is the tone at its worst, embodied in quasi-liturgical modes: "and he / he who was," "he who is other must be the final mystery, who lives under the law of the dead father," "she who is in the mirror," "she who pondered all these things silently..."

Though Dahlen loves pronouncements, no one seems to love them more than Rae Armantrout. The device, when pompous, delivered ex-cathedra, rages as viral matter throughout Language poetry. Here are a couple of examples proffered by Armantrout: "Emphatic / precision / is revealed as / hostility." "A list may pantomime / focus." This one from Lisa Houston has a lighter mood: "Food eaten by the silent can resemble rapid streams, as can similar drugs." And Brian Barry: "Goatness eats from inside out / feasts on the stuff that makes the man..."

8.

In *Nemesis*, lew daly writes of "technique, and produces what Fritz Perls, in *In and Out of the Garbage Can*, used to call a "mind fuck." And daly has energy; one feels excitement as he spins through his numerous feints, slights of hand, and riffs of principles of language. His premise is that between "languages" there is space for "feeling" new verse "techniques." Immediate materials come from "a setting down" and whatever we find "at hand." I interpret this to mean that daly *sets down* abstractions and matter from his own psyche which he furnishes with details from physical settings. There's a flux resulting in an "ecclesiolatry" transpiring between these worlds, a "vision" endorsing "the materiality / between." Obviously, the conundrum intensifies, as daly proceeds. If he weren't so bright, and the rhythms of his verse so satisfying, I would sneer at his tortured, elusive, arguments. The mystical baggage introduced with "ecclesiolatry" culminates in the delicious word "cruciate," subtly flavoring daly's meditation on language as creative act and elevating it. Yet, daly's assertion that there is a "new technique" reveals that he has fallen into the conceptual trap that other Language Poets do—rather than be specific about a newly discerned "truth," you merely state it as truth, leading us to confusion and irritability. If he means to direct us to rely more on open ranges between our pre-received notions and a literal universe of specific objects around us, I am with him. How would a pure aesthetician handle such a theme? The structure of his argument would surely be clearer than daly's, and he would not, as daly does, turn lovingly towards the images of "salts" and second chances. I do, though, love the wind-off, although I don't know what daly means by it:

> Clearly the new technique, on-
> ly as strong as the theft
> of its salts, the weakest
> set, is a second chance

So, it is possible for a poet writing in the Language mode to win me over. Readers interested in more of daly may order *nemesis*, the book in which this poem appears, from Burning Deck Press.

9.

Another poet, Stephen Rodefer, contrasts with daly, in that Rodefer, though far more loquacious, seems driven towards sheer "writing" as self-fascination rather than self-revelation. Sure, he's full of vitality and has a way with puns, surreal juxtapositions, and bland narrative strategies. He's at his worst when lines go utterly slack and fall between typing exercise lines and facile alliterations. Here's one of his worst moments: "Many winds against wind will dinner turn, sewing ear to ear, end to end, saying yet let law reign in cave." He's cute here, and arrogant, and bad. One of his various chapters, or set pieces, "Avery," opens this way:

VEXATIOUS SCENE, protean parody, demolishing
sea, discern me in this thick mist-breathing night, your
undisclosed hemisphere, edifice shed. Tamping soil,
lying head, bent low, issued far, so fairly creature. Icy
shell, grooved inarm, I am horse — because your
speech foretells the ingenuity. From mid-breast I am
like a giant in your size. Look how great your seizure is
to correspond unto a part. What was beautiful, in being
ugly, makes affliction fiery, read for great marvel
adjoined to this, above the middle of the shouldered
wood.

I won't bore you with counting up all the long vowel "e" rhymes, evidence
of severe viral damage, possibly terminal: scene, protean, parody, sea, me,
breathing... The trappings are cheap-shot epical: "protean," demolishing sea,"
"undisclosed hemisphere," "mist-breathing night." One expects to see Niobe
stride forth grasping her children, or Aeneas pursuing Dido through the palm
trees. And how do we read the phrase "so fairly creature?" Is this yet another
instance of bad writing where a poet wants a phrase to squint more than one way?
The creature is "fair," yes. But why the adverb "fairly?" Are readers supposed to
supply the indefinite pronoun, correcting the syntax? Is "fairly creature" a
compound invention, some sort of new love species. A horse, we soon find is
involved, "in arm" [inarmed?], we find. I gather that the speaker [the horse], is
of sufficient hands so that the sweetie [who seems no more substantial than a
"vexatious scene"] reaches the horse's "grooved in arm" at "mid-breast." Consider this line: "Look how great your seizure is to correspond unto a part." That's
wretched, either as experimental poetry, as ordinary syntax, or as an observation
felt and designed to engage a reader. Ugh! My guess is that few Language Poets,
if they are truthful, can read much of this, and Rodefer's book is lavish with stuff
this bad and worse. The book, incidentally, is *Passing Duration*, 1991.

10.

Jed Rasula, in "The Tent of Times," provides the perfect culture for
producing verse viruses. He informs us that as he wades "in & out" of a dream
he comes "on bits of broken glass, / floating in silt like bubbles." He also finds
transmitters, eggs that glow and "wring the gaze," red ants, "priapic stones,"
hands resembling "bulls in a pasture," water snakes in a trough, "a little tub where

islands fit." Mystical and mythical objects float about: "a shell of the soul," Athena's shield, "*Amore* splashing," "Mithraic honey," Ananke twisting "her fate device," and "archaic compulsions." Even on land objects conglomerate, "glued to memory's hive / of heat seeped in through an open wound." The very "ground fills up with stones—the inner earth creeps out. / Flakes & shards, concepts, glues, / something grows." Beneath all this runs the motif of language, of words, of meanings. There are allusions to mad King Lear: Rasula sucks "the air out of Lear" and crusts, blears, and gnaws at the "drift" he intuits. And the word *intuit* is a clue. For a poet like Rasula, the psychic jumble rolls with the swell and drifts towards some unifying theme or idea, possibly too arcane for merely rational minds is the perceiver. Both the poet and his reader must trust Rasula's intuition. No matter how adventitious the connections among the bits of Rasula's flotsam and jetsam, there are "meanings." Fortunately, Rasula's psyche welters with fascinating salvage, and I am willing to examine it without caring whether my feet are on firm sea bottom or not. Lesser poets, though, are apt to irritate when what accrues is merely a collection of broken egg shells, garden pebbles sparrow bones, and fly wings left over from a spider's dinner—objects of little consequence.

In "The Person," Lyn Hejinian is mildly associative. Each of her stanzas presents ideas which she then obfuscates. Some are ideas about language and the aesthetic properties of verse. She likes being conceptual, and is often complacent. She says she translates her "thought / into jump-language" as a way of doubling "fate." Jumpstart cables? Hejinian sets up one idea—here she ends a stanza with "fate"—and then jumps across or sparks over from the next stanza to an anode in the preceding stanza. Hejinian believes that an altruistic poet who knows "what to want" will be "free." Most of her flotsam and jetsam consists of feverish shibboleths of a schoolmarmish sort. The result is an embarrassingly dull philosophizing. Here are some examples:

"Each sensation is witness to the congestion of its glance..."
"Elation can manifest itself from time to time in finding..."
"Music is rational in a thing that affects me..."
"Things see their argument go to and fro before my eyes..."
"Sound is a sentence of water..."

Her yoking of disparately floating elements (copulating frogs follow "the judgment and the matching method," which follows "balls of these intentions," which follows "light and nightmares") seems merely pedantic, despite little whiffs of surprise (the fucking frogs) which emerge and then quickly vanish. My complaint is not that Hejinian rarely completes a thought—certainly our minds naturally billow with partially formed impressions and ideas, most of which we barely notice—but that her thoughts are trite.

More successful than either Rasula or Hejinian is Bob Perelman whose linguistic romps are intelligent and brisk. Sufficiently modest, he avoids pomposity. He opts for a semblance of sense and plays freely among puns, syllabic sound-echoes, and word designs. Here, he combines humor, narrative hints, and aesthetics:

> Assertion:
> The object can only be created by the senses.
> So beat me with your light-saber
> make me watch and direct bad movies!
> The end is form-fitted space.

To him words are "human persons, / appetitious meanings," the "flesh" he'll sell himself for. He interrupts himself. He appears to struggle for insight, falling back on a form of declension: "I sing you hear / they. . . " His concluding "Coda" displays winsome playfulness blended with a serious statement on education, poetry, and civilization:

> the education wants the poem, like a sidewalk, waterpipes under
>   the street, wires overhead in every direction, grass
>   and cement under foot, cars, no cars in alterity
>   of sincere disposition
> And my time is gone in the smooth
> code I send before.
> Good night. Good night.

His "Sentimental Mechanics" is a three-stanza romp that borrows moments from Poe ("never") and incorporates child talk with its cute illogicality ("I need to know, what it was / my mommy said. The ice cream melted, / I was in my head"). There are references to old films (Humphrey Bogart) and to Tennyson's "Charge of the Light Brigade" ("Theirs not to reason why, / Theirs but to do or die"). Stanza two reveals his commitment to finding "another word," a linguist's dream of discovery, like a geneticist who imagines stumbling at last on whatever submicroscropic scrap truly constitutes life: "There's got to be another word. / There's not another world."

11.

Much of this writing is "automatic," an infantile behavior regressing to kindergarten and elementary school days when bright kids scribbled flotsam and jetsam from their amoebic minds on paper, showed them to teacher, and if they were sufficiently surreal and bizarre, the kids was seen as a genius. Coprophiliac, yes, and fecal, for the feeling persists that whatever grotesquely drops from one's psyche, child or adult, since they are *yours* are to be prized, and, if possible, not flushed away or thrown out in the garbage. You may even find people to think they are scribbles of genius, and some may even publish you! I fear, alas, that much Language Poetry I read is too often automatic, spun forth from ill-educated, ill-practiced poeticules who've probably only vaguely heard of Keats and Dryden, and not at all of Ben Jonson, Christopher Marlowe, Wyatt and Surrey, Algernon Charles Swinburne, D. H. Lawrence (as critic), W. H. Auden, and Robert Graves. Drastic liposuction treatments are needed, and speedily.

12.

Among a surprisingly disparate olio of poets showcased in the new journal *Cathay* devoted to such writing, one poet in particular strikes me. Ray Jordan attempts to wed Language to the Shakespearean Sonnet. His "129," despite its arithmetical title (Language Poets like seeing themselves as linguistico-scientists), is both interesting and inept. The end rhymes would grace the effort of a bright grade schooler scribbling to impress his teacher. Check these pairings: swelling lust / churning trust; keep it straight / favorite bait; it saddened me so / smokeless fire of woe; the wax of extreme / in the dream. The flow of lines from trimeters to nonameters seems due to chance, and, generally, the longer the lines the worse the writing. These two are the foulest:

> & don't forget the silver spoon which effectively lured the mad
> or the inverted candle burning all but lionless it saddened me so

Now, don't misread me: I'm excited by the idea that poets fill old wineskins with new wine; yet, I do expect quality; but Jordan's woefully lacking. How do responsible editors let such dreck pass? Are their sensibilities numbed by all the Language scribbling sent to them?

13.

Among the Language poets who neutralize Language viruses in their works are Barbara Guest and Rosmarie Waldrop. Waldrop is intellectual, chiselled, and cool; Guest is inventive, humorous, and warm. Both are full of surprises. You'll find residues of most of the viruses I've isolated and complained of; but these poets control, even overwhelm, and transform what appears as rot and disease in lesser poets. Guest and Waldrop should be acknowledged as among our most original poets, coteries and fashion notwithstanding.

Guest's *The Countess From Minneapolis,* first published in 1967, appeared recently in a new edition, and what a joy it is. In "Prairie Houses," ostensibly about rabbit, mole, and snake burrows, Guest turns the tables, for the habitations (seen as "hard-mouthed houses with their / robust nipples the gossamer hair") anticipate human dwellings despoiling the prairies. The bumps (earth-breasts) of creature burrows are breasts among the "gossamer" prairie grasses. Guest's transition to human dwellings depends on the writer as "scientist," a common feature of Language Poetry. Guest is medical, architectural, and engineering. She also reflects the Language Poet's fondness for Stein's alliterations and other verbal pyrotechnics. Even when Guest's scientific references are overt, and the phrase-ology complex, Guest maintains the energy of her lines; ie., she never writes badly, uses padding, or flaunts cliches:

> On the earth exerting a wilful pressure
>
> something like a stethoscope against the breast
>
> only permanent.
>
> Selective engineering architectural submissiveness
> and rendering of necessity in regard to height,
> eschewment of climate exposure, elemental
>   understandings,
> constructive adjustments to vale and storm
>
> historical reconstruction of early earthworks...

Again in the Language mode, Guest is fond of surreal, koan-like questions: no answers are expected. Here she launches a sardonic thrust at those pretentious philosophical questions of essence usually asked of gurus and angels:

> The problem proposed to the lemon tree. When

will your green fruit turn yellow? When shall I
understand Minneapolis?

Guest loves linguistic permutations. Delicious is her prose poem on
domestic problems between a hero Eofirth and his wife. The latter recalls how
splendid Eofirth was when he "led her in a northern country to the first wild
strawberry." The piece concludes as the wife pleads not to be abandoned. The
olio of cross-cultural references is brilliant: Christianity, Strindberg, and film-
making. I love the line "Who have commanded dwarfs." Here is the last half of
the piece:

> She hid under the quilt refusing to hear his impas-
> sioned, "I'll immigrate! I'll immigrate!" savaging the room.

> Don't Eofirth, she cried, abandon me to these
> nerveless plains. This forgetful river. You who have made
> Christ swing from a tree. Who have commanded dwarfs.
> Never forget the loneliness of Strindberg in Paris. And
> never, like that other well-known exile, film the politics
> of loss.

Another poem spins riffs on Anglo-Saxon poetry. Guest's mix of anachronisms and the antique is both fastidious and loving. Her "kennings," imitative
of the old Anglo/Saxon normative foot, are inventive, and she favors puns, viz.,
weird as it echoes the Anglo-Saxon *wyrd,* or Fate:

(SCOP —A POET) WIDSITH
Scoping along the Mississippi. I a Scop. Coasting the
Myth-West, musing the margins, earth yearned river
wracked, grieving and groping, I a Scop making my weird.

The idea of a Countess in Minneapolis is rare, and Guest devotes several
prose poems to this classy self. I may be mistaken, but I discern echoes of Ronald
Firbank's ladies as they inhabited his arcane, artful, humorously exotic stories.
Firbank's *The Flower Beneath the Foot* is particularly apt. Guest's Countess even
reads European fiction, referring to the "exoticism of reading a British novel
while visiting Duluth." Earlier, a friend advises her to obtain "a sophisticated
cat," which she does. Here is poem #21. I envy "hen's teeth in the rain!"

"This street reminds me of scarceness, even loss like

searching for hen's teeth in the rain," murmured the
Countess to herself as she picked her way slowly down
Hennepin Avenue. "I feel frightfully sad somehow and
truly lost. I wish I had a glass of sherry right now, only
that would never do. I mean I couldn't drink it here on
the corner. Look at that gutter. So muddy. The wind's
from the Southeast which should mean...I never know
what it means. The prairies confuse me so. Perhaps Liv
will have a hot bath ready when I finally reach home. That
and the new frock from New York with the twin reveres.
I wonder how reveres shall look on top of mutton sleeves.
There's venison for supper. And the St. Louis Dispatch
with luck should have arrived." The Countess hesitated
for a moment as the sidewalk drifted into dirt and her
grey eyes filled with dust.

Few poets match Rosmarie Waldrop for intelligence. In lesser hands, her
scientism would be paltry. Her latest book *Lawn of Excluded Middle* is lavish with
Language Poet techniques. Here are samples of her arithmetical-scientific
Language Poet self: "What's left over if I subtract the fact that my leg goes up from
the fact that I raise it?" "It is possible, I admitted, to do physics in inches as well
as in centimeters, but a concept is more than a convenience." "Busy moving
ahead, I can't also observe myself moving, let alone assess the speed of full steam
minus fiction and sidetracked in metric crevices. It's hard to identify with the
image of an arrow even if it points only to the application we make of it."
"Meaning is like going up to someone I would be with, though often the distance
doesn't seem to lessen no matter how straight my course."

Waldrop's readers participate in a "physics" of esthetics based on a poetic
and painterly rather than a scientific, verifiable truth. This should surprise no
one, for science denies the freedom to fracture or dismiss grammar (as a relic not
congenial to avant garde writing), as do Language Poets when they are at all clear
on the issue. What confounds and complicates is the annexing of "scientific"
approaches to language by poets who boast that despite a science of linguistics,
the poet who "foregrounds" language (that's the jargon) assumes there is a
"science" of poetry, of verse, with lasers operating on their behalf. It's as clear as
a boil on Sam Johnson's neck that such pretensions reduce to a scary truth that
these poets are really old-fashioned, pursuing, finally, what Holly Prado, in a
perspicacious letter to me on these matters calls "a sense of human warmth and
body in the work."

We pick our way through Waldrop's work, reminded often of de Chirico's paintings or DuChamps' graphics, with various geometric forms and lines visible, defining objects and landscapes as a way of spinning mental connections. A superficial math gives the illusion of specificity. And, of course, one should not overlook Waldrop's profound involvement with similar poetries in France, particularly those of Emmanuel Hocquard and Edmond Jabés, both of whom she has lovingly translated, the four for Jabés published by the Wesleyan and Chicago University Presses.

"Logic," Waldrop says, "is no help when you have no premises." And throughout this feminist work ("The Lawn of Excluded Middle," Waldrop writes, "plays with the idea of woman as the excluded middle. Women and, more particularly, the womb, the empty center of the woman's body, the locus of fertility."), she asserts numerous premises, often haltingly, as a way of restoring the power that logic once had in her life and in Western thought. One senses that her pursuit is never concluded, evidenced by her descent into disturbing images: "I have read that female prisoners to be hanged must wear rubber pants and a dress sewn shut around the knees because uterus and ovaries spill with the shock down the shaft." When a swallow lurches into a window pane, Waldrop moves from the specifics of the event to a generalization about humans. Her final line could be restated as a theorem, or premise, to be etched in gilt and displayed on a poetry temple wall, one given over to geometric symbolisms. What I'm saying is that a good poet knows how to deliver apothegms without stultification and pretension. The poem follows:

> We know that swallows are drawn to window panes, etching
> swift lurching streaks across and sometimes crashing. I picked
> up the body as if easing the vast sky through a narrow pulse
> toppling over itself. Caught between simulacrum and paradox,
> the hard air. Even if a body could survive entering its own
> image, the mirror is left empty, no fault in the glass breaking the
> evenness of light.

14.

When I began assembling this piece—I'd written on some of these poets in *Hunting the Snark: A Compendium of New Literary Terms*, in four *Great American Poetry Bake-off* volumes, and in the *Black and Blue Guide to Literary Journals*—wanting to be fair, I read and reread both older and newer work. While I see more activity than ever—more journals feature Language Poets, more writers conferences star them, more and more writing programs are directed and populated by them, and more presses publish their works—the quality as my biopsies have shown remains dismal. The virus will hit its apogee and then, we hope, crumble, much as the vaunted Post-Structuralists and their clones are zooming out of fashion. In the English Department at the University of California, Irvine, where I teach, and where Derrida, Lyotard, Hillis Miller, and acolytes hold forth, I understand that there is trouble recruiting first-rate graduate students—like Arnold's Scholar Gypsy, fearing contamination, they are fleeing elsewhere, to programs less sterile and more energetic, to Michigan, Duke, and U Cal Berkeley. Of course, assuming that I am wrong, and Language Poetry continues to grow in visibility and influence, there will always be those rare poets of the caliber of Barbara Guest and Rosmarie Waldrop, most of whose work transcends all the gross excesses and mannerisms of the Language mode.

INDEX

INDEX

INDEX

INDEX